PEDAGOGY AS CREATIVE PRACTICE IN ARCHITECTURE

Architectural education in the United Kingdom performs a difficult balancing act: meeting the requirements of professional accreditation bodies and preparing students for practice, while also offering a meaningful education for those who do not intend to become architects. Increasingly, professional pressures frame architectural education as training rather than as an exploratory, experimental process – one that equips students to face unpredictable future challenges in the profession and beyond.

In response, many educators develop a *hidden curriculum*: an implicit set of values, methods and priorities that sit alongside formal learning outcomes. This hidden curriculum tends to privilege curiosity, criticality and open-ended inquiry, often through interdisciplinary and art-based approaches. Working in the gaps between what can be specified and what must be discovered, they complicate the "university-to-practice conveyor belt" narrative and widen what architectural education can be.

This book shines a light on those creative pedagogical practices – working within, and often despite, systemic pressures – and shows why they matter for the vitality of architectural education at a time of deep uncertainty across higher education. It is organised into two parts: **Discussions**, which offer in-depth explorations of current challenges, and **Insights**, which present a selection of case studies. Together, they argue for architectural education as a space that cultivates imagination, agency and adaptive ways of thinking – qualities essential for shaping futures that are not yet known.

This book provides essential reading for educators and advanced students of architecture.

Kasia Nawratek is a Senior Lecturer at Manchester School of Architecture, a registered architect and a writer. Her research brings posthuman approaches to the climate crisis into dialogue with literary and narrative methods of architectural investigation. Grounded in Mikhail Bakhtin's concept of polyphony, her teaching nurtures inclusive, dialogic studio cultures and frames speculative design as a form of world-building. She edited *Space and Language in Architectural Education: Catalysts and Tensions* (Routledge, 2022). Her pedagogical work was recognised with the SCOSA Innovation in Architectural Education Award (2024). Alongside her academic practice, she writes fiction in Polish: her children's book *Kresek, Bartek i całkiem zwyczajny początek* won the Kornel Makuszyński Award (2017), and her YA novel *Ja, świnia* was published in 2023.

Christopher Little is a Senior Lecturer in Academic Development at Manchester Metropolitan University's central University Teaching Academy. Chris offers academic development consultancy at Manchester Metropolitan and co-leads the university's Advance HE Recognition provision. His leadership in this area of staff development and recognition was crystallised in 2024 with the award of Principal Fellow from Advance HE. His research interests include academic literacies, undergraduate research cultures, assessment and feedback and inclusive teaching practices, and he remains research active in all of these areas.

PEDAGOGY AS CREATIVE PRACTICE IN ARCHITECTURE

Inspiration and Resistance During Change

Edited by Kasia Nawratek and Christopher Little

Routledge
Taylor & Francis Group
LONDON AND NEW YORK

Designed cover image: Zhaoyilin Zhang

First published 2027
by Routledge
4 Park Square, Milton Park, Abingdon, Oxon OX14 4RN

and by Routledge
605 Third Avenue, New York, NY 10158

Routledge is an imprint of the Taylor & Francis Group, an informa business

British Library Cataloguing-in-Publication Data
A catalogue record for this book is available from the British Library

Library of Congress Cataloging-in-Publication Data
Names: Nawratek, Kasia editor | Little, Christopher
(Christopher William Richard) editor
Title: Pedagogy as creative practice in architecture: inspiration and resistance during change / edited by Kasia Nawratek and Christopher Little.
Description: New York: Routledge, 2026. |
Includes bibliographical references and index.
Identifiers: LCCN 2026008954 (print) | LCCN 2026008955 (ebook) |
ISBN 9781041089599 hardback | ISBN 9781041089551 paperback |
ISBN 9781003647720 ebook
Subjects: LCSH: Architecture—Study and teaching—Great Britain |
LCGFT: Essays | Case studies
Classification: LCC NA2185 .P43 2026 (print) | LCC NA2185 (ebook)
LC record available at https://lccn.loc.gov/2026008954
LC ebook record available at https://lccn.loc.gov/2026008955

ISBN: 9781041089599 (hbk)
ISBN: 9781041089551 (pbk)
ISBN: 9781003647720 (ebk)

DOI: 10.4324/9781003647720

Typeset in Optima
by codeMantra

CONTENTS

CONTRIBUTORS

Matthew Bradshaw is a University Teacher at Sheffield University School of Architecture and Landscape and a practising architect at Chiles Evans + Care Architects in Sheffield. He has been teaching on the undergraduate architecture course since 2006 and is currently co-leader of the Year One programme. His teaching is informed by his varied professional experience, an understanding of the challenges and opportunities of the construction industry and a practice of design through iterative making and testing.

Luke Bushnell-Wye studied at the Universities of Cambridge, East London and Liverpool. With over ten years' experience in architectural practice and education, he teaches mainly first-year undergraduates and has been central to developing a seminar course focused on sensory awareness, core concepts and empathetic design thinking. His interests span liminal thresholds in student work, architectural representation in literature and the profession's use of language when addressing lay audiences and early-stage students.

Wei Shan Chia's work as an architect and educator centres on the intersection of craft, iteration and "learning through making". As the BA Architecture Programme Co-Lead and Year One Lead at the University of Sheffield, she is focused on foundational design pedagogy and champions inclusive approaches to architectural education. In addition to her academic work, Shan is a Director at CW2/Architects.

Emily Crompton is a Senior Lecturer and architect at Manchester School of Architecture (MSA) where she leads MSA LIVE, the Live Projects programme and the Foundation course. Alongside her teaching, Emily is interested in how cities can include minoritised groups and how the role of the architect is entangled with that. Building on her research into the LGBT+ Centre in Manchester, she uses archival and participatory design methods to understand the changing contexts of designing inclusive spaces. Previously Emily was the project coordinator on the "Ambition for Ageing" research project which involved creating innovative engagement methods and working closely with residents and organisations. She curates a project known as the Library of Engagements which archives methods of engagement concerning spaces, buildings, neighbourhoods and cities. She is a registered Architect with ARB, a founding member of QuEAN (Queer Educators in Architecture Network).

Anna Gidman is a Senior Lecturer and undergraduate programme lead at Manchester School of Architecture. As an architect, she is interested in natural materials in construction and is a coordinator of the Architects Climate Action Network (ACAN) Natural Materials group. Her interests lie in studio where she teaches postgraduate students in the atelier Some Kind of Nature, which responds to the climate crisis through a post-humanist framework which foregrounds relationships and decentres humans. Architecturally, this translates into a strong focus on context, care, multifunctionality and expression through space, materiality, technology and time.

Mark Hammond is Senior Lecturer and Interim Research Lead at Manchester School of Architecture (MSA), Manchester Metropolitan University. His research focuses on urban ageing and spatial justice, with a specific interest in housing inequality and ageism in the built environment. He teaches in the And Architecture atelier at MSA, where students are encouraged to engage with participatory and design-research methodologies to address social inequities and global challenges.

Samuel Holden is a Senior Lecturer at Manchester School of Architecture working at the intersection of critical theory, urban studies and political history. His current teaching and research focus on the relationship of socialist politics and neoliberalism, with particular attention to the role of local government, urban regeneration and the UK Labour Party.

Mel Lacey is an Associate Professor of Teaching and Learning at Sheffield Hallam University. She teaches across the Biosciences and Chemistry undergraduate and postgraduate degree programmes. Her research includes Molecular Microbiology, Pedagogy and Public Engagement of Science. She leads the Accessibility of Science Research Group in the Biomolecular Sciences Research Centre and the interdisciplinary Sheffield Hallam Blue Spaces Network.

Christopher Little is a Senior Lecturer in Academic Development at Manchester Metropolitan University's Central University Teaching Academy. Chris offers academic development consultancy at Manchester Metropolitan and co-leads the university's Advance HE Recognition provision. His leadership in this area of staff development and recognition was crystallised in 2024 with the award of Principal Fellow from Advance HE. His research interests include academic literacies, undergraduate research cultures, assessment and feedback and inclusive teaching practices, and he remains research active in all of these areas.

Malcolm Miles is a writer and researcher on critical theory, culture and society. His most recent book is *Art Rebellion* (2023). Previous books include *Paradoxical Urbanism* (2021), *Cities and Literature* (2019), *Limits to Culture* (2017), *Eco-Aesthetics* (2014), *Herbert Marcuse* (2011) and *Cities and Cultures* (2007).

Scott Miller is a trained modelmaker whose work spans architectural, commercial and display models, as well as exhibition curation, design and construction. He is currently the Workshop Technical Manager of the B15 Modelmaking Workshop at Manchester School of Architecture. He obtained a degree in Modelmaking in 2011 from the Arts University Bournemouth and a PGCert in Higher Education from the University of Manchester in 2021. His interests lie in the preservation, theory and promotion of modelmaking in design education. Alongside his role at MSA, he is the project lead of the Architect Index of Modelmaking.

Kasia Nawratek is a Senior Lecturer at Manchester School of Architecture, a registered architect and a writer. Her research brings posthuman approaches to the climate crisis into dialogue with literary and narrative methods of architectural investigation. Grounded in Mikhail Bakhtin's concept of polyphony, her teaching nurtures inclusive, dialogic studio cultures and frames speculative design as a form of world-building. She edited *Space and Language in Architectural Education: Catalysts and Tensions* (Routledge, 2022). Her pedagogical work was recognised with the SCOSA Innovation in Architectural Education Award (2024). Alongside her academic practice, she writes fiction in Polish: her children's book *Kresek, Bartek i całkiem zwyczajny początek* won the Kornel Makuszyński Award (2017), and her YA novel *Ja, świnia* was published in 2023.

Jonathan Orlek is a Senior Lecturer in Architecture at Liverpool John Moores University. He is an architectural researcher and practitioner, often working at the intersections of art, architecture and ethnography. His research explores artist-led organisations and spaces, community-based prototyping, housing and urban practices of care. He is also a director of social enterprise architecture collective Studio Polpo.

Lucretia Ray, graduating from the University of Liverpool, worked for more than a decade in architectural practice, specialising in the educational and industrial sectors. Ten years ago, she returned to the Liverpool School of Architecture, where she teaches widely across its accredited programmes. As coordinator of the first-year undergraduate course, she has devised a pioneering four-part teaching module that nurtures the students' basic architectural skills and includes seminars on empathetic and critical thinking. Lucretia leads a large and diverse team of studio tutors; she has distinguished herself in facilitating their career progression by identifying their dormant skills and providing them opportunities to grow. Her scholarship includes a strong focus on the design of appropriate learning and teaching environments for neuro-diverse architecture students.

Rachel Schwartz-Narbonne is a Senior Lecturer in Environmental Chemistry at Sheffield Hallam University. Her transdisciplinary research spans organic geochemistry, analytical chemistry and microbiology weaving through science public engagement, community-science methodology and social artscience practice.

Cith Skelcher is an Architect and Senior Teacher at the University of Sheffield's School of Architecture and Landscape. Cith worked with Cottrell and Vermeulen Architecture for ten years specialising in educational and community-based projects and participatory processes, and she continues to draw on this experience in her teaching, seeing architecture as a social practice. Cith has played an instrumental role in supporting inclusive and feminist pedagogy within the school through her teaching practice and leadership roles and through the co-creation of repositories such as the Inclusive Learning Tool Kit and the SSoA Feminist Library, with the broader goal of democratising access to the rich cultural capital of institutions for all.

Tanya Southcott is a Lecturer in Architecture and Design at the University of Brighton. She studied architecture at the University of Waterloo and McGill University in Canada and holds a certificate in heritage conservation planning from the University of Victoria. Tanya sits on the Steering Committee for the Architectural Humanities Research Association and co-leads the Architectural and Spatial Histories strand of the Centre for Design History at the University of Brighton. She uses her research, advocacy and teaching experience to promote the importance of humanities in architectural education and in the wider profession.

Julia Udall is an architectural educator, researcher and practitioner, who has taught at postgraduate level since 2008, and currently leads Year Four MArch and is the Post Graduate Research Tutor for Architecture. Her research is characterised by transdisciplinary working to address entwined societal and ecological crises. In this work the ecosocial is understood both as an area of investigation and methodological approach, that is collaborative, exploratory, rigorous and situated, with a strong feminist ethical underpinning. Julia leads the pan-European LIfe-centering Cultural HEritage Network (LICHEN), which mobilises innovative art and design approaches to support communities to reconnect with nature through care for their cultural landscape and local economies. Her Future Observatory Design Accelerator Project "Co-Designing a Positive Energy District with SADACCA" supports the development of the energy infrastructures required for green transition, by working with and from the energetic infrastructures of solidarity and care that underpin joyful neighbourhood life.

Rob Vinall is a Senior Lecturer and Practitioner working across interior, spatial and architectural design. He has over a decade of experience in higher education, with a focus on practice-led pedagogy, studio culture, learning through making and student belonging. He holds an MA from the Royal College of Art and maintains an active practice across architectural and set design. His research explores material and pedagogic conditions of learning, with attention to space, making and the formation of confidence and identity. His work also examines the intersections of identity and space, with an interest in queer spatial phenomenology and lived experience.

Stefan White is Professor of Architecture at Manchester Metropolitan University and a Director of the Architecture Research Office which addresses global challenges through Advanced and Applied architecture-led transdisciplinary research (A3RO). Arguing that architecture is essential for collectively inventing and implementing solutions to global social and environmental challenges, he champions an affective, Deleuzian approach to pedagogy, research and practice. Understanding creative processes as driven through joyful engagement with difference, he sees them as essential in generating new relations of knowledge and being with potential for change and emancipation. Over two decades, he has led highly participatory creative processes exploring the outer limits of architectural practice and pedagogy: impacting directly on the lives of many thousands of Greater Manchester residents; serving as a prominent prototype for citizen engagement across the university; and a research paradigm for regional, national and international approaches to addressing geographical health inequalities among older people.

ACKNOWLEDGEMENTS

We would like to thank Dan Jary of the Sheffield School of Architecture and Landscape, whose mentorship and friendship have shaped this project from the start. Dan was part of this book's earliest conversations and worked with the editors in its formative stages; this book's punk spirit owes a great deal to his thinking, his humour and his refusal to accept the narrowing of what architectural education can be. Above all, we are grateful for his kindness and empathetic approach to teaching, which has quietly shaped the ethos of so many educators and continues as a living legacy.

INTRODUCTION

Kasia Nawratek and Christopher Little

When the idea for this book was first discussed, we used to describe it as a "punk book". We'd try to explain what it would be about, but the moment we said "punk book", people's eyes lit up – and we had their attention. That subversive, anarchic charge was exactly what we were looking for; it's also what persuaded many contributors to join the project.

It is therefore worth asking why the punk element felt so enticing to architectural educators and what it reveals about the condition of architectural education in the UK in 2025. The impulse to play with the rules – to treat play as a strategy, to deploy creativity in an environment that neither expects nor seems to value it, where it can often feel that everything is driven by metrics and statistics – is a natural response from people whose professional identities are rooted in creative inquiry.

Our earliest conversations also surfaced a shared feeling among architectural educators of being under siege from all sides: constantly forced to reinvent their practice, and to contort themselves to meet the expectations of universities and professional bodies. The ever-shifting goalposts of UK academia – notably the diverging academic career paths that require staff to plan their futures along either teaching-focused or research-focused pathways, create a working environment in which no one can ever be "good enough". This is not unique to architecture schools, but architecture's already fraught position is further complicated by the presence of two professional accrediting bodies, the Architects Registration Board (ARB) and the Royal Institute of British Architects (RIBA), which, as of late 2025, are apparently "at war" (Spocchia, 2025) over the protection of the title versus the activities carried out by the architect. The opening salvo was the RIBA president, Chris Williamson, resigning from ARB registration (Williamson and Gordon, 2025).

DOI: 10.4324/9781003647720-1

This uncertainty is not confined to the UK, nor can it be dismissed as an "overseas problem". Reports of the Trump administration's decision to exclude architecture from professional degrees (Ravenscroft, 2025), and to limit funding, and therefore access to the profession, echo uncomfortably close to home. In the UK, the Labour government's decision to cut funding for architectural apprenticeships for over-21s from January 2026 will directly affect access to the final stage of architectural training at master's level, now requiring self-funding or employer support (Cruise et al., 2025). Level 7 apprenticeships were meant to widen participation by offering a practice-based alternative route into the profession, making qualification more viable for lower-income and mature students and aligning with the ARB's ambition to open the profession to students from disadvantaged backgrounds.

Architecture schools are watching these shifts closely. Any change in accreditation or funding triggers enormous work: rebranding and restructuring programmes inside the slowly turning cogs of university systems. Architecture schools across the country are currently grappling with the latest ARB change in accreditation (ARB, n.d.), under which undergraduate programmes will no longer be ARB-accredited from December 2027, and the undergraduate course will no longer be required for registration (RIBA, n.d.). The shift to Master's-level accreditation will change the architectural education landscape in the UK and, hopefully, as intended, will make routes into the profession more accessible. The timing, however, could hardly be more precarious. Universities are looking for savings wherever possible, while often failing to recognise the labour- and resource-intensive nature of design studio-based courses.

There is a deeper conflict at play, reaching down to the roots of the idea of the university. The European model, based on Humboldtian principles of academic freedom and the combination of teaching and research, understands teaching as an active, dialogic creative activity involving both teachers and students. It also frames education as a process of self-actualisation and personal development (Östling, 2018, p. 43). This model is increasingly confronted by the neoliberal university, in which employability, ever-growing cohort sizes, measurable outcomes and commercialisation define modern UK institutions.

In this context, it is not difficult to see how architecture is uniquely positioned – and uniquely tested – along the fault lines between these two models. As a discipline that depends on the individual realisation of creative potential traditionally associated with the profession yet is constrained by professional expectations for ready-for-practice graduates, architecture becomes a relatively small laboratory in which the Humboldtian model collides with the neoliberal one.

However, it is important to acknowledge that any apparent alignment between the architect as a lone creative genius and the Humboldtian ideal of holistic individual development is, at least in part, an unhappy accident. Rather than opening the profession up, it reinforces deeply entrenched and exclusionary assumptions about who an architect is, what they do and how they practise. The familiar image of architecture as an "old boys' club" is not just a stereotype: the recently published Fawcett Society report (2025), commissioned by RIBA, documents persistent structural barriers faced by women in the profession. It found that women are systematically paid less, contend with exclusionary workplace cultures, and see their careers disproportionately disrupted when they become mothers or carers. Most disturbingly, around half of the women surveyed reported experiencing misogyny or harassment at work.

The Workshop

In response to this fractured situation, architectural educators contributing to this book often choose to work within imagined institutions, partially ignoring – or actively subverting – dominant institutional narratives. This is probably why the idea of the "punk book" resonated so strongly in the early discussions. To make space for those discussions, we began the process of creating this book by inviting all interested potential contributors to take part in an all-day workshop, designed to provide dedicated time and space for conversation and creativity.

The workshop was devised with Professor Dan Jary, a colleague and mentor, now retired from the Sheffield School of Architecture and Landscape. Like this book itself, especially its subversive streak, it emerged through years of conversations with Dan, as we charted our growing disillusionment and compared notes on the never-ending game of reinvention, played out in an ever-shrinking space for experimentation.

The choice of venue was intentional: we used Live Works, the Sheffield School of Architecture and Landscape's "urban room", a space away from campus, in the city centre. The call for this book referenced institutional and professional pressures, as well as a "hidden curriculum" and the "resistance" of architectural educators facing those challenges. We also invited two types of contributions: longer academic texts aimed primarily at research staff, and shorter insights aimed primarily at teaching staff. This was intended to recognise the diverging pathways in UK academia, and the uneven time available for scholarship, particularly for colleagues on teaching-focused contracts.

The workshop took place on 3 July 2024 with 15 participants from universities across the UK and we planned it as a day of reflection and creative action. The reflection was structured around important pedagogical texts chiming with the themes of this book. We used excerpts from *Pedagogy of the Oppressed* (Freire, 1970), *Dumbing Us Down: The Hidden Curriculum of Compulsory Schooling* (Gatto, 1992), *Radical Pedagogies in Architectural*

Education (Colomina et al., 2022), *Starting a Free School of Architecture* (Forde, 2020), and *The Undercommons* (Harney and Moten, 2013). Participants formed small groups, and each was given an excerpt to read and discuss. We asked them to take their discussions out of the Live Works base and experience the city. After discussions, we asked participants to form a creative response to the readings and discussions, again, engaging with the city space.

It was intended, in part, to mirror the process of architectural inquiry in the design studio: students engage with theoretical frameworks through reading, respond to them creatively, and test ideas through contextual, often situated, engagement with a site. The participants were immediately on board with the premise, and there was a palpable sense of taking the workshop's playfulness very seriously. What emerged was not casual "fun", but focus: a deep commitment to the discussions and to the creative responses they generated.

One highlight was a memorable performance by Malcolm Miles, cosplaying university management in a riff on Paulo Freire, paper tie and all, lobbing cheap sweets at the audience. Alongside this were poems, ephemeral chalk street art, and a Live Works glass-door intervention bearing the word "Average", which baffled and delighted curious passers-by. The time we spent together reading, debating, making and laughing gave real weight to the final discussion, and it shaped several ideas that later surfaced in this book. We believe this book would be different, and perhaps less rich, without the workshop. Many of the threads that run through these chapters emerged on that warm July day in Sheffield, and they continue to hold this book together. As the collection will show, the core ethos of the workshop lives on. Our collections centre upon notions of dialogue, environmental responsibility and authenticity by creating practices and spaces for staff and students to produce unexpected and meaningful outputs.

We can hear the echoes of the more philosophical discussions covered at the workshop in the first section of this book, "Discussions". Here, our contributions discuss the precarious and crucial position of architectural educators in encouraging alternative perspectives on notions of uncertainty, polyphony, precedents and ecological awareness. There is also a clear "punkish" element to how some of our contributors to this first section utilise traditional "academic' structures like dissertations and studios to subvert and provide space for counterculture. Anyone who has ever attended anything like our exploratory workshop will be familiar with the journey of "what if" that Gidman takes us on in her fictionalised Other School.

As with all good discussions, the workshop did not just remain in the abstract. Contributors shared numerous examples from their practice of where they live out these theoretical contestations and debates in their daily practice. Many of these examples from the event are present in our "Insights" section, which typically brings together shorter, teaching-focused examples of creative practice. The studio, as a site of education, but also of contestation, is discussed in detail by several contributions, exploring its impact on the belonging of Foundation year students and what happens when we expand the boundaries of the studio all the way to the beach. Contributions discuss the transformative potential of feminist practice and the ways in which reflective teaching practices can help students unfold and explore their identities. We also end our collection with a manifesto advocating for making as a method of inquiry. These vignettes of practice were sprinkled throughout our event in July 2024 and helped to move discussions from the abstract to the concrete and back again.

Summary of Chapters

This book is split into two sections: "Discussions" brings together Chapters 1–7, while Chapters 8–13 are grouped into a section titled "Insights".

Chapter 1 sees Malcolm Miles chart and critique the development of Higher Education since the late nineteenth century. Miles explores the tensions between neoliberal approaches to HE and the pressures which exert themselves upon contemporary Architectural Education. This chapter posits three alternative approaches to architecture, seeking to reframe contemporary debates and questions in this area.

Across Chapter 2, Kasia Nawratek shares the parallels and intersections between her creative writing and architectural practices. Here, fiction which explores edgelands and a volumetric conceptualisation of landscape is echoed in architectural education practices using creative writing and linguistic methods. This chapter explores temporal, linguistic, spatial and translative perspectives foregrounding a practice which is caring, quietly subversive and transformative.

In Chapter 3, the leaders of Manchester School of Architecture's "And Architecture" atelier critically explore the role of precedents and precedent studies in architectural education. Here, Hammond, Holden and White show the value of encouraging students to apply precedents from outside of architecture to help students to explore positionality, ultimately developing and extending students' architectural identities and practices.

Chapter 4 details Udall, Lacey, Orlek and Schwartz-Narbonne's revelatory practice in working with soil. Here, we learn of their innovative design studio which not only develops students' architectural abilities, but also their ecological awareness and literacy. Through the analogy of "snorkelling in soil", they reveal that this practice leads to an increased environmental awareness among their students and a growth in students' perceptions and accommodation of environments and non-human actors within the design process.

In Chapter 5, Tanya Southcott explores creating space for subversion and contestation within the academic dissertation. As Southcott details, the dissertation is often positioned as vehicle for developing research and writing skills through specialist research studies. Here, however, this chapter charts the ways in which the dissertation becomes a space for individual student activism, providing a space for students to develop and contest discursive positions within the architectural discipline.

Chapter 6 sees Cith Skelcher raise and explore the future of the studio within architectural education. The studio is exposed here, with Skelcher calling for a critical appraisal of the inherent systemic barriers and inequalities in studio teaching. It is argued that only by doing this can we fully realise the transformative potential and pedagogical value of studio teaching.

In Chapter 7 we visit Anna Gidman's "Other School" – a fictional and idealised architectural school. Here, we take a thought-provoking tour through the Other School, exploring what a contemporary school of architecture may look like if academic regulations were more flexible, if learning and environment design were meaningfully co-created with students and if schools of architecture truly became civic hubs for the local community.

Chapter 8 sees the start of the "Insights" section. This chapter is written reflectively by Christopher Little and explores the process of being invited into the collection as an editor and as a non-creative academic. As an outsider to architectural practice, Little reflects upon the challenges facing university educators in 2026, before reflecting upon the innate sense of hope, care and resistance shown not just in this collection but in the workshop noted above. This chapter discusses the ways that creative architectural education practice offers moments of connection, student engagement, challenge and risk, contradicting common sector expectations.

In the first practice-focused "Insights" contribution, Chapter 9 sees Wei Shan Chia and Matthew Bradshaw discuss their "Life's a Beach" project at Sheffield School of Architecture and Landscape. Here, they detail how building sandcastles and protective beach tents provides space for students to explore the types of roles and challenges they may face in practice projects once qualified. This chapter discusses the processes of constructing their castles and tents, before seeing their castles reclaimed by the sea and repurposing the tent materials in the local community.

In Chapter 10, Rob Vinall discusses the role of the studio in fostering explorations of belonging and identity in Foundation Year students. Informed by experiential and open space learning, Vinall's chapter notes how the foundation studio site itself becomes more than a learning space, becoming a pedagogical space for experimentation, community and identity-development.

Lucretia Ray and Luke Bushnell-Wye, in Chapter 11, explore the reflective teaching processes through which they help students to unfold and shed "academic armour". Here, the discussion seminar course foregrounds critical reflection and creative thinking. Their practices centre upon discussion of topics such as experience, desire, participation, aurality and perception, to name a few.

Chapter 12 sees Emily Crompton of Manchester School of Architecture explore the ways in which feminist and queer pedagogical principles develop and expand students' considerations of inclusive architectural possibilities. Crompton details this practice by dissecting a series of revelatory teaching moments or "a-ha moments". Here, we see the impacts of challenging students' preconceptions around space and power, repositioning thereafter as relational, fluid and ethically programmed.

Finally, Chapter 13 sees Scott Miller's "Manifesto for Making" exploring how iterative modelmaking fosters inclusive and transformative learning. The manifesto calls for better recognition of technical staff as educators and integrated studio-workshop cultures. Here, Miller advocates for reinstating physical making as a core component of architectural education, not as nostalgic craft but as a vital complement to digital design.

Ten Years Later

As we finish the manuscript in early 2026, it is now just over ten years since the publication of *Radical Pedagogies: Architectural Education and the British Tradition* (2015), edited by Daisy Froud and Harriet Harriss. That book mattered to us: it was a milestone in UK debates on architectural education and, when we began work on *Pedagogy as Creative Practice*, we were told, more than once, that it follows in *Radical Pedagogies'* footsteps.

We agree. Rereading it brings a kind of joyful recognition when the accounts chime so closely with our own experiences, followed by a pang of realisation about how the last decade has unfolded. The UK context is eerily familiar, but the pressures have intensified: rising tuition costs, accreditation changes, and the discipline's ongoing – seemingly permanent – identity crisis. Schools are pulled and stretched thin between practice, regulation, and the university. In that sense, *Radical Pedagogies* sits at an uncannily similar moment to ours: facing accreditation reform while being pressed from all directions.

The most striking realisation comes when Harriss writes about "the endless questioning how we make architectural education 'better'" and notes that

> Better is simply no longer good enough, and it doesn't address the fundamental challenges that today's educators and students face. These require new reserves of imagination, tenacity and the ability not just to dream but to deliver. (…) Professionalism must go beyond compliance-driven tropes of credentialism that maintain the status quo. In other words, maybe we need to do more than just accept, or tweak, the established system.
>
> *(Harriss, 2015, p. xii)*

From the vantage point of early 2026, challenging the status quo, and even the ambition to make architectural education "better", can sound like an unattainable luxury. We remain hopeful and ambitious, but "better" can feel just out of reach when it would require time, attention and labour that have been tied up elsewhere: administrative duties, heavy teaching workloads and the ongoing pressure to conduct research.

And then there is the pandemic, with its long wake. When we finally returned to something like normality, changed, transformed, but proud to have weathered the storm, we expected calmer sailing ahead. That did not happen. Instead, as many universities began making cuts, our jobs were on the line.

Reading Harriss's words now can feel like assuming the role of the glamorously world-weary character in William Gibson's *Agency* (2020), who remarks with eerie precision:

> "They're still a bit in advance of the pandemics, at least." (...) "Nothing before the 2020s has ever seemed entirely real, to me. Hard to imagine they weren't constantly happy, given all they still had. Tigers, for instance".
>
> *(Gibson, 2020, p. 53)*

Our lost tigers are the working conditions that make it possible to exercise creativity – to question, to experiment, and to respond meaningfully to a status quo that increasingly demands compliance rather than imagination.

Where we differ is in geography. In the epilogue, Harriss and Froud note their London-centrism (p. 194). Our collection deliberately shifts the centre of gravity northwards: nine of the thirteen chapters discuss pedagogy in Manchester, Sheffield and Liverpool. This is hardly accidental. Both editors are based at Manchester Metropolitan University and have longstanding professional links to the region.

Looking ahead to the next ten years, and hoping someone will write the follow-up, we wish for ourselves, the discipline, and schools of architecture to get our tigers back. We believe that what we do in architectural education is not separate from the so-called real world of practice. We are not looking down from the heights of an ivory tower: we are down-to-earth, using an ever-diminishing space for critical reflection to question, challenge and improve the status quo.

References

Architects Registration Board (ARB) (n.d.) *Tomorrow's architects: FAQs*. Available at: https://arb.org.uk/information-for-schools-of-architecture/tomorrows-architects-faqs/ (Accessed: 30 December 2025).

Colomina, B., Galán, I. G., Kotsioris, E. and Meister, A.-M. (eds.) (2022) *Radical pedagogies*. Cambridge, MA: The MIT Press.

Cruise, M., Clare, W. and Wilson, S. (2025) 'Level 7 apprenticeships are making architecture more inclusive – why cut their funding?'. *BD Online*, 29 June. Available at: https://www.bdonline.co.uk/opinion/level-7-apprenticeships-are-making-architecture-more-inclusive-why-cut-their-funding/5136757.article (Accessed: 30 December 2025).

Fawcett Society (2025) *Build it together: progress & planning towards gender equity in the architecture sector*. Available at: https://www.fawcettsociety.org.uk/Handlers/Download.ashx?IDMF=264609e1-2821-4a28-ae74-93dbbc00a6a4 (Accessed: 5 November 2025).

Forde, T. (2020) 'Starting a free school of architecture', *Charrette*, 6(1), pp. 121–143. Available at: https://www.ingentaconnect.com/content/arched/char/2020/00000006/00000001 (Accessed: 28 December 2025).

Freire, P. (1970) *Pedagogy of the oppressed*. Translated by M. B. Ramos. New York: Continuum. (Originally published 1968).

Froud, D. and Harriss, H. (eds.) (2015) *Radical pedagogies: architectural education and the British tradition*. Newcastle upon Tyne: RIBA Publishing.

Gatto, J. T. (1992) *Dumbing us down: the hidden curriculum of compulsory schooling*. Philadelphia, PA: New Society Publishers.

Gibson, W. (2020) *Agency*. London: Viking.

Harney, S. and Moten, F. (2013) *The undercommons: fugitive planning and black study*. Wivenhoe: Minor Compositions.

Östling, J. (2018) *Humboldt and the Modern German University: an intellectual history*. Translated by L. Olsson. Lund: Lund University Press.

Ravenscroft, T. (2025) 'Architecture no longer considered a "professional degree" in US'. *Dezeen*, 24 November. Available at: https://www.dezeen.com/2025/11/24/architecture-degree-not-professional-usa/ (Accessed: 30 December 2025).

Royal Institute of British Architects (RIBA) (2025) *Build it together: Progress and planning towards gender equity in the architecture profession*. Available at: https://www.riba.org/campaigns/policies/build-it-together-gender-equity-in-architecture/ (Accessed: 5 November 2025).

Royal Institute of British Architects (RIBA) (n.d.) *Changes to studying architecture*. Available at: https://www.riba.org/learn/become-an-architect/studying-architecture/changes-to-studying-architecture/ (Accessed: 30 December 2025).

Spocchia, G. (2025) 'RIBA's war on ARB: 90% of profession in support, AJ survey says', *Architects' Journal*, 15 December. Available at: https://www.architectsjournal.co.uk/news/ribas-war-on-arb-90-of-profession-in-support-aj-survey-says (Accessed: 30 December 2025).

Williamson, C. and Gordon, A. (2025) 'RIBA president: Why I resigned from the ARB', *Architects' Journal*, 16 December. Available at: https://www.architectsjournal.co.uk/news/opinion/riba-president-why-i-resigned-from-the-arb (Accessed: 30 December 2025).

Discussions

1

UNCERTAINTY AS AN EDUCATIONAL METHOD

Malcolm Miles

England is a backward place in which to teach or practice architecture (and much else). The malaise is not recent – a prejudice against intellectuals is ingrained in English culture – but the rise of neoliberalism renders the built environment and institutions of higher education subject to market values amid increasingly nasty culture wars. Knowledge is reclassified as redundant – or subversive – expertise while, historian Tony Judt writes, "the panoptic control that the modern state can exercise over its subjects has continued to expand" (2010, p. 107).

Higher education is where such restrictive, anti-rational currents should be resisted. Instead, marketised, competitive managerialism has replaced administration for the public good as its organising principle, reversing the ethos of the post-war Welfare State (and longer histories of liberal reformism and socialism). Now, the need is to reclaim higher education for critical practices in architecture, and in the arts, humanities and social sciences generally, whereby received imperatives are rejected, alternatives examined and a radical imagination grows. Below, I outline the difficulties faced by higher education in the arts, humanities and social sciences today, reconsider their more progressive inheritances, and cite cases of alternative approaches in architectural discourse: a subjective sense of place; spatial co-production and a proposal for a new, transdisciplinary Bauhaus.

Backwards and Forwards ...

The arts, humanities and social sciences threaten the neoliberal order because they refuse to manufacture solutions, instead re-writing questions and re-investigating the contexts from which the questions emerge. They

DOI: 10.4324/9781003647720-3

combine a pursuit of knowledge for its own sake – which is a classical legacy, separating pure thought from utility – with a (useful) desire to make a better world. Squaring this circle is problematic but produces a space between the polarities of pure rationality and utopian desire: not a grey area, more a kaleidoscope, a way to extend the horizon of the possible. Critical theorist Slavoj Žižek writes,

> ... state and business institutions complain all the time about how humanities serve no purpose, and how universities should be made to serve the needs of actual life (i.e. of capital). But what if this, precisely, is what makes our enormous education system so precious? It serves no clearly defined goal, it just multiplies useless culture, refined thinking, sensitivity to art, etc?
>
> *(2023, p. 51)*

Indeed, this should be celebrated, including the absence of a predefined goal: that is, a non-teleological scrutiny of realities (plural) which is incompatible with a system of predetermined ends and prescribed – usually entrepreneurial – outputs.

The new managerialism regards this as day-dreaming, invalid in the immaterial economy of late capitalism in which the arts are subsumed in the cultural industries sector (with public relations, advertising and financial services). Architecture is similarly subordinated to urban redevelopment, exemplified by prestige projects presented in suave digital animation. This starchitecture, and the celebrity status and wealth of winners in art and architecture, attracts students who are aware of the declining public sector. Of course, other pedagogies are available: development architecture; social housing; co-design; and the re-purposing of buildings in city centres, the latter a growth area post-Covid. These offer engagement rather than glamour, in which context, architect Jeremy Till describes participatory urbanism "as an opportunity to reformulate, and thus resuscitate, architectural practice" (2009, p. 25).

That reformulation began some decades back, as in Walter Segal's modernist designs for self-build housing in Lewisham; and in the fusion of aesthetics and industry in the Bauhaus, first in Weimar then in Dessau. Power-relations and privilege are not always challenged: architect Peter Sulzer asserts that only the architect can "develop an ordering structure ... it cannot be done by the users" (2009, p. 159) but he admits that part of the architect's role is in gaining permissions, using professional clout as much as design skills (p. 160). The role of facilitator has a parallel advance in planning practice and discourse, described by planning academic Leonie Sandercock as "knowing through dialogue" (1998, p. 76). It means that local, tacit knowledge is valued as equal to technical and intellectual knowledges, refusing the elitism of the classical separation of abstract from useful knowledge while retaining the value of knowledge over prejudice or dictate.

Knowledge was key to the European Enlightenment but identified with power. For Thomas Hobbes, the lack of "a common Power" to keep people in awe produces only chaos, with "no commodious Buildings ... no Arts; no Letters; no Society", only fear and likely violent death ([1651] 2017, pp. 102–103). Against that grimness, notions of an innately good human nature such as Jean-Jacques Rousseau's idea of a once-pure humanity since corrupted, or efforts towards realisation of universal Reason as eventual freedom and happiness, are leaps of faith, not deduction. There is no panacea. Still, Matthew Arnold wrote of culture as a defence against social chaos after the fracturing of organised religion, looking to an educated middle class as its vehicle (1869). The expansion of university education since then might be read as extending the base for precisely that project, cultivating critically imaginative practices – my own is theory – to contribute to a better world. I write this chapter in that spirit, realising that this retains the paradox of a non-teleological approach (learning as self-justifying end) merged with a useful, and politicised, end (a better world). But the new managerialism has no interest in philosophical problems, fixated on league tables, brand-images, quantitative rather than qualitative data, benchmarks and borrowed, if out-dated, macho-management.

The Knowledge Mill

The rot was evident by the millennium. To give two anecdotal instances: a colleague in an architecture school said the Millennium Bridge in Newcastle-Gateshead should not have won the 2002 RIBA Stirling Prize because, lacking a roof, it was not a building. A year before, at a conference on higher education in art and design, a keynote speaker from a business school said universities should model themselves on a well-known supermarket: a narrow, mechanistic definition of the field and an already-pervasive marketisation.

Architectural discourses offered alternative approaches: Iain Borden's *Skateboarding, Space and the City* (2001) on skateboarding as embodied architecture; *Non-Plan*, edited by Jonathan Hughes and Simon Sadler (2000), on participatory urbanism; Leonie Sandercock's *Towards Cosmopolis* (1998) on planning for multicultural cities; *Occupying Architecture*, edited by Jonathan Hill (1998), on adaptations of spaces and meanings; *Architecture and Revolution*, edited by Neil Leach, set in post-Cold War Europe (1999); *Architecture of the Everyday*, edited by Steven Harris and Deborah Berke (1997) on the quotidian; Peter Hall's *Cities of Tomorrow* (revised, 1996) on urban visions; and Beatriz Colomina's *Privacy and Publicity* (1996), a feminist critique of Le Corbusier. Contextually, geographer Doreen Massey (1994; 2005) did much to introduce the ideas of French Marxist sociologist Henri Lefebvre to urban theory, and sociologist Richard Sennett explored the relation of urban space to the human body in *Flesh and Stone* (1994). The above are only a few of the titles contributing to lively debates in the approach to the millennium. *Strangely Familiar* (1996), edited by Borden, Joe Kerr, Jane Rendell and Alicia Pivaro, included a representative range of contributions from feminist and post-colonial positions, and off-beat stories of past and cities and city lives. Among emerging tendencies were an emphasis on transdisciplinary knowledge and participation (Blundell-Jones, Petrescu and Till, 2005); urban ecology (Rawes, 2013); multi-sensory perceptions (Degen, 2008); and conceptual architecture (Rendell, 2007).

Those were resistant voices. They remain, but the market has won. At first, the aim of liberal education – a better world – was merely re-directed in a narrower, functionalist way. Zizec cites the Bologna reforms – beginning in 1999, standardising academic qualifications in the European Union – as subordinating learning to economic and social needs, "to make it useful in relation to the concrete problems we are facing ... producing expert opinions meant to resolve the problems posed by social agents" (2011, p. 411). He reads this as an attack on the public use of reason when the real need is to reflect critically on how problems emerge, "to re-formulate them, to discern a problem in the very way we perceive such problems" (2011, p. 411). He also cites the selective phasing out, in Britain in the 2010s, of state funding: "higher education in arts, humanities and social sciences will become a market deal between universities and private individuals who wish to pursue such subjects entirely at their own cost" (2011, p. 411). In effect, this is a reductive return to eighteenth-century bourgeois efforts at wealth accumulation and class domination. The difference now is that the merchant class has been replaced as driver of enterprise by global capital in its opaque, often violent, and all-pervasive form.

Marketisation and managerialism have won. Education is work-training; research is product development; universities are outlets in a knowledge mall where experiences and solutions are all. Judt writes, "the market-as-metaphor dominates conversation. Deans and heads of departments are constrained to assess output and economic impact when judging the quality of someone's work" (2010, p. 117). Except that managers have little interest in content; much can happen beneath the radar.

Grim Times

There is a history of anti-intellectualism and anti-modernism in English culture, if perhaps less in higher education. Hungarian immigrant Georges Mikes wrote, in *How to Be a Brit,* "In England it is bad manners to be clever" ([1946] 1981, p. 32). Writing on the arrival in Britain of avant-garde intellectuals fleeing Nazi Germany in the 1930s, architectural critic Owen Hatherley notes Bauhaus director Walter Gropius' revulsion at the weather and the food; and that, "Great Britain, as seen through the eyes of these newly arrived refugees … [was] insular and monocultural, cold and emotionless" (2025, p. 22). Things have changed, he says, apart from the bad housing, but the changes are uneven. On the one hand, a flourishing, critical discourse of the built environment continues (exemplified above), still to an extent informed by Bauhaus ideals of social and technological progress; on the other hand, there is a widening wealth gap, precarious employment (including in universities) and a disregard for learning.

Zizec notes (above) that the arts, humanities and social sciences are casualties because they deal in questions, not answers, *in contingencies, not certainties* and might accurately be viewed by servants of market totalitarianism as resistant. Political scientist Wendy Brown writes of a grim scenario in North America, too,

> After more than a century of public education construed and funded as a medium for egalitarianism and social mobility and as a means of achieving a broadly educated democracy … public higher education … is increasingly structured to entrench rather than redress class trajectories. As it devotes itself to enhancing the value of human capital, it now abjures the project of producing a public readied for participation in popular sovereignty.
>
> *(2015, p. 184)*

Similarly, for critical theorist Nancy Fraser, "extending liberal arts education from the elite to the many was nothing short of a radical democratic event" (Brown, p. 184) while its reversal reveals the market as the sole "site of veridiction" in human activity (p. 67) while "economic principles become the model for state conduct, the economy becomes the primary object of state concern and policy, and the marketization of domains and conduct' is disseminated" (p. 62). Dark times, indeed, when, "financialised capitalism is … governance without … the fig leaf of consent" and private wealth occupies the state (Brown, 2023, p. 130).

Things get worse when the managerial device of permanent crisis is introjected. As political theorist Isabel Lorey, citing sociologist Robert Castel (2003) argues, precarity is like "a virus that permeates everyday life, dissolving social ties and undermining the physical structures of the individual" (2015, p. 51). Neoliberalism becomes "a normalised political-economic instrument" (2015, p. 39). Judt argues, too, "Our disability is *discursive*: we simply do not know how to talk about these things anymore" (2010, p. 34, original emphasis). But he adds that this is not instinctive, which I read as suggesting an exit in a leap of radical refusal. For Lorey, too, "in dealing with *contingency*, the possibility arises … of being able to leave and start something new … of exodus and constituting" (2015, pp. 104–105; original emphasis).

Higher education has a key role in renewing and extending critical positions, especially in the arts, humanities and social sciences. In that context, architectural education may reconsider what constitutes a building or a city, whether housing is a noun or a verb, and whether both practice and education might beneficially be extricated from the cultural industries with their burden of urban branding and redevelopment. Sociologist Justin O'Connor argues that, in any case, the sector is past its sell-by date: "largely absent from the visions being proposed as a way out of the interregnum" (2024, p. 78). In contrast, for O'Connor, "the everyday economy is about the continual making and remaking of places and our goal should be the retention of this public value for communities" (2024, p. 223). Paolo Gebaudo writes, too,

> After years in which democratic decision-making has been appropriated by technocrats and businessmen [sic], the present organic crisis of capitalist democracies calls for the establishment of new democratic institutions by means of which political communities might recover some control over their destiny.
>
> *(2021, p. 11)*

Instead of romanticising the *polis*, this means seeing and producing it in new ways. These include collective-collaborative practices like Assemble, winner of the Turner Prize in 2015; and reconsiderations of spatial agency in a fusion of design, construction and occupation. If this appears utopian, I cite philosopher Simon Critchley,

> … it is part of the duty of philosophy to construct concepts that allow us to imagine that another city and another world are possible, however difficult that may be to achieve in practice.
>
> *(2012, p. 93)*

And the obligation, too, of higher education.

Legacies

Although universities in Europe began as theological institutions, and were in that sense vocational, in the late nineteenth century the idea of transferable knowledge – as product of pure research, applicable in any field – informed their expansion. This widened access to professions, mainly for men; and encouraged free enquiry, following the Kantian ideal of free thinking based on disinterested judgement (free from vested interests). This was the position advanced in Germany by sociologist Max Weber, seeking education's freedom from political influence; and by Wilhelm von Humboldt, founder of Berlin University, who saw universities as giving scope for the fuller evolution of humanity. Journalist Stuart Jeffries glosses, "the subject of knowledge was … the speculative spirit. Universities … must lay open the whole body of learning" (2021, p. 97). Brown, too, writes of, "the core of the Humboldtian model of education … [as being] internally unbiased and independent of external influence" (2023, p. 63). In parallel, aesthetics, then a recent branch of philosophy, pursued the ideal of art for art's sake.

At the same time, there were extensive efforts at self-improvement, especially but not only in literacy, in working-class communities across Europe. In England, institutional support was provided by the Guild of St George, founded by art critic John Ruskin in 1871, with courses in design and craft supporting rural economies. In London, Canon Samuel Barnett proposed university settlements in working-class areas, serving "a common purpose of improving the lives of the people" (1888, p. 101). Arguing that "the Settlement would be common ground for all social classes … the students would exchange ideas and form friendships … the residents would mingle freely in the crowd" (p. 103). Barnett, with his wife Henrietta, founded Toynbee Hall in East London in 1884 as an educational vehicle for social change. Then in 1905, the Workers' Educational Association was established, with branches across Britain. By the mid-century, literary scholar Richard Hoggart, within the emerging field of Cultural Studies, reported, "The economic barriers to knowledge have been largely removed" (1958, p. 321), as 150,000 people participated in "the liberal, non-vocational study of humanities … organised by voluntary bodies and university extra-mural departments" (p. 320).

Perhaps it was no coincidence that Clement Atlee and William Beveridge, founders of the Welfare State, had attended Toynbee Hall. But the task was not simply to extend access to higher education, it was also to widen fields within it, to see knowledge as deriving from and in turn re-shaping the whole of society. Economic historian R. H. Tawney argued in a lecture in 1933 that history had not hitherto understood economic factors in social change; although there was empirical material, the construction of a pattern or argument was missing ([1933] 1978, pp. 48–54). Interpretation, he said, is indispensable for history as the study of "the life of society" (p. 54). This required an inter-disciplinary approach entailing "the economic foundations, the political superstructure and the dynamic of ideas" of any period (p. 64).

Tawney supported the Workers' Educational Association, and saw widening educational access as redefining the university as an institution for "those who are not studying for the purpose of any profession except that of a reasonable and humane conduct of life" (1966, p. 84). The Atlee government (1945–1951) pursued such humane ideas, in context of advances in technologies and social equality celebrated in the Festival of Britain in 1951, by widening access to higher education. In 1945 there were 50,000 university places; by 1961 this had risen to 107,000, with much of the expansion in new universities. Historian David Kynaston notes that curricula did not change, apart from increased provision for science (2007, p. 462), but that graduates were seen as "the elite of tomorrow" (2013, p. 220). This sounds conservative in retaining the model of an elite, now a technocratic class; yet the point was also to radically widen access to it. In one way, then, the post-war Welfare State is a late version of liberal reformism's attempt to buy off insurrection by providing better conditions: housing, public transport and sewers in the nineteenth century; housing, health and higher education in the twentieth. But, in another way, like the genii let out of the bottle, learning breaks boundaries; the newly available higher education was not work-training but an exemption from the pressures of employment enabling free, non-prescriptive enquiry.

In contrast, under neoliberalism education is transactional. Fraser writes, "central banks and global financial institutions have replaced states as the arbiters of … consequential rules that govern the central relations of capitalist society" (2023, pp. 127–128). Brown reflects that "'fearless, critical analysis of values, consideration of the knowledges necessary to form them … and identification of their importance to individual and collective freedom and futurity – these are hardly the principles by which most university curriculums are designed today" (2023, p. 107). This is one reason to recall those other, liberal, utopian and socialist histories of learning which were foundational to the expansion of higher education in the British Welfare State. As said above, this squares the circle of free thinking and social benefit (or social engineering): learning in the arts, humanities have intrinsic worth; and is a vehicle for social mobility (such as mine, a grammar schoolboy from the suburbs who went to art school). So, while Jeffries writes, "when knowledge became like money such stories were obsolete" (2021, p. 97) that depends on the extent to which the memories are buried rather than reconsidered. Besides, the project, like Enlightenment, is yet incomplete.

Centres and Margins?

Applying Tawny's ideas to architectural education would introduce technological, political, social and cultural frameworks. The newly available higher education of the Welfare State was explicitly not work-training, and the benefit of a non-productivity-led regime might well be remembered now. Additionally, since the 1970s, most discourses have been reframed by feminism and post-colonialism. From Lefebvre, too, the power-relations of spatial practice have been interrogated. All this leads to challenges to received conceptualisations such as centre-margin, subject-object and teaching-learning.

In this vein, Sandercock looks to what she calls voices from the borderlands,

> ... people who dwell in cultures of displacement and transplantation, to cultures with a long history of repression, to people who have been marginalised for hundreds of years, but who are now insurgent, and who are turning their very marginality into a creative space for theorising.
>
> *(1998, p. 111)*

For Sandercock, such voices articulate difference, now a commonly used term in cultural and social theory, and in areas of planning practice. But this also reminds me of the role of people conventionally called users in planning and architecture (who are dwellers, experts on their own places), and Lefebvre's construct of lived space: spaces which people adapt, appropriate and overlay with association, memory, desire and familiarity. Lefebvre argued that space is historically specific, multivalent and variable. Lived space is always in tension with the Cartesian space of plans: the "representations of space" of "scientists, planners, urbanists, technocratic subdividers and social engineers" (1991, p. 38) which are uniform, unlimited, and defined by geometric coordinates, not by experience.

For René Descartes, writing in the 1630s, during the Thirty Years' War, such space, like the fields of geometry and mathematics, provided certainty in a world torn by religious conflicts. But its price was a new orthodoxy. Lefebvre writes,

> Within the spatial practice of modern society, the architect ensconces himself [sic] in his own space. He has a *representation of this space*, one which is bound to graphic elements – to sheets of paper, plans, elevations, sections, perspective views of façades, modules, and so on. This *conceived* space is thought by those who make it to be *true*, despite the fact – or perhaps because of the fact – that it is geometrical ... locus of the objectification of plans.
>
> *(1991, p. 361, emphasis original)*

If Sandercock draws attention to voices from the borderlands (which are not borderlands to people who inhabit them), Lefebvre looks to the relation of subject and object, which is also centre and margin, to render it resistantly reversible. That is, urban redevelopment inscribes new centres which marginalise adjacent neighbourhoods; but the experiences of people who live and work in such neighbourhoods enhance their centrality when voiced.

The difficulty is that such voices are relegated as anecdotal: tacit knowledge. The same power-relation informs the conventional city plan, the architect's master plan and the use of linear perspective to render space as distancing vistas. Massey writes, "the privileging of vision impoverishes us through deprivation of other forms of sensory perception" (1994, p. 232). Further, the purpose of devices such as the god's eye view of the city plan is to ensure a detachment which de-humanises space, as if uncontentious, while unequal power-relations are lent a veil of neutrality through old devices like statues and memorials, or new ones like surveillance, crisis and the introjection of market values.

By the 2000s, radical ideas abounded in planning, architecture and urban design practices, and across the arts, humanities and social sciences in education. The resulting revisioning of urbanism revolved around contingency and mutability. In 2006, Sandercock wrote,

> ... negotiating peaceful intercultural coexistence, block by block, neighbourhood by neighbourhood, will become a central preoccupation of citizens as well as urban professionals and politicians. The right to the city is the right of all residents to presence throughout the city, the right to inhabit and appropriate public space, and the right to participate as an equal in public affairs, to be engaged in debating and designing the future of the city and creating new ... ways of being together.
>
> *(2006, p. 48)*

Sandercock may romanticise struggle but there are two important points: the attention to local scale; and the implication that not all voices will be in agreement: an agonistic politics. This implies co-subjecthood. For Lefebvre, "appropriation is defined by ... the priority of use and value over exchange and exchange value; a community that works space for its own use; collective management of the produced space" (2014, p. 95).

The idea of a community producing its own space, incidentally, echoes the radical pedagogy evolved by Paulo Freire in adult literacy groups in Brazil in the 1960s, arguing that "critical and liberating dialogue, which presupposes action, must be carried on with the oppressed at whatever stage their struggle for liberation has reached" (1972, p. 41). Freire's method was to ask students to share their life experiences, valuing their tacit knowledge while inviting reflection: "it is necessary to trust in the oppressed and in their ability to reason" (1972, p. 41). This extricates learning from the power-relation of explaining the world to those assumed to be unable to do so themselves. Freire writes,

> Narration (with the teacher as narrator) leads the students to memorize mechanically the narrated content ... turns them into containers, into receptacles to be filled by the teacher. ... Education thus becomes an act of depositing, in which the students are the depositories and the teacher

> is the depositor. ... This is the banking concept of education, in which the scope of action allowed to the students extends only so far as receiving, filing, and storing the deposits.
>
> *(pp. 45–46)*

Knowledge emerges through a shared, "restless, impatient, continuing, hopeful inquiry people pursue in the world, with the world, with each other" (p. 46). In architecture in the global North, this translates into the "alternative creative spaces" which architect Robert Hollands sees, "beyond the egalitarian art squats and collectives of the 1960s" including "community interest companies, charities, partnerships, volunteer-led, social or cultural enterprises, not-for-profit companies" (2023, p. 64).

This is not learning from the borderlands, but learning in situations in which centre-margin, object-subject relations are creatively re-thought. For Lorey, "the first step in this direction is disobedience, the refusal of servile virtuosity" (2025, p. 105). Since managerialism expresses little interest in content rather than metrics, higher education may yet offer modes of enquiry which emphasise contingency over solutions, and ground content in uncertainty.

Sites – Osnabrück

Psychoanalyst and writer Hélène Cixous visits Osnabrück, a prosperous, bourgeois city where her Jewish mother lived until 1933. Witches were previously drowned there earlier. The synagogue was burned in 1938, some of its stones now parcelled in wire cages:

> ... I walk a few metres and I am standing before the wire mesh ... tightly packed with blond stones. On each side ... two clean, well-buffed engraved copper tablets. The metal pages tell the same story twice ... Once I made people believe, people looked at me fervently, like the cinema when it began, I lived in the most pleasant and richest district ... A bare space between two houses. Imprisoned in wire mesh ... what remains ... bones strewn on the ground after the fire. A neat collection of bone. Like hens, the well-kept ruins in their coop of rubble.
>
> *(2022, pp. 64–65)*

The voice moves from first-person author to mute stones, the focus from present to past. Cixous begins, narrating the writing of this book and her visits to Osnabrück,

> The book had already begun, I was running, I was remembering I was forgetting I was seeing: no sooner had I found than I lost, I misplaced, more

> and more, I was going down the streets … in 1648, in 9, in 1561, in 1942, in 2020 … in the middle of Troy's ramparts.
>
> *(p. 3)*

And, in a free-floating text,

> Only on my third expedition – from innocent visit I've progressed to an increasingly well-mapped campaign, henceforth I go like Champollion, ebullient at just the thought – did I "see" the Old Synagogue, but not really, I mis-saw it by accident, I saw without seeing it … I felt a cloud darken my right eye … I find myself in the obsessive state of mind of the nineteenth-century archaeologist who thinks he's found the sacred site of the originary scene … I cross mountains valleys tides, I grow old …
>
> *(p. 28)*

This is text, postmodern in its self-referencing; also, a purposive use of the first-person and equally purposive un-marked transition to other, abstracted voices. It stretches syntax and punctuation as signifiers; and offers a more or less factual account of her visits, shaded by her mother's move from Nazi Germany to an Algeria later afflicted by further conflict.

The roles of subject and object are problematised: Cixous is a subject (self), and an actor in the situation she experiences and observes. And the spaces in which she goes are also active agents (subjects). Space and place are inter-produced, stated and dis-integrated.

Elemental Building

Elemental is an architectural practice in Chile, concerned with social housing and the co-production of built environments. A pilot project was the design and construction of houses for squatter families in the centre of the port city of Iquique, in 2000, on the plots they had occupied for decades and within a budget of $7,500 per dwelling (including infrastructure). It was important not to evacuate dwellers to the city margins where land was cheaper, which meant that the budget could cover only half of the construction costs. Elemental's response was to build part-houses: the essential structure with services, kitchen and bathroom. Completion, allowing for adaptation, was handed to dwellers:

> With the tradition and skills of self-building that squatter families acquire through need, they would be able to in-fill and complete the house given a well-designed framework from which to start. … as the houses are added to over time, they gain value and their rather stark original design is softened through occupation and use.
>
> *(Awan, Schneider and Till, 2011, p. 144)*

This is, roughly, what occupiers of Le Corbusier's model housing scheme in Pessac, near Bordeaux, did through extensions, in-fills and decoration, much to the consternation of architectural purists (Boudon, 1972). A similar model was used in South African townships, from the 1990s onwards, providing basic elements for people well-versed in building squatter houses from scrap materials. Architect Chinedu Umenyilora writes, "the architect designs the seed, and the self-builder creates the flower" (2000, p. 217).

In all cases, dwellers are spatial agents, taking on themselves the task of making a built environment which is home, and a facet of the image of the city. Architect Doina Petrescu calls such processes *bricolage*, borrowing the term from anthropologist Claude Levi-Strauss; she sees it driven by desire:

> Driven by desire, participatory design is a collective bricolage in which individuals (clients, users, designers) are able to interrogate the heterogeneity of a situation, to acknowledge their own position and then go beyond it, to open up new meanings, new possibilities, to collage their own collage into other collages, in order to discover a common project.
>
> *(2005, p. 45)*

For the squatters at Iquique it might be thought that the aim was simply shelter. Yet on what basis are these dwellers aesthetically disenfranchised, or taken as unable to socialise their situation?

New Bauhaus?

Finally, a report by Christian Bason from the Danish Design Centre, Rowan Conway from an innovation network, Dan Hill from the Swedish innovation agency, and Mariana Mazzucato, Professor of the Economics of Innovation and Public Value at University College London: *A New Bauhaus for a Green New Deal* (2021).

The Bauhaus was a school of art, design and architecture identified with progressive socio- cultural formations and an internationalism aligned to the Left. Bason, Conway, Hill and Mazzucato "retrofit" the idea of the Bauhaus (2021, p. 2), asserting that the technology exists for a green society but that the obstacles are "behavioural, cultural, political and economic". This reminds me of Herbert Marcuse's claim in 1967 that "the material and intellectual forces which could be put to work for the realisation of a free society are at hand,' but blocked by vested interests" (1970, p. 64).

The report seeks cooperative methods, transdisciplinary expertise and an open, participatory spirit to enact their aims. Bason *et al* also say that while design can do much, the need is to redesign economics, too. Optimism merges into received constructs:

> The imaginative capacity of design, art and architecture actively creates possible futures, making tangible and motivating the numerous diverse

> and complex scenarios implicit in the Green Deal. Europe's skillset here is unparalleled.
>
> *(2021, p. 3)*

The report asserts that the New Bauhaus could develop a toolkit for design, aiding clients as well as architects while re-working "the cultures that shape public life" (Bason et al., 2021). This could imply participative construction; or an elite view, improving the worlds of others for them. It is the problem faced by Freire (above). The key factor is that all knowledges – tacit, technical and intellectual – are equally valid. This is not to deny the value of academic and professional skills – that would be nonsense – but that knowledges require appropriate modes of practice.

The report is well-intentioned, and architects and planners can (and do) lend weight to the efforts of communities to gain better, more equitable spaces. I also agree that, when it is difficult to imagine what does not yet exist there is a need for prototypes to demonstrate material possibilities, and for pilot schemes to demonstrate viability. Interestingly, the co-authors opt for retrofit as a new architectural practice:

> The New Bauhaus must fully embrace the recent and burgeoning interest in a design focused on care and culture as much as form and function, reversing the 20th century's extractive modes by working with retrofit, repair, restoration and regeneration.
>
> *(p. 4)*

This reduces carbon emissions and invites broad participation because, unlike a new site, inhabited sites have resident publics with stories to share. The need for planning remains, but this includes radical planning, when the planner engages with mobilised communities to represent their ideas to the authorities. The report adds, "the white cubes at Dessau [the purpose-built second home of the Bauhaus] stand for blank voids, ready to be filled with vibrant, novel colour" (p. 7). Similarly, perhaps, a university can be "flipped inside-out" (p. 7) as it enters the public sphere of agonistic contestation.

No more silos, either technical or professional. Instead, transdisciplinary co-design. This is where the report voices a key sentiment:

> The divergent thinking of artists can help continually reimagine and refresh our futures, requiring us to sometimes dwell in the messy unknown. We need spaces, physical and digital, built and imagined, in which we can safely disagree in public, in which we can *pursue uncertainty fruitfully*.
>
> *(p. 11, my emphasis)*

Uncertainty, continual re-framing of questions, as a basis for architectural education is a path to designing buildings and using materials, but also to constructing meanings. For Petrescu, "participation should be understood as a progressive and evolving process that constructs itself inferentially … adjusting its aims according to the newly created situations" (p. 53). There are no guarantees; the future has no grand design.

This resolves the squared circle of free enquiry and social benefit inasmuch as the means (enacting espoused values) already constitute, and directly produce, the outcome. The means *are* the end. I give the last word to critical theorist Raymond Geuss:

> First, meaning (and consequently knowledge) is essentially contextual; second, meaning must be a collective, that is, a social phenomenon; third, there is no final all-encompassing framework which puts everything together; finally, the absence of such a framework … does not entirely destroy the phenomenon of local meaning.
>
> *(2020, p. 163)*

References

Arnold, M. ([1869] 1889) *Culture and Anarchy*. Smith Elder and Co.

Awan, N., Schneider, T. and Till, J. (2011) *Spatial Agency: Other Ways of Doing Architecture*. Routledge.

Barnett, S.A. and Barnett, H.O., (1888) *Practicable Socialism: Essays on Social Reform*. Longmans Green.

Bason, C., Conway, R., Hill, D. and Mazzucato, M. (2021) *A New Bauhaus for a Green Deal*. Available at: www.ucl.ac.uk/bartlett/public-purpose/publications/2021/jan/new-bauhaus-green-deal (Accessed: 26 November 2025).

Blundell-Jones, P., Petrescu, D. and Till, J. (eds) (2005) *Architecture and Participation*. Spon Press.

Borden, I. (2001) *Skateboarding, Space and the City*. Berg.

Borden, I., Kerr, J., Rendell, J. and Pivaro, A. (eds) (1996) *Strangely Familiar: Narratives of Architecture in the City*. Routledge.

Boudon, P. (1972) *Lived-In Architecture: Le Corbusier's Pessac Revisisted*. MIT.

Brown, W. (2015) *Undoing the Demos: Neoliberalism's Stealth Revolution*. Zone Books.

Brown, W. (2023) *Nihilistic Times: Thinking with Max Weber*. Harvard.

Castel, R. (2003) *L'Insécurité sociale*. Seuil.

Cixous, H. (2022) *Well-Kept Ruins*. Seagull Books.

Colomina, B. (1996) *Privacy and Publicity: Modern Architecture and Mass Media*. MIT.

Critchley, S. (2012) *The Faith of the Faithless: Experiments in Political Theology*. Verso.

Degen, M. M. (2008) *Sensing Cities*. Routledge.

Fraser, N. (2023) *Cannibal Capitalism: How Our System Is Devouring Democracy, Care and the Planet – and What We Can Do About It*. Verso.

Freire, P. (1972) *Pedagogy of the Oppressed*. Penguin.

Geuss, R. (2020) *Who Needs a World View?* Harvard.

Hall, P. [(1988] 1996) *Cities of Tomorrow*. Oxford, Blackwell.

Harris, S. and Berke, D. (eds) (1997) *Architecture of the Everyday*. MIT.

Hatherley, O. (2025) *The Alienation Effect: How Central European Emigrés Transformed the British Twentieth Century*. Allen Lane.

Hill, J. (ed) (1998) *Occupying Architecture: Between the Architect and the User*. Routledge.
Hobbes, T. [(1651] 2017) *Leviathan*. Penguin.
Hoggart, R. (1958) *The Uses of Literacy*. Penguin.
Hollands, R. G. (2023) *Beyond the Neoliberal Creative City*. Bristol University Press.
Hughes, J. and Sadler, S. (eds) (2000) *Non-Plan: Essays on Freedom, Participation and Change in Modern Architecture and Urbanism*. Architectural Press.
Jeffries, S. (2021) *Everything All the While Everywhere: How We Became Postmodern*. Verso.
Judt, T. (2010) *Ill Fares the Land*. Penguin.
Kynaston, D. (2007) *Austerity Britain, 1945–51*. Bloomsbury.
Kynaston, D. (2013) *Modernity Britain: Opening the Box, 1957–59*. Bloomsbury.
Leach, N. (ed) (1999) *Architecture and Revolution*. Routledge.
Lefebvre, H. ([1974] 1991) *The Production of Space*, translated from the French by D. Nicholson-Smith. Blackwell.
Lefebvre, H. (2014) *Toward an Architecture of Enjoyment*, L. Stanek (ed), translated from the French by R. Bononno. University of Minnesota Press.
Lorey, I. (2015) *State of Insecurity: Government of the Precarious*. Verso.
Marcuse, H. (1970) 'The end of utopia', in J. Shapiro and S. M. Weber (eds), *Five Lectures: Psychoanalysis, Politics and Utopia*. Beacon Press, pp. 62–81.
Massey, D. (1994) *Space, Place and Gender*. Polity.
Massey, D. (2005) *For Space*. Sage.
Mikes, G. ([1946] 1981) *How to Be a Brit*. Penguin.
O'Connor, J. (2024) *Culture Is Not an Industry: Reclaiming Art and Culture for the Common Good*. Manchester University Press.
Petrescu, D. (2009) 'Losing control, keeping desire', in P. B. Jones, D. Petrescu and J. Till (eds), *Architecture and Participation*. Taylor & Francis, pp. 43–61.
Rawes, P. (ed) (2013) *Relational Architectural Ecologies: Architecture, Nature and Subjectivity*. Routledge.
Rendell, J. (2007) 'Site-writing: Enigma and embellishment', in J. Rendell, J. Hill, M. Fraser and M. Dorrian (eds), *Critical Architecture*. Routledge, pp. 150–162.
Sandercock, L. (1998) *Towards Cosmopolis*. Wiley.
Sandercock, L. (2006) 'Cosmopolitan urbanism: a love song to our Mongrel cities', in J. Binnie, J. Holloway, S. Millington and C. Young (eds), *Cosmopolitan Urbanism*. Routledge, pp. 49–64.
Sennett, R. (1994) *Flesh and Stone*. Faber and Faber.
Sulzer, P. (2009) 'Notes on participation', in P. B. Jones, D. Petrescu and J. Till (eds), *Architecture and Participation*. Taylor & Francis, pp. 149–160.
Tawny, R. H. [1914] (1966) 'An experiment in democratic education', in R. Hinden (ed), *The Radical Tradition*. Harmondsworth, Penguin, pp. 74–85.
Tawny, R. H. [1933] (1978) 'The study of economic history', in J. M. Winter (ed), *History and Society: Essays by R H Tawney*. Routledge & Kegan Paul, pp. 47–65.
Till, J. (2009) 'The negotiation of hope', in P. B. Jones, D. Petrescu and J. Till (eds), *Architecture and Participation*. Taylor & Francis, pp. 23–42.
Umenyilora, C. (2000) 'Empowering the self-builder', in J. Hughes and S. Sadler (eds), *Non-Plan*. Routledge, pp. 210–221.
Zizek, S. (2011) *Living in the End Times*. Verso.
Zizek, S. (2023) *Surplus-Enjoyment*. Bloomsbury.

2

BEASTS SLEEPING FURIOUSLY

An Investigation into Transdisciplinary Creative Practices on the Intersection of Creative Writing and Architecture

Kasia Nawratek

Untangling the Weave

This chapter traces the trajectory of two seemingly separate practices of mine: a pedagogical, research-informed practice in architectural academia and a creative writing practice. On the surface, they occupy two distinctly different activity spheres, separated by language and crafting tools. My work in academia is almost exclusively communicated in English, whereas my creative writing is in my mother tongue, Polish.

Yet, when inspected closely, this perceived duality disappears and a different picture emerges: creative practice appears as a tangled flow of ideas, a complex weave where individual strands grow stronger and more visible with time, only to subside and become a support for newer threads. To separate them, would be to never fully grasp their complexity and how they inform and feed each other. On a more personal level, it could also be said that the weave represents not so much a way of thinking as a way of being as an academic, an educator, a writer and a person.

I untangle this weave using four perspectives – temporal, linguistic, spatial and translative – to capture my creative practice in its different iterations and their complex interrelationships.

The temporal perspective is the most straightforward, as it recounts how my practices developed over time. A quick glance at the chronological order of events reveals an alternating pattern: intensive periods of creative writing falling in between stages of my pedagogical practice (usually between jobs, allowing for a period of uninterrupted space for creativity). To some extent, this dispels the myth of the possibility of parallel practices, where deep concentration can be shared between multiple projects at a time. While I

DOI: 10.4324/9781003647720-4

could write a short story alongside full-time work (Nawratek, 2019), novels required uninterrupted stretches of time needed to submerge myself fully in a single language and a single project (Nawratek, 2016; 2023). Temporally, the strands don't run side by side but take shifts – each thickening for a time while the other recedes.

The linguistic perspective reveals a different kind of division. My creative writing (children's and young adult books) is in Polish, whereas my academic and research texts are in English. Before my move to academia, I was a practising architect, but this practice was also almost entirely in English, making it my "professional" language. As my second language, English does not afford me the same boldness in breaking linguistic rules with ease, which I do frequently in my creative writing in Polish. Adherence to rules characterises my writing in English, whereas my Polish constantly scouts the edges of language conventions in search of innovation and idiosyncratic expression for my characters.

In both languages and across practices, I seek to retain a distinct voice. In my creative writing, I predominantly speak through the first-person narrator, telling the story from the point of view of the protagonist. As this text proves, I feel most at ease when expressing my thoughts this way, but in academic writing the first-person voice has gained legitimacy not that long ago, mostly in the humanities, and is not equally welcome across disciplines. The figure of the disembodied, objective and dispassionate scientist still looms large over embodied, gendered and diverse voices. I follow in the footsteps of feminist writers, such as Doreen Massey, to find my voice in academia without losing my identity, both as a person and as a writer.

The linguistic perspective could easily open onto a broader discussion of the relationship between English and Polish, how their structures influence each other, and how processes of translation, in turn, shape my way of thinking. While a full exploration lies beyond the scope of this chapter, it is important to note that I am far from alone in this constant pull between languages: according to the 2021 Census, 612,000 people speak Polish as their main language in the UK (Office for National Statistics, 2022), making it the most commonly spoken language after English (or Welsh in Wales). My own weave of languages and voices is thus part of a wider, multilingual fabric of diasporic experience.

The two further perspectives – spatial and translative – are more complex and, in some ways, echo two modes of engaging with the world: through language and through image. A productive tension runs between them. Paul Ricoeur located the roots of creativity in language (Kearney, 1988), suggesting that the word precedes the emergence of the image, and that the gap between the two is where the mystery of creativity resides. In my own practice this tension is sharpened by the tools associated with my different roles: as a writer, I construct and inhabit worlds primarily through language; as a trained architect, I begin with images and visual representation, using words mainly to clarify, frame, and summarise what the image proposes.

Spatial Threads: Embodied Geometries

In my pedagogical practice, I use architectural, space-oriented tools to investigate the spatial perspective, and the starting point for these investigations is my relationship with landscape. This strand emerges as a leading force shaping the weave of ideas and has the biggest impact on all my practices.

My spatial perspective is rooted in my childhood experiences of freely exploring my neighbourhood and later shaped by my architectural training. In both cases, my spatial awareness was developed by using the body as a probe, resulting in an embodied understanding of distance, scale, boundaries and thresholds.

The original territory of exploration that shaped this awareness is the post-socialist, post-industrial city during a time of change. The city of Katowice is the capital of the Upper Silesia region in Poland: a historical and geographical region located mostly in south-western Poland, with a small part over the border in Czechia. Upper Silesia is a post-industrial extractive landscape known for heavy industry and coal mining, with its own language and distinct cultural identity. According to the 2021 Census (Statistics Poland, 2023), there were over half a million Silesians, and over 400,000 people declared that they used Silesian at home.

The Upper Silesian landscape is post-industrial and highly urbanised, with remnants of historical heavy industry and coal mining still present. It is also rich in green areas: many slag heaps are now overgrown or have been turned into parks. The most famous example is Silesian Park, which began to be created in the early 1950s on around 620 hectares of recultivated post-industrial wasteland. Despite its industrial profile and history, Upper Silesia is also rich in forests, which in 2023 covered around 30% of its area (Państwowe Gospodarstwo Leśne Lasy Państwowe, 2024). The statistical data simply confirm what my childhood experience already suggested: this was a landscape of industrial infrastructure, working and defunct, integrated with nature, painstakingly recovering lost ground.

During my formative exploratory years, my neighbourhood was a typical high-rise residential complex built in the 1970s and 1980s, huddled around an older coal mine that was its functional and visual centre of gravity. A few streets flanking the coal mine were occupied by older red-brick buildings, the traditional *familoki*, named after the German *Familien-Block*: multi-family residential buildings with their window frames painted red. The neighbourhood's boundary was blurred by no-man's-lands: a coal mine wastewater reservoir, a brickyard sticking another chimney up into the air, a historic park flanked by allotments, a railway line, and a stretch of meadows peppered with ruins of houses demolished years earlier to make way for the ever-delayed new road.

These peripheral spaces were especially enticing for children precisely because they were forbidden by adults, and marked by warning signs hanging on ineffective, rusty chain-link fencing. Their semi-illicit status amplified our bodily alertness: every step was a negotiation with risk, curiosity, and the porousness of boundaries. They were synonymous with adventure and potential.

The coal mine announced itself above ground with two chimneys and a headframe: inhumanly scaled, partly mobile structures – fascinating and unsettling – surface embassies of the underworld. But it also made itself known through the body. Tremors below travelled upward into the concrete high-rises, which shuddered and swayed with the moving ground. Even with reduced extraction, Upper Silesia still shakes – a reminder of dormant power beneath. The tremor is brief and terrifying: glasses rattle, cupboard doors swing open, sometimes furniture shifts. The higher the building, the wider the sway. The mine has a voice too, a whiny siren that used to stop the neighbourhood in its tracks. In the past, at its sound, miners' families gathered at the gate, waiting for news. The air often carried a metallic tang, leaving a bitter aftertaste. Sound, movement, smell and taste inscribed the landscape into the body.

Together – the tremors, the siren, the otherworldly landmarks – rescaled the world beyond the human. The underground became vast, dark and unknowable: a place of risk and death, and the storehouse of "black gold", the literal and economic fuel of the region. It reached down into the Earth and back into deep time, to the human-free past of giant tropical ferns. Dwarfed by the underground, the landscape on the surface gained a whole new dimension, vast and unknowable, making human beings and their silly surface pursuits seem insignificant in comparison.

These experiences trained me, long before formal education, to think of landscape not as a flat surface but as a thick section: layered, unstable, extending downwards, upwards with smoke plumes and backwards in time. In what follows, I turn to a more explicitly geometric understanding of landscape through volumetric accounts of territory.

Spatial Threads: Volumetric Landscapes

This geometric understanding of landscape finds resonance in a series of cartographic and theoretical approaches that explicitly move beyond the idea of territory as a flat, horizontal surface. My first point of reference is the classic image by Ian McHarg from his influential work Design with Nature (1969), where territory is represented as a layered "cake", a complex system composed of multiple, interacting strata. Each layer (geology, physiography, hydrology, soils, vegetation, wildlife, socio-cultural, socio-economic, infrastructure and climate) is independent yet acts in dynamic relationship with the others. McHarg's drawing offers a visual nudge towards a volumetric understanding of landscape.

A more recent strand of thinking relates to the military use of maps, developed and perfected during the First World War with the use of aerial photography to capture the dynamic military situation, with the aerial view becoming "a metaphor for the surveillance, control, and projection of military power across the landscape" (Waldheim, 2016, p. 142).

Jeremy W. Crampton notes that "territory is not just horizontal" (Crampton, 2011) and goes on to describe the spatial framing of landscape as "volumetric". He draws on the work of architect Eyal Weizman, whose analysis of the West Bank (Segal, Tartakover and Weizman, 2003) frames territory as a three-dimensional volume, where layers of underground and overground infrastructure and security corridors, woven through and over each other, create a multilayered and folded structure of strategic, ethnic, functional and political territories. This multilayered understanding of territory is needed to make sense of conflicting territorial claims (Weizman, 2023).

Stuart Elden's work on the West Bank and on Israel's border with Lebanon (2013) invokes Peter Sloterdijk and his preoccupations with air and the determination of human existence through spatialised relationships, conceptualised as spheres of various sizes representing different types of situatedness and relationships that determine our existence in the world (Sloterdijk, 2009a, 2009b). He makes a case for thinking "about volume, through volume, with volume – rather than simply the vertical to make sense of the complexities of territory today" (Elden, 2013, p. 35).

Stephen Graham, in "Vertical: The City from Satellites to Bunkers" (2016), challenges the idea of the city as a flat territory and insists on a fully vertical reading of urban space, treating it as a volume that stretches from mines and tunnels deep underground to the upper layers of the atmosphere, where satellites jostle for position in an increasingly crowded sky.

For all this geometric (volumetric) understanding of space, I still come back to Doreen Massey's approach, where she defines places not merely as "areas with boundaries around", but as "articulated moments in networks of social relations and understandings ..." (Massey, 1994). Taken together, these accounts push landscape away from a neutral backdrop and towards a thick, contested, relational volume – much closer to the dynamic, deep and multilayered Upper Silesia of my childhood than to the flatness of a conventional map.

In my pedagogical practice, this volumetric and relational view of landscape underpins the tools I use with students: deep-mapping exercises using both visual and narrative devices through which they learn to "read" and represent space.

Spatial Threads: What Hides Underground

In an attempt to bind these ideas – a volumetric sense of space and an understanding of place grounded in social relations and culture – I would like to invoke a painting by a local Silesian artist, Teofil Ociepka (1891–1978), his work titled "Elektrociepłownia" ("Combined Heat and Power Plant"), held in the Museum of the History of Katowice.

Ociepka was a primitivist painter who worked as a power plant machinist at a coal mine until his retirement (Kitowska-Łysiak, 2007). The painting depicts a typical Upper Silesian landscape, with a headframe in the background and industrial buildings under a stormy – or smoke-filled – sky. Into this familiar scene, Ociepka inserts a giant beast with an open maw: a dragon-like animal fused with the machinery that produces heat and power, a hybrid of mythical body and human-made technology. Here, myth, an underground presence, works in concert with machines.

Looking more closely, the painter's tenderness is evident in the depiction of the beast. The monster is big and scary, yet it also has the softness of a mole's fur and the ready-to-dig paws of a burrowing animal. The spikes along its back, by contrast, are stone-like and sharp; its eyes turn towards the sky, and its teeth seem to guard the flame held inside its throat.

Silesian writer Szczepan Twardoch, author of the 2014 novel "Drach", has used a similar metaphor. In an interview (Sobolewska, 2014), he has described Silesia as a body shaped by coal extraction: in the novel, the narrator is the titular *drach*, a dragon, and the coal mine is its body.

In my own book "Kresek, Bartek i całkiem zwyczajny początek" (2016) the coal mine is personified as an old, grumpy but powerful monster living deep underground. Its tantrums shake the underground world, threatening the buildings where the main character, a nine-year-old boy named Bartek, lives. This is his greatest fear, the collapse of his whole neighbourhood following the earth tremor caused by the bad-tempered coal mine monster. This story is not merely hypothetical. In my neighbourhood, ten-storey buildings, after years of tremors, had to be straightened using hydraulic jacks, as they were all leaning at an imperceptible but ultimately dangerous degree.

An underground monster personifies a mythical understanding of the Silesian landscape. Ociepka's almost domesticated depiction and Twardoch's more visceral and darker imagination both capture the dark side of the mine's presence: its unpredictability, its untameable nature and the constant threat of death that accompanies those who work underground and their families. In my children's book, death appears in the story of a dog waiting in vain for his human, who leaves for a shift in the mine and never returns. Death is always present in the shadows of daily life, the underground beasts claiming their due with an inevitable and frightening regularity.

In Upper Silesia, the mythical dimension of the underground is rooted in deep time, predating humans and grounded in the Carboniferous period: a time of beasts, perhaps still present in the world beneath our feet and entwined with death and risk still accompanying modern extractive practices.

The underground as the mythical dimension features prominently in some of the earliest known stories. The perilous journey to the underworld, the domain of death, is a story repeated across cultures and times: a human travelling deep underground and returning to the surface of the Earth. There are many variations of this story, and the return is never guaranteed. Katabasis, a descent to the underworld, is a common theme in classical literature: the story of Orpheus and Eurydice; Persephone joining her husband, Hades, the god of the underworld, for half the year during winter, only to return in spring to her mother Demeter, the goddess of harvest. "Anna In w grobowcach świata" ("Anna in the Catacombs") by Olga Tokarczuk (2006) is a retelling of the even earlier Sumerian myth of Inanna, the goddess of harvest and war, who visits her sister, the goddess of the underworld, and returns to the world of the living. Tokarczuk imagines the myth out of time, locating it in a futuristic city, a palimpsest of vertical constructions with foundations embedded in tombs and ruins of the previous iterations of the city.

Robert Macfarlane, in "Underland: A Deep Time Journey", proposes three ways in which we use the underground: shelter, yield and dispose (2020, p. 8). In the Silesian context, "yield" stands for coal, wealth and pride, while "dispose" names the fear – the unspoken fear of death – that is pushed down into the depths along with waste and danger, taking shape of the monster patiently waiting for new sacrifices.

This vertical, volumetric understanding of space, grounded in the landscape and its stories, is part of my identity, developed during my formative childhood years. My own personal axis mundi is still firmly located in my neighbourhood exerting its pull wherever I am, and grounding me in the world.

Spatial Threads: Edgeland Children

If the vertical axis of my childhood was anchored in underground depths, the horizontal axis ran close to the Earth's surface. It traced the routes my small body cut through the neighbourhood: across wastelands, over and under fences, along tracks that never appeared on any official map. I followed illicit shortcuts into the neighbourhood's forbidden corners, immersed in ruderal foliage, alert to nettles but also to the far more dangerous human presences that frequented the same paths. On foot, I stitched together a sideways geography of Silesian edgelands: the rocky shore of the wastewater reservoir, the unofficial path through the allotments, the gap in the fence behind the brickyard leading to the park, triangulated by the headframe and chimneys that served as orientation points.

This is the horizontal axis of edgelands.

"Edgelands", the term first introduced by Marion Shoard (2000) and later expanded by poets Michael Symmons Roberts and Paul Farley (2012), is the name I use in an attempt to describe, and therefore to grasp, spaces that slip in and out of focus whenever I try to fix them within a stable classification. Their defining quality is semantic ambiguity: a spatial and linguistic zone in-between, on the edge. This ambiguity resists precise definition and instead invites a network of proximate terms and references in which edgelands may, or may not, appear. For this purpose, I also draw on Richard Mabey's "The Unofficial Countryside" (Mabey, 2010), Gilles Clément's wider category of the "third landscape" (2022), and Alan Berger's "drosscape" (2006).

The vertical axis discussed earlier is an embodied, internalised orientation, an awareness formed from within, in sync with the biological systems of my body. The horizontal axis, by contrast, is realised through movement and play, and it draws language into the act of making space. Michel de Certeau, in "The Practice of Everyday Life" (1984, p. 97), makes a direct link between walking and language: "The act of walking is to the urban system what the speech act is to language or to the statements uttered". The paths I walked were not simply routes; they were statements – situated, tactical and repeatable in ways that gradually produced a legible world.

This linguistic angle carries an unexpected political charge. In my previous discussion of edgelands (Nawratek, 2022), I referred to Boris Groys' account of money (or numbers) as a mediating language in capitalism (Groys, 2010): a medium that enables compromise by flattening differences into a single scale of value. Language, however, does not flatten so easily. It multiplies meanings, produces frictions, and opens space for ambiguity, precisely the kind of instability that can disrupt rigid, closed capitalist narratives.

From this perspective, the attempt to describe edgelands becomes a small act of rebellion: it makes a gap in the dominant narrative, allowing other meanings to appear, persist, or survive an all-front assault. Their semantic ambivalence is what allows edgelands to function as "reservoirs of meanings" (Jorgensen and Tylecote, 2007, p. 458): open to multiple values inscribed by multiple users outside established power structures. In my view, they are among the last lines of defence against the capitalist city, because their ambiguity gives people agency to define them as what they need them to be in any given moment. This also signals another interpretative opening: non-humans reclaiming edgelands as habitats, inscribing themselves into these spaces through a fully embodied redefinition. I will return to this thread later, in the discussion of my pedagogical practice.

It is no surprise, then, that edgelands became integral to my creative practice. This is where I shaped a large part of my identity and established a bond with the world through unsupervised exploration on foot. Thinking with Gareth Doherty's distinction between the aerial image (the horizontal) and the vertical transect produced through fieldwork (2019), my childhood explorations inserted my body into the map. The horizontal axis is usually associated with the map – an abstract, flattened view. The transect, by contrast, is a cut made at the scale of the walking body: a way of binding landscape to lived experience. My personal transects through the neighbourhood were not drawn but walked, and they assembled a very different image of the city from the one available in official cartography.

Research on children's ability to roam and explore – their "home range", defined as the distance they are allowed to travel from home (Woolley and Griffin, 2015), suggests that this range has dramatically shrunk over recent decades. In the 1980s, when I was growing up, my home range was relatively wide. It expanded to further neighbourhoods when I rode my bicycle, forming a connected web of locations and paths: a personal network of territories. No structured playground, with its safe surfaces and apparatus, could match the complexity of this terrain. Playgrounds are pretend worlds, carefully framed and risk managed. In contrast, edgelands are stages that can be endlessly appropriated: places to perform stories, to world-build without limits.

My mental map of the neighbourhood was therefore not a bird's-eye diagram, but a sequence of spaces remembered through the body: places where nettles stung, where teenagers gathered to drink, where dogs roamed loose, where the path narrowed and demanded negotiation with others. Risk, effort, and encounter, not just distance, shaped this horizontal axis.

Edgelands offered anonymity and a loosening of social scripts, but they also demanded cooperation, awareness, and the development of tacit rules: who controls which patch, how to approach older teenagers (or when to avoid them), when to hide, when to show off and how to avoid the unwanted adult gaze. In this sense, the horizontal axis of edgelands is not a backdrop but an active process of becoming through exploration, an arena where agency is rehearsed and actualised in and through the landscape.

For me, this process was inseparable from the vertical axis described earlier. The same coal mine that anchored my personal axis mundi was also responsible for the shape of the terrain that constituted my horizontal playground.

A volumetric understanding of space plays out across these two axes: reaching down into the deep time of the Earth below and extending into the edgelands on the surface. It is therefore not an abstract theory, but a lived condition.

Translative Threads: Designing with the Trouble

So far, I have untangled the weave of my practice through temporal, linguistic and spatial perspectives. In concentrating on the spatial one, I have developed a volumetric understanding of landscape: a vertical axis rooted in the underground and a horizontal axis traced by embodied movement through Silesian edgelands.

The final perspective, which I call translative, refers to my academic practice in architectural education and research. Translative describes an oscillation between creative practice and pedagogy, where ideas, methods and sensibilities developed through writing are translated into teaching and research, then translated back again – altered by students' questions and interpretations, as well as by institutional constraints. Here, my creative practice and situated identity do not sit alongside teaching: they actively shape it.

The key concept here is context, understood in architectural terms as a specific place with material, measurable and tangible characteristics, but also as a knot of cultural, social, economic, political and historical relations. Context also means the positioning of the designer – architect, student, teacher – as a whole person, with their own histories, bodies, (multiple) languages, ambitions and insecurities.

In my pedagogical approach to architectural projects, this layered understanding of context is one of the key tasks awaiting students in the studio. It is also the decisive moment in positioning their work, because the propositional part of the project depends on how the site is read and how the architect locates themselves in relation to it. The narrative that emerges here sets up the world-building exercise of the architectural proposal: a version of the world with the project in it.

In my teaching, this is where techniques from literary world-building enter the design studio. Students are asked not only to analyse the site, but to construct a situated narrative of the place they are engaging with – as architects and as creative individuals. My role is to support them in developing their own practice, rather than modelling it on mine. This is an intimate, bespoke process, and a risky one: it requires students to confront their own positionality, and to test it.

Mikhail Bakhtin's idea of polyphony (Bakhtin, 1984) is useful here. Writing about the novel, he contrasts monologic narratives, where every character ultimately serves the author's viewpoint, with dialogic (polyphonic) ones, where different voices express genuinely competing ways of seeing the world. In this kind of writing, conflict isn't something to be resolved; it's what makes the world on the page feel fuller and more inclusive.

For architecture to respond to the needs of many rather than a privileged few, design processes need similar polyphonic strategies. Polyphony and dialogism offer a way to flatten hierarchies in the studio: the architect's voice is no longer perched at the top of a power pyramid but inserted into a web of relationships where human and non-human, present and absent actors can all speak. The design process becomes a dynamic, dialogic situation of shifting dependencies rather than a single authoritative storyline.

In this sense, my pedagogical practice uses polyphony not to "fix" the world, but to understand it. Conflict becomes a design driver: students are invited first to identify different voices, then to trace the conflicts between them. They make these tensions visible and explore how they play out in space, rather than rushing towards premature resolution. This is what I call "designing with the trouble" in direct conversation with Haraway (2016), and it marks my movement towards post-humanist approaches informed by Braidotti (2013), Tsing (2015), and others.

These names point towards feminist narratives of sustainability, but I am wary of adopting the sustainability label without examining it. Too often, sustainability in architecture is reduced to a technological problem to be solved, whereas a translative, polyphonic approach insists on sustainability as a systemic and contextual issue, one that cannot be reduced to a technical fix.

Birmingham: Language, the Cut and Early Experiments in Polyphony

This translative practice took a first, concrete shape in Birmingham. Walking along the canal, I had a sense of getting "under the skin" of the city. In the nearby Black Country, canals are called "the cut", an apt image: a deliberate incision through the urban fabric, a scar tissue softened by nature colonising every scrap of land along the cut's edges.

Together with poet Derek Littlewood and with the guest appearance of Black Country poet Liz Berry, I led a transdisciplinary workshop in which students worked across poetry, literature, filmmaking and architecture, using the Birmingham canal as the shared site of investigation. This is when the idea of edgelands began to inform my thinking about cities. The poets opened conversations about language, local accents and dialects. Their work revealed a diversity within English that often surprised international students and destabilised assumptions about a single "proper" language of professionalism.

Using Bakhtin's polyphony, students moved from theory into practice through a multilayered process of translation. They brought Romanian, Persian, English and Russian into the project (Nawratek, 2022), discovering that exact translation between languages was impossible. Subtle shifts in meaning exposed the different ways in which each language sees the world, and, consequently, how our engagements with space depend on the language we inhabit at a given moment. The project thus became an exercise in linguistic and spatial polyphony at once: a group of students encountering a place, and each other, through many partially overlapping, partially incompatible world-descriptions.

In retrospect, Birmingham marks the moment when the translative perspective crystallised. Literary concepts: polyphony, world-building, translation, were no longer simply metaphors for my own thinking; they became operative tools in the studio, structuring how students read sites, narrate contexts and negotiate conflicts.

Sheffield: Edgelands, More-than-Human Cities and the Climate Crisis

The second key location is Sheffield. My first impressions as captured in my phone notes in 2015 were of a doubly "post" city – post-industrial and post-apocalyptic:

> As if it fell into the valleys between those hills, got stuck, put down roots, and then the greenery just slid down from the hill tops, channelled through the streets and again bubbled up in all the random places.

I noted weeds, dry grass and poppies. The red-brick familiarity of Kelham Island immediately recalled the *familoki* of my Silesian neighbourhood: different cities, separated by thousands of kilometres, shaped by the same forces of industrialisation and more recent deindustrialisation. As industry retreated, it left voids that were quickly claimed by nature. Plants "bubbled up" in overlooked, unattended spaces, creating a post-industrial edgeland landscape. Once again, I gravitated towards the canal, extending the fascination that had begun in Birmingham. This time, however, the focus shifted more decisively towards a more-than-human perspective.

Previously, nature had appeared in my thinking as background: a green filler in sectional drawings, an ambiguous "green" feature of the landscape, without much appreciation or understanding of its qualities. The Sheffield canal refused that reading. It presented itself as a complex web of relationships in which post-industrial infrastructure and architecture, spontaneous vegetation, non-humans, and humans co-produced a complex urban ecosystem.

Here, the edgeland ceased to be only a human playground or metaphor. It became a site where the climate crisis and ecological renewal are materially negotiated. In my teaching, this meant asking students to consider the canal as an urban ecosystem and attend to the agencies of non-humans alongside those of human actors, often with conflicting interests (Nawratek, 2021). The question was no longer simply how to regenerate a derelict site, but how to work within a landscape already busy with more-than-human forms of occupation and repair.

A clear new direction emerged from Sheffield: a translative practice that connects post-industrial edgelands, polyphonic narratives and more-than-human concerns in response to the climate crisis. The next step, in Manchester, would build on this trajectory rather than start anew.

Manchester: The Manifesto

In Manchester, I found a welcoming home for my literary experiments in architecture. I keep experimenting across research-focused modules (dissertation and research methods for postgraduate students) and design studios across undergraduate and postgraduate courses. The post-industrial thread that started in Birmingham, wove through Sheffield and tied me to Manchester. It is on the man-made island of Pomona that this thread binds me to the place most tightly.

Pomona Island was a stage for some of my most daring pedagogical experiments. An archetypal edgeland, it never ceased to be an enticing space for exploration: tied to the canal and part of Manchester's industrial and trade history. Now poised to be developed, but defiantly "empty" and overgrown, it is waiting for capitalist forces to take over once again.

In students' eyes, Pomona became a person, represented by a desk or an altar filled with manufactured personal artefacts (Woodhead et al., 2022) telling a story of Manchester districts as squabbling siblings. Another group of students saw the island through the lens of the ultimate Other – perhaps another species, perhaps an extraterrestrial (Price et al., 2022). More recently, I chose Pomona again as a site for final master's and undergraduate studios. Narratives around memory, what we choose to remember, and how, drive our work on Pomona this year as a place of memory, but also wilful forgetting, allowing it to navigate the capitalist narrative of profit and growth.

Design studios are part of the *Some Kind of Nature* atelier which I lead, a vertical teaching structure comprising students from the final undergraduate year, two years of Master of Architecture, and the final year of the Master of Landscape Architecture. My interest in urban biodiversity started in Sheffield and gained momentum in Manchester, where the atelier began in 2021 with a focus on sustainability. This, however, proved limiting: on the one hand, it did not capture the full scope of the atelier's approach and, on the other, the perception of the atelier was constrained by how "sustainability" was understood by others.

In search of a better framing, I formulated the Some Kind of Nature manifesto in 2024. Although I wrote it, I must credit all tutors and students of the atelier over the years, who all contributed to its formulation through discussions in and beyond studio. The manifesto frames the atelier as rooted in post-humanist philosophy, shifting the focus from the subject to relationships, foregrounding dialogic methods with conflict as design driver.

> Our design process is contextual, care-ful, open to multiple, often conflicting voices (Mikhail Bakhtin's polyphony) and entangled (Donna Haraway). We are collaborative, transdisciplinary and dialogical.
>
> Architecturally speaking, this manifesto translates into a strong focus on context, multifunctional briefs, and an in-depth understanding of tangible expressions of human and non-human relationships expressed through space, materiality, technology and time.
>
> *(Nawratek, 2024)*

The key concept binding together the post-humanist approach, care methodologies and design is time. The temporal dimension is important in the architectural context, where it extends the architectural project far into the future and requires an expiry date for every building and careful planning for its lifespan. It foregrounds care and maintenance as activities as important as design process and requiring an architect's attention and skill. It also echoes the vertical axis grounding me in the world, reaching into the deep time and rescaling the understanding of time to planetary proportions.

Care and maintenance come with bodily costs for cleaners and maintenance workers, because buildings designed without care will age at huge cost, not only in materials and energy, but also in labour performed in often unsafe and demanding conditions. The adventures of Guadalupe Acedo, cleaning the Koolhaas-designed house, illustrate the disparity between the glossy image of high-concept architecture and the reality of hauling a vacuum cleaner up the stairs as depicted in the 2008 documentary "Koolhaas Houselife" directed by Ila Bêka and Louise Lemoîne.

This leads us to extend care to architects themselves and to recognise the conditions of architectural production, where gender, socio-economic and racial inequalities structure hierarchical and exploitative working environments. When this lens is expanded to the wider web of people involved in producing architecture, including construction and maintenance workers, we are forced to think differently about the design process and its embedded inequalities. From this perspective, architects also have a role in shaping "care infrastructures" – the social, spatial and institutional arrangements that support caring life (The Care Collective, 2020).

Buildings age quickly, and demolition often appears to be the easier, and therefore preferred, option, rather than reuse. For the old-fashioned idea of the sole genius, the "master-architect", there is little allure in working with a structure that is already there. It requires carefulness, dialogue and flexibility: a perceived softness that is often judged as not inventive enough, and therefore not fit for the "truly" creative architect.

A not-so-subtle gender framing can also be detected in this reasoning, as the traditional (I would say old-fashioned) architect is by default a privileged male. This is also how we educate architects: to be sole creators, working independently and realising their vision without compromises. And yet we also recognise that architects never work alone (unless they self-build for themselves), and that a different approach – collaborative and careful – is needed. This creates a tension in the architectural education, where outdated, deeply rooted attitudes and ideas of who an architect is and how they work, still shape how we teach.

> We use conflict as an important design driver, but our intention is not to resolve it but to use it to deepen our understanding. We don't see ourselves

> as problem solvers, as this position can lead to reductive and potentially harmful interventions.
>
> *(Nawratek, 2024)*

The repositioning of the architect–designer is driven by the dialogic method, where conflicts are seen as a useful tool for understanding, not something to be eradicated.

> Therefore, we don't solve, we respond. We don't intervene, we propose.
>
> The shift in language reflects the shift in our understanding of the architect's role: from vertical (hierarchical) to horizontal (collaborative).
>
> *(Nawratek, 2024)*

The translative aspect – ideas explored in creative practice, translated into spatial inquiry, and back – describes a constant oscillation between methods, languages and tools. It is one practice, rooted in the same ideas, but realised through different kinds of craft; at times, these modes intersect and borrow from one another.

The Weave Untangled

In this chapter, I aimed to capture the full spectrum of my practice and how its different elements influence each other. The weave, consisting of my creative writing practice and the ideas it engages with, is positioned as a driving force for a unique pedagogical approach, enriched by a creative writing practice in a different language.

My experience as a migrant working across languages, a writer and an architect comes together in a practice actualised through teaching and writing. The theoretical framework, grounded in philosophy and literature, allows me to explore the ideas I am interested in: the embodied relationship with landscape; the formative experiences of childhood related to space; and the act of creation as a gesture, a moment of becoming with the world – a way of being in the world and relating to it. The translative element is at the centre of the creative process: it is where positionality in relation to the world finds an active way of interacting with it.

I could not capture my practice in full; the question of how my pedagogy relates to my writing remains unanswered. It may require more space and time, as another book, brewing in the background, will finally emerge.

As with the monsters of the Silesian underworld, the hills of Sheffield appear to me as ancient beasts, now sound asleep, dreaming in sync with the city. The fast-moving weather fronts strike their backs, but they don't stir, and the city is safe, clinging to their bodies.

References

Bakhtin, M. (1984) *Problems of Dostoevsky's poetics*. Translated from Russian by C. Emerson. Minneapolis: University of Minnesota Press.Bêka, I. and Lemoine, L. (2008) *Koolhaas Houselife* [Film]. Paris: BêkaFilms.

Berger, A. (2006) *Drosscape: Wasting land in urban America*. New York: Princeton Architectural Press.

Braidotti, R. (2013) *The posthuman*. Cambridge: Polity Press.

The Care Collective (2020) *The care manifesto: the politics of interdependence*. London: Verso.

Clément, G. (2022) *Manifesto of the third landscape*. Translated by M. Bee and R. Fèvre. Lund: Trans Europe Halles (TEH Series on New Imaginaries, 3).

Crampton, J.W. (2011) 'Cartographic calculations of territory', *Progress in Human Geography*, 35(1), pp. 92–103. doi:10.1177/0309132509358474.

de Certeau, M. (1984) *The practice of everyday life*. Translated by S. Rendall. Berkeley: University of California Press.

Doherty, G. (2019) 'The vertical and the horizontal: combining ethnographic and geographic methods in understanding landscape', in Braae, E. and Steiner, H. (eds) *Routledge research companion to landscape architecture*. London: Routledge, pp. 203–214. doi:10.4324/9781315613116-15.

Elden, S. (2013) 'Secure the volume: vertical geopolitics and the depth of power', *Political Geography*, 34, pp. 35–51. doi:10.1016/j.polgeo.2012.12.009.

Farley, P. and Symmons Roberts, M. (2012) *Edgelands*. London: Vintage Books.

Graham, S. (2016) *Vertical: the city from satellites to bunkers*. London: Verso.

Groys, B. (2010) *The communist postscript*. Translated by T. Ford. London: Verso.

Haraway, D.J. (2016) *Staying with the trouble: making kin in the Chthulucene*. Durham, NC: Duke University Press.

Jorgensen, A. and Tylecote, M. (2007) 'Ambivalent landscapes—wilderness in the urban interstices', *Landscape Research*, 32(4), pp. 443–462. doi:10.1080/01426390701449802.

Kearney, R. (1988) 'Paul Ricoeur and the hermeneutic imagination', *Philosophy & Social Criticism*, 14(2), pp. 115–145. doi:10.1177/019145378801400202.

Kitowska-Łysiak, M. (2007) *Teofil Ociepka*. Culture.pl. Available at: https://culture.pl/en/artist/teofil-ociepka (Accessed: 30 December 2025).

Mabey, R. (2010) *The unofficial countryside*. Wimborne Minster: Dovecote Press.

Macfarlane, R. (2020) *Underland: a deep time journey*. London: Penguin Books.

Massey, D. (1994) 'A global sense of place', in Massey, D. (ed) *Space, place and gender*. Cambridge: Polity Press, pp. 146–156.

McHarg, I.L. (1969) *Design with nature*. New York: John Wiley & Sons.

Nawratek, K. (2016) *Kresek, Bartek i całkiem zwyczajny początek*. Warszawa: Agencja Wydawnicza Ezop.

Nawratek, K. (2019) 'Sklep miętowy', *Zwykłe życie*, 20.

Nawratek, K. (2021) 'Hope in the burning world', in Pelsmakers, S. and Newman, N. (eds) *Design Studio 2021, Volume 1: Everything needs to change – architecture and the climate emergency*. London: RIBA Publishing, pp. 86–97.

Nawratek, K. (2022) 'Mapping the creative edge: dialogic pedagogies in architectural education', in Nawratek, K. (ed) *Space and language in architectural education: catalysts and tensions*. London: Routledge, pp. 79–98.

Nawratek, K. (2023) *Ja, Świnia*. Warszawa: Wydawnictwo Dwukropek.

Nawratek, K. (2024) *Some kind of nature: design studio manifesto*. Unpublished course document, Manchester School of Architecture, Manchester Metropolitan University.

Office for National Statistics (2022) *Language, England and Wales: Census 2021*. Available at: https://www.ons.gov.uk/peoplepopulationandcommunity/culturalidentity/language/bulletins/languageenglandandwales/census2021 (Accessed: 3 December 2025).

Państwowe Gospodarstwo Leśne Lasy Państwowe (2024) *Raport o stanie lasów w Polsce 2023*. Bedoń: Ośrodek Rozwojowo-Wdrożeniowy Lasów Państwowych. Available at: https://www.bdl.lasy.gov.pl/portal/Media/Default/Publikacje/raport_o_stanie_lasow_2023.pdf (Accessed: 4 December 2025).

Price, R., Shendurnikar, S., Zhang, Y. and Yang, Y. (2022) *Alien Gaze*. Student project (Research methods module), Manchester School of Architecture, Manchester. Unpublished.

Segal, R., Tartakover, D. and Weizman, E. (eds) (2003) *A civilian occupation: the politics of Israeli architecture*. London: Verso.

Shoard, M. (2000) 'Edgelands of promise', *Landscapes*, 1(2), pp. 74–93. doi:10.1179/lan.2000.1.2.74.

Sloterdijk, P. (2009a) *Terror from the air*. Translated by A. Patton. New York: Semiotext(e).

Sloterdijk, P. (2009b) 'Airquakes', *Environment and Planning D: Society and Space*, 27(1), pp. 41–57.

Sobolewska, J. (2014) 'Szczepan Twardoch opowiada o swojej najnowszej powieści „Drach"', *Polityka*, 25 November. Available at: https://www.polityka.pl/tygodnikpolityka/kultura/1600119,1,szczepan-twardoch-opowiada-o-swojej-najnowszej-powiesci-drach.read (Accessed: 4 December 2025).

Statistics Poland (2023) *National Population and Housing Census 2021. Population: size and demographic-social structure in the light of the 2021 Census results*. Warsaw: Statistics Poland. Available at: https://stat.gov.pl/en/national-census/national-population-and-housing-census-2021/final-results-of-the-national-population-and-housing-census-2021/size-and-demographic-social-structure-in-the-light-of-the-2021-census-results,6,1.html (Accessed: 4 December 2025).

Tokarczuk, O. (2006) *Anna In w grobowcach świata*. Kraków: Znak.

Tsing, A.L. (2015) *The mushroom at the end of the world: on the possibility of life in capitalist ruins*. Princeton, NJ: Princeton University Press.

Twardoch, S. (2014) *Drach*. Kraków: Wydawnictwo Literackie.

Waldheim, C. (2016) *Landscape as urbanism: a general theory*. Princeton, NJ: Princeton University Press.

Weizman, E. (2023) 'Archaeology, architecture and the politics of verticality', in Parker, I. (ed) *For Palestine: essays from the Tom Hurndall Memorial Lecture Group*. Cambridge: Open Book Publishers, pp. 123–142. doi:10.11647/OBP.0345.09.

Woodhead, M., Li, H., Desouza, Q. and Laming, J. (2022) *Pomona's Desk*. Student project (Research Methods module), Manchester School of Architecture, Manchester. Unpublished.

Woolley, H.E. and Griffin, E. (2015) 'Decreasing experiences of home range, outdoor spaces, activities and companions: changes across three generations in Sheffield in north England', *Children's Geographies*, 13(6), pp. 677–691. doi:10.1080/14733285.2014.952186 (Accessed: 4 December 2025).

3

COMFORT BEYOND LIMITS

Precedents for Creativity

Mark Hammond, Samuel Holden and Stefan White

Comfort beyond Limits: Precedents for Creativity

> I had this perception of architecture as a plan, as columns, as a house, as a building. I feel like I was clamouring for something that felt safe and familiar, but reductive.
>
> *Mohsin Ali*

> The past six years, we've all been training or been taught up to just use CAD and whatever. Anything digital and then now it's like when you wanna go back to drawing, it's a forgotten skill. Like no one really talks about it anymore.
>
> *Kyra Jennings*

Precedent studies are a well-established element of architectural teaching and learning. The analysis of existing building designs has long been seen as an important tool for exposing students to demonstrable examples of good practice, as a way of building up a body of ideas and influences that students can draw upon when they move into professional settings. Clark and Pause's seminal 1985 publication "Precedents in Architecture" still reflects how precedents are predominantly used in architectural education, with this book espousing the benefits to studying the form, geometry and aesthetic of buildings as a means of developing one's own architectural sensibilities.

The limitations of this approach, in light of the increasingly diverse roles that architecture students move into after graduation, are becoming increasingly visible. In Clark and Pause's preface, they note that, "Without apology, we make no attempt to discuss the social, political, economic or technical

DOI: 10.4324/9781003647720-5

aspects of architecture. The domain of design ideas lies within the formal and spatial realm of architecture" (Clark and Pause, 1985: v). As educators, we see that this narrow view of the precedent continues today, supported by the proliferation of image-based resources for sharing building design examples; websites such as ArchDaily and Dezeen, and increasingly decontextualised media such as standalone images posted on Instagram or Pinterest. The social, political and economic implications of the architects labour are at best implied and more commonly erased, leaving the precedent as an imperfect tool of architectural inculcation – a way for students to understand what a "good building" is through repeated exposure, without understanding the underlying processes and potentials of the architect to address professional or societal challenges.

While we don't dispute that there is some benefit to students from analysing the formal, aesthetic and technical qualities of buildings, we argue that this interpretation of precedent is misaligned with the more experimental and flexible interpretation of architectural education explored in this book. Much like critical pedagogy's concern with decentring of the teacher as an authority figure in the learning process (See Giroux, 1988; Freire, 2005), we contend that this experimental turn requires us to decentre "the building" within the use of precedents. This is not to say that we should ignore the need, value and skill that come with good building design, rather we should be supporting students to value the creative and exploratory processes that underpin diverse forms of architectural practice. We believe this requires students to be more personally and emotionally involved, challenging their internalised sense of limits, in order to manifest solutions that match the conditions they find themselves practising within (White, 2017). To address this, we suggest that precedents from outside of the discipline of architecture can play an important role in questioning the normative assumptions within the profession. In analysing work that has no obvious architectural application the learner is invited to identify a connection between the example, its architectural potential and themselves as individuals. In this chapter, we will explore how using a wider range of precedents, particularly process-driven artistic practices, can provide opportunities for architecture students and graduates to expand their creative toolkit, and extend their understandings of what they, as would-be architects, are capable of and ultimately finding ways to deploy our identities, experiences and ethics through our practices.

Supported by a novel theorisation of precedents within architectural pedagogy, this chapter presents critical reflections by staff and students in the "And Architecture" atelier at Manchester School of Architecture. "And Architecture" is a research-led design studio that seeks to explore the positive difference that architects and architecture can make to society. We believe that for widespread social inequities (such as poverty, racism or ableism) to be addressed, we must challenge the normative role of the architect and architecture in reproducing societal injustices. These injustices are manifested within the profession itself, with very low numbers of global majority groups and women progressing through education to prominent positions in the profession for example. However, more broadly, the built environment predominantly privileges those who are economically advantaged and physically active with architectural design rarely supporting the spatial desires of even highly prominent under-represented groups. For example, Jan Gehl's promotion of good city design does not seek to address the fundamentally different experience of safety that urban environments provide for women.

This chapter uses illustrated case studies from within the atelier to reveal firstly, the impact of engaging differently through precedents on students' personal and architectural comfort zones secondly, the significance of different methods for successful and inclusive design processes and thirdly, the impact of this process both within and outside of graduates' "architectural" career paths.

The Differences Precedents Can Make

The term precedent, simply meaning "what has gone before", is perhaps most commonly used in the legal profession. Legal precedents ensure that agreed interpretations of law from previous cases are used to form the basis of new judgements, ensuring consistency from case to case and giving legal professionals the confidence that their actions are sensible. In architecture, this legal analogy seems to hold true – architects investigate "successful" cases to understand what a sensible response to their own project might be. Precedents are used to provide the architect not just with inspiration, but legitimacy and viability – if someone else has done something, and it worked for them, then surely it will work for me too.

The issue with this analogy is that legal precedents assume that the underpinning laws are unquestionable and unchanging, and the only concern is how to apply it correctly. There is no such consensus in architecture about what, as a profession, we are trying to achieve. By its very nature, a precedent is something that has been created and so represents what is *possible* but cannot provide us insight into the *potential* of architecture – the ideas that sit just beyond the horizon of the profession as it is today, showing the world as it might be tomorrow. To achieve the latter, our use of precedents needs to shift from successful outcomes to emergent processes that offer a route for architects to act creatively in response to the societal challenges they seek to address.

To understand the potential of architecture, we must first explore the ways that architects develop constrained, habitual behaviours. Stevens (1995) discusses the way that education conditions architects to think and act in particular ways and argues that a student's success is defined by how similar to their (often male, white, middle class) tutors they can become. This process seeks to reinforce the legitimacy of certain behaviours, asking would-be architects to set aside what makes them different to conform to a set of professional expectations. This argument reflects similar points made by philosopher Gilles Deleuze (1994), who argues that engaging in "habitual" ways of thinking is not just a benign act, but a process that systematically and deliberately eradicates "difference" from our understanding of the world, and in doing so reinforces existing power structures within society. While the act of research and learning within a precedent study implies a conscious attempt to break from habit, the source material is only ever representative of the status quo – the underpinning financial, political and professional power structure that enabled the building to be realised. This underexposure of different approaches can cause designers to assume that any outcome failing to match an imagined ideal must be an error, to be corrected or concealed (White, 2017).

We argue that the way precedents shape norms within architecture is an example of what architectural historian Robin Evans calls the "translation analogy" (Evans, 1997). Evans compares the process of designing a building to translating a text from one language to another. He suggests that the design process is the translation of the architect's thoughts into drawing and from drawing to building. The translation analogy is conveniently and routinely internalised by architecture students, who assume these translations are precise and controlled, and indeed that they are the ones in control of these processes. This infers that students of architecture learn which ideas are correct (through education including precedents) and that creative design is merely the translation of these correct ideas into a built reality. A building precedent offers the promise of a predictable, rational input to a linear design process, and implies that a neat translation from idea to resolution can be achieved. Evans rejects this idea and instead argues that translation is always imperfect, messy and transformative. Rather than freeing architects to be creative, the translation analogy places significant restrictions on them. It obfuscates the intangible creative processes that are necessary to understanding the potential of architecture to make a difference. This enables students and professionals alike to stay in their comfort zone, confident that they will produce an acceptable outcome, yet limiting their ability to employ their personal differences for creative or social purposes. This raises questions about the kinds of precedents we focus on, and indeed how they can actively disrupt the idea that architecture is merely a linear, mechanical process.

Critical pedagogy explicitly challenges this reproduction of norms and the idea of "banking knowledge", where teaching is understood as an exercise in transferring insights from teacher to learner – a process that privileges and reinforces normative behaviours and inhibits the emergence of "difference" (hooks, 1994; Freire, 2005). The transfer of knowledge from precedent to learner, similarly one-directional, amplifies this bias as it relies on examples actually being constructed. It perpetuates the world as is, unfair and unequal, rather than the world as it might be. If we agree that precedents as a concept are a valid pedagogic tool, but their application in architecture lends itself to a loss of experimentation, we must consider instead whether there are different ways that the model can be applied to support learners' capacity to act differently, and to make a positive contribution to society.

Challenging the erasure of difference is a key element of critical pedagogy, given that normative, habitual thinking reinforces many of the social inequalities that require redress. This is exemplified in queer, feminist, critical race and disability scholarship, where a recognition of difference is central to any attempt to address systemic marginalisation from a latent but unspoken "social norm" (Butler, 1993; Ahmed, 2006; McRuer, 2006; Boys, 2014). The limiting and suppression of difference leads to institutional biases and unconscious discrimination, but in doing so also undermines the potential of architecture to realise novel approaches and outcomes.

To address this erasure of difference, we argue that precedents need to offer the tools and opportunity for architects to reimagine the ways they can generate and express ideas. Rather than offering solutions to similar design problems to those an architect might face, precedents need to offer an invitation for architects to be different, and to extend their capabilities and add turbulence to otherwise undisturbed design processes. Critically, these precedents need to challenge the normative ideas of what successful architecture is, and to invite a greater diversity of perspectives and experiences into new forms of architecture practice. Rather than seeking to minimise difference, we contend that precedents need to invite architects to reconcile who they are with what they do as designers. To achieve this, we suggest that we begin exploring precedents entirely outside of the architectural canon. Such precedents resist any attempts to immediately translate the precedent back into the comfort zone of architectural habit. In our own teaching practices as part of the "And Architecture" atelier, we invite students to explore art practices as methodological precedents, which we use to emphasise the production of the unexpected, critical and innovative discoveries, rather than to demonstrate the legitimacy or ability of their architectural proposal.

Precedents in Practice: "And Architecture"

The "And Architecture" atelier is a studio cohort spanning bachelor's and master's levels, including both Architecture and Landscape Architecture students. Our final year Master of Architecture students develop a single year-long design thesis. We ask these students to develop design-research projects that respond to issues of spatial inclusion and develop a bespoke design-research methodology to achieve this. These methodologies are used to identify and/or generate relationships with user groups or audiences affected by the selected issues as well as to specify sites where meaningful interactions could occur.

We observe that students often attempt to replicate creative processes from their prior education, repeating a linear narrative of research (sites, users, building programme), from which they attempt to persuade us that their eventual design brief and resolution are rationally defined. To challenge this, we ask students to background these traditional forms of site/user/material analysis and instead begin by engaging with "difference". This means using methodological precedents which are likely to be unfamiliar to their practice of architecture and using these to explore self-selected social and personal issues related to differences of identity, ability and advantage between individuals and populations.

The students are initially asked to select a particular method from a selection of artistic precedents to explore an issue they are interested in. In the first few weeks, we provide a list of possible precedents, including but not limited to performance artists (Francis Alÿs, Tania Bruguera), collage artists (Martha Rosler, Cold War Steve), video artists (Ant Farm, Stealth Unlimited, William Kentridge) and installation/artefact artists (Cyrus Kibiru, Julie Becker, Erwin Worm). At first, we invite students to blatantly copy their precedent artist, and each week to add a new precedent until the methods they are producing have merged, separated and deviated so strongly from the source materials that they become undoubtably the students' own creation. In fact the methodological reproduction is a repetition of the affective mechanism of the original and will inevitably lead to the production of different outcomes when applied in new contexts with new elements. As students progress through the course, they may seek out and introduce their own artistic precedents or repeat methods that resonate with them.

Students are asked to produce a series of "performances", using a weekly cycle of "Practice> Performance> Potential". First, they must be explicit about the artists' precedents they investigated and how they are being utilised in their own work (practice). Second, they document what they made and how it was experienced (performance). Third, they reflect on their learning and how it might lead to something new (potential). We ask for this cycle to be repeated weekly (as a minimum), to promote students acting without hesitation and without fear of making "a mistake". This process expects that the student will "perform" the method in response to both their issue of interest and build on and extend their existing capabilities.

We use the term "performance" because it requires the student to consider the audience for their work, which we reinforce should not be limited to their tutors. In doing so, precedents allow us to consider form that creative outputs can take as well as content, and how as an architect you can engage and affect other people within and outside of the profession. Understanding how to affect an audience becomes the central methodological focus for students to develop a design-research approach, as the power to make a difference as architects is determined by our ability to convince others of the need and potential of our practices. This process of affective exploration seeks to iteratively problematise an emerging question, a process which is necessary because in contrast to an exploration of the *possible*, there is no predefined or identifiable solution in the discovery of *potential*.

In the next three sections, we will demonstrate our approach to using precedents within the "And Architecture" atelier using case studies from students' work. These examples will, in turn, explore how the use of non-traditional precedents helped challenge students' methodological conformity, imagine new ways of practising architecture and support students to explore their personal identities and experiences within their work. Taken together, these case studies reveal how the use of process-driven artistic precedents can generate unexpected and novel spatial outcomes that push students beyond their own, both self- and institutionally imposed, limitations.

As an example of this approach, Eleanor Nurse's work in semester 1 explored housing inequality and its relationship to capitalism in Manchester. She undertook a recreation of Julie Becker's "I must create a masterpiece to pay the rent" (see Museum of Modern Art, 2019). Becker's work entails a scale model home, developed through an in-depth ethnography of her time in Los Angeles, as a reflection on contemporary capitalism with themes of gentrification, dispossession and nightmares. Akin to Becker, Eleanor used reference images, from a critical investigation into rental conditions in Manchester, to recreate a featured apartment. Eleanor's model is intricately detailed with a red potty beside the toilet, a radiator harbouring mould behind and a dank pink towel. The model, particularly when combined with the reference images and Eleanor's video which features a soundtrack of everyday domesticity, affects an emotional response from the viewer. The viewer is forced to acknowledge that it is a representation of actual living conditions in Manchester. This process led her to reflect on the role of the architect in reproducing housing inequality, and the lack of autonomy in the profession to resolve societal tensions. As a result, rather than trying in vain to "solve" the issue of housing inequality in her project, she instead explores these issues with a more allegorical lens, integrating yet more artistic and architectural precedents (Adam Curtis, Lebbeus Woods, Superstudio) over the course of her thesis.

Beyond Comfortable Methods

Kyra Jennings was concerned with the difficulties faced by people with skin conditions and associated social anxiety, an issue derived from personal experience. Kyra began her project by using a variety of precedents to investigate and develop her thinking in this space, focusing initially on the work of artist

Noemi Lakmaier. Lakmaier, who uses a wheelchair, is a live performance and installation artist whose work concerns "othering" and often uses her own body as a key element of her performances. In her piece *One Morning in May*, she chose to crawl for a journey across a deprived area of London, becoming covered in dirt as part of a visceral performance of the difficulties faced by disadvantaged people when they engage with the city (Lakmaier, 2012). Critically, the work explored how the audience – people who saw her in the street – reacted to what she was doing. Kyra decided to adapt this precedent, covering her face in emollient and proceeding to have her social interactions filmed on a night out in central Manchester.

> But before I did that, that walk, I was really, really nervous. I was nervous the whole way anyway… all my peers were obviously like, no, you should just go for it. And I'm so glad I did because that's actually when the narrative came about.

This exercise presented a significant personal challenge to Kyra, but the selection of the precedent, the deployment of Lakmaier's method and her performance designed in response were obviously all in her hands. She sought the support of her peers to be able to face the challenge to go beyond her personal social comfort zone, which involved potential ridicule in a social setting. The performance was, unlike Lakmaier, recorded as video from a first-person perspective, putting the audience of her film in her position throughout. The audience sees the glances of strangers, the double-take expressions of bar staff, the odd person staring. Her film is an affective performance because anyone watching could identify with the social struggle for acceptance presented in her public journey.

> I put loads of thick emollient on my face, and I went on this walk and that was when the narrative all came about. I had that breakthrough for my project where I'm trying to reimagine spaces that tackle social stigma, and it allows people who feel any type of anxiety to feel more comfortable to go into these social settings…

This performance was pivotal in her project because it not only provided a novel route to explore users, sites and issues, but critically was able to break down her own internalised sense of limits. By engaging with a methodological approach that was so far outside of her comfort zone, appreciating how generative these activities were, and experiencing validation by her peers and tutors, Kyra continued to explore her issues in creative, personal or interpersonal methods. Later in her project, however, the gravitational pull of architectural norms crept back into her project and the need to produce a design led her back to her comfort zone.

One week in studio, Kyra presented a hastily drawn sketch of a building elevation. Apologetically, she explained that Revit, the computer-aided design software she used, had crashed the day before, and that she had lost a week's worth of work. The sketch, in her mind, was a way of showing what her Revit drawing looked like, rather than a creative output in its own right. The hand drawing, which took one tenth of the time to make as her computerised drawing, was lively and experimental, providing a much greater sense of her project than we had seen in previous weeks.

> Thankfully, my Revit broke, and Mark was like well, why don't you just start drawing? I was like yeah, but drawing is for first years...why would I do it in 6th year? ... I had no choice, so I did start a drawing and thankfully I did.

Despite our explicit call for creative methods, and the success of her earlier work, Kyra was still so tied to "traditional" architectural methods for translation of programme and site into spatial proposition that she could only countenance the use of even something as prosaic as hand-drawn orthographic projection when she had no choice. Her comment, *drawing is for first years,* further reveals students' internalised perception of a linear and proper way to both learn and generate spatial form. Kyra perceived that hand drawing was lesser because it was taught earlier in her architectural education. This example demonstrates how deeply internalised Evan's Translation analogy has become within architectural education. This self-policed conservatism was highlighted further when in discussions about this situation, she reflected that *if I had it my way, I'd just be an artist, to be honest.* With this realisation and positive reinforcement from the tutor team, she reiterated her confidence to explore her creative potential. Subsequently, Kyra spent two weeks developing increasingly sophisticated hand drawings, later experimenting with collaging elements onto the design and projecting scenes through the tracing paper with her drawings on. These approaches were critical in developing and communicating her vision which she would not have had the opportunity to try had she not been forced, through technical failure, to break out of her comfort zone (Figure 3.1)

Different Ways of Doing Architecture

> It was really hard for me to let go and start not using what I always use as crutches, and start being more intuitive. It's probably the first time in my life I've ever done that. I think, even though it's a really difficult process... I can't argue with how successful that has been in articulating [the nature of diasporic space] even though it's completely different to my usual language or style.
>
> *Mohsin Ali*

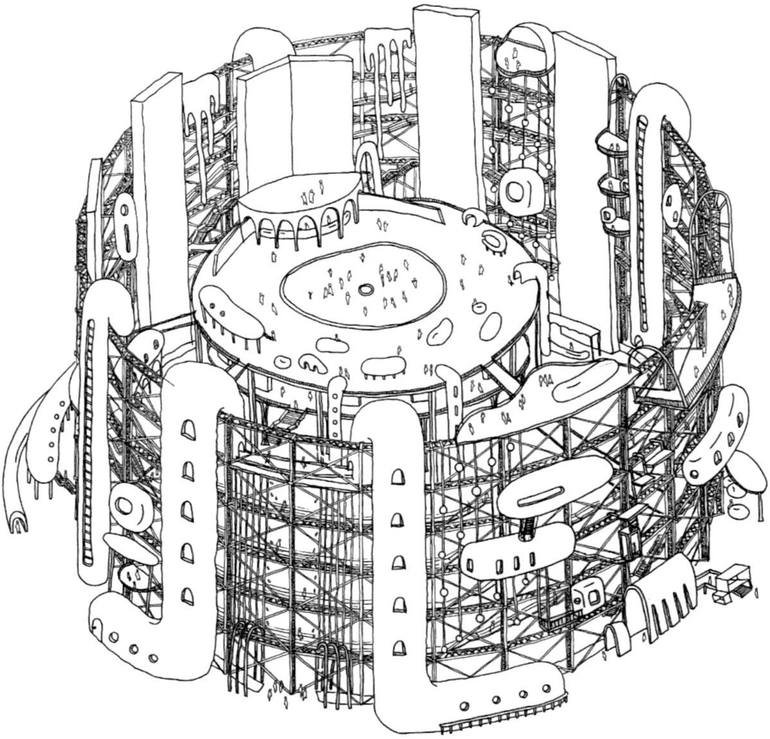

Figure 3.1 Kyra's hand-drawn axonometric of a disused gasholder converted into a nightclub (Credit: Kyra Jennings).

Mohsin Ali's studio project explored how architectural methods can be used to translate the complex, immaterial experiences of post-colonial migrants into more accessible, tangible forms, concluding with the design of a diasporic theme park "Assimiland". Mohsin, born in Bradford to Pakistani migrants, was already comfortable developing artistic outputs, but had not previously used them to develop architectural design projects before. In semester 1, Mohsin had an eclectic range of precedents, which iteratively drew out new ideas about diaspora, hybridity and dichotomy. He began with a visceral performance of two characters, "Self" and "Other", in a tense dialogue. The video of two people, facing each other, is overlaid with a discordant soundscape of Mohsin's own diasporic audio memories (ranging from Scooby Doo and Kanye West to news coverage of the 2004 Iraq War and 1963 Indian film Grashati). Like Kyra's performance,

Mohsin referenced Noemi Lakmaier's use of body and voyeurism, but created something clearly different from the seed precedent. Mohsin's early investigations were affective and showed great confidence and bravery – one highlight being a video of himself wearing a kandura while visiting sites of discomfort (three pubs and an airport), which combined Tania Bruguera's performative approaches and an interest in ethnographic research.

Later however, tensions began to emerge as he struggled to embed these artistic methods into an architectural project that met the professional criteria of the course. In semester 2, he proposed creating a diasporic archive within a Bradford library, the first iteration of which was competent but limited. The layout, created through conventional geometries of rectangular shelves and semi-circular walls, was depersonalised, and failed to draw in the rich personal reflections that had been so successfully documented in his earlier work. His precedents had ceased to disrupt his own design process, with archive becoming the building programme rather than a mechanism for exploring diaspora spatially. His first attempt to create a diasporic archive was, in Mohsin's view, a failure because his architectural habits (which sought solutions and optimisation) overwhelmed his artistic identity (which sought spontaneity and delight).

> This point in the process was definitely driven by fear for me. I was just on the edge of letting go, but it got really ugly before it started being good. I feel like I was clamouring for something that felt safe and familiar, but reductive. So, after that I realised in need to jump into the void a little bit more, submitting to the fact that my work could be a more methodological project, a conceptual project, a conversation, which resonated a lot more with what I wanted to get out of my thesis.

Mohsin quickly addressed this by consciously leaning into his artistic precedents as a way of disrupting his architectural process, which he acknowledges was leading him to create designs that he didn't really want to make. As a final year student, he already knew that he could design a competent building to answer a question posed by a design brief. What he didn't know was the potential of architecture to problematise the question, to use design processes to create space to extend himself intellectually. For the next iteration of his design, he went back to using archival material as a methodological driver, rather than seeing the archive just as a programme that his design needed to house. Taking inspiration from Oliver Jeffers (2007) children's book "The Incredible Book-Eating Boy", whose illustrations are made entirely of scans and collages of other existing books, he explored how he could use the forms and aesthetics of archival material to actively generate the forms and aesthetics of his space. He took items from his father's attic, which he felt embodied his and his father's diasporic identity, curating them into two-dimensional panels or small three-dimensional dioramas and then tracing over them to generate the massing and features of his eventual theme

Figure 3.2 Mohsin's initial design for Assimilland, incorporating elements directly traced from his father's possessions (Credit: Mohsin Ali).

park design. The architectural limitation that Mohsin fought by using this method was fear of illegitimacy – how can a process of balancing archival objects on top of each other, tracing over it and calling it a building possibly be taken seriously? The architecture he proposes through these means is far more sophisticated, engaging and meaningful than his attempts to rationally work through his design to turn a programme into a form (Figure 3.2).

Through this process, Mohsin was able to better reconcile his architectural and artistic modes of practice, and to redefine what he understood as legitimate architectural practice. This is not to say that everything Mohsin does in the future will use archival dioramas to create form, but rather that he knows that it is possible to take methodological precedents and use these productively to be an architect that employs his skills and passion as an artist instead of denying them due to fear of difference. This allows him to respond to his own vision about his future professional career:

> I believe the practice of art is integral to my personal and professional path moving forward… I've had this looming RIBA accreditation hanging over me throughout my education, but I'm worried my work is going to be

> reduced to plans and sections as the only language we can talk about architecture... artists [...] amaze me with their ability to explore the absolute potentials of doing things differently, going to the absolute peripheries of their minds to do it [...] gave me this desire to go out there and explore how I practice architecture differently.

After graduation, Mohsin moved to Saudi Arabia to set up an art and research-led architectural practice, Third Space* Studio, and soon after joined the curatorial team at Hayy Jameel, a leading art gallery and creative hub in Jeddah, whose collection and initiative focuses on issues of diaspora and identity in the global south. Mohsin works with artists directly and reflects on how his knowledge of artistic precedents contributes to his current role.

> I had a really great awareness of like thinking through methodology and artist methodology... and also the critical social thematics as well. What I do all day now is talk to artists about their methodologies! About how they can be translated into different forms, whether its public programming, exhibition spaces, or talks. There is a criticality, but also a spatial production to this. I don't know...maybe being a curator is a bit like being an architect... I'm still discovering my personal curatorial practice.

Mohsin's career path was foreshadowed in his studio portfolio. When asked to produce a "cultural capital" CV for himself set in 2050, a task informed by the precedent of Katerina Ruedi's (1998) critical reflection of her own career, Mohsin stated his desire to work at a gallery, in a role that blurs and extends architectural, research and curatorial practices. Mohsin, like many students, noted at the time how few people had ever asked him what he wanted to achieve through his education, beyond a tacit assumption that he would become a building designer. For all the architectural precedent studies that Mohsin inevitably undertook during his five years of education, it is notable that it was the artistic ones that have had the determining contribution in him defining a new architectural space to practice within.

Being an Architect and being Yourself

> In five years doing architecture never once was the whole Mongolian part of me explored. So, then I was like, OK, now it's time to do that. I was making videos about the culture, about people, and about family. I didn't really know where it's going to end up.
>
> *Uka Luvsansambuu*

Uka Luvsansambuu used artistic methods to develop a contemporary vernacular for Mongolia which was then deployed to connect the urban periphery of the capital city, Ulaanbaatar. One of Uka's performances involved an ethnographic collation of cultural artefacts in the theme of belonging/identity from five Mongolian families living in the UK. The performance merged two unconnected artistic precedents; Zadie Xa's "House" exhibition, which combines visual cultural elements of Korea within a conventional Korean home (See Whitechapel Gallery, 2022); and Yayoi Kusama's "Infinity Mirror Rooms", which creates immersive mirrored rooms to reflect mental state while asleep (See Applin, 2012). Uka's performance itself was the collation of these cultural artefacts into a single space with audio picked by the five families. The piece highlighted the tensions between living in the UK and a romanticised longing for Mongolia.

Uka expanded this analysis of Mongolian migration across his family's journey. This narrated the transition from the rural nomadic herder lifestyle to semi-rural communities consisting of multiple "ger" (Mongolian variant of a yurt), to the urban inhabitation of Soviet blocks, and finally to the UK. Urbanisation in the Soviet era had led to large numbers of Mongolian's becoming sedentary within the Stalinist apartment blocks. In the post-Soviet era, these blocks had gone into private ownership overnight and over time had been accompanied by sprawling suburbs where small plots of land housed a permanent Yurt for the residents working in City occupations.

By reflecting on the lived experience of his family and the relationship between urban form and cultural transformation over time he was able to develop a design guide for contemporary Mongolia which he deployed in his final proposal. His work connected the yurts of the "ger" district of Ulaanbaatar to the soviet apartments of the city centre through a wall that, instead of dividing, connected communities through a variety of physical and social infrastructure. By re-engaging with the people of Mongolia, specifically by imposing Mongolian ways of living onto the original Soviet plan, Uka proposed a culturally appropriate redevelopment of the block. The contextual sophistication of his proposals was generated through his continual engagement with the cultural specifics of Mongolia and using this to critique the standardised modes of planning that had been applied across the Eastern Bloc. His grounded and articulate proposals build on his personal understanding of the issues and have an intense specificity which lends them contextual meaning, providing real insight into how contemporary nomadic and urban life in Ulaanbaatar might be reconciled or negotiated.

The use of non-traditional precedents in Uka's project was critical in creating space for Uka to explore his own identity through his architectural practice. It gave space for a project to emerge that was more than an objective study of Mongolian vernacular or society, but something deeply personal that no other student on the programme could have achieved. The methods used allowed Uka to see his architectural practices as being collective, rather than individual – working with his family and other Mongolians to articulate a vision that would have been, at best, prosaic had he adopted a more linear approach of research (Figure 3.3).

Figure 3.3 Uka's illustration, documenting the cultural and architectural transformations of Mongolia (Credit: Luvsansambuu Luvsansambuu).

Conclusion: Comfort beyond Limits

The experience of the students illustrated in this chapter demonstrates a common struggle to transcend an internalised set of norms on what the correct way to practice architecture is. This traditional precedent of practice has the effect of confirming great robustness and security on behaviours conducted under its auspices, but at the same time serves to restrict the imaginative potential of those who are most invested in it. Because these models falsely present creativity as linear, rational and correct only when done in a certain way, students often self-censor – viewing deviation as unprofessional or even shameful ("drawing is for 1st years"). This suppresses both imaginative work and expressions of cultural, personal and methodological differences. This is of existential concern for the profession, with the potential to stagnate the work of the architect and leave them unprepared for the challenges not just of tomorrow, but of today.

The students' deviation from architectural norms and habits should not be understood in isolation from wider societal movements that marginalise "difference". We read Kyra, Mohsin and Uka's life experiences, shaped by their backgrounds and intersectional identities, as playing a role in shaping their internalised understanding of their social position, which is critical in determining what they *feel* they are able to achieve and aspire to (Bourdieu, 1992). In a predominantly male, white, privileged profession, architectural precedents can reinforce this sense of limits – that experimentation is for the elite, and that the best we can aspire to is to replicate the great work of others. While similar issues exist in the world of art, we found it much easier to decolonise our curriculum by selecting precedents from artists from diverse backgrounds and experiences. Almost everyone can make art and share it with the world, whereas making a building is much more exclusive. Precedents are much more than just fodder for students to pinch formal ideas and can instead be a route to discover avenues to explore and release socially repressed aspects of their identity, attitudes and existence (exploring the *whole Mongolian part of me*) for the first time. By embracing non-traditional methods (Kyra), challenging what architectural practice means (Mohsin), and being confident about integrating personal experience into work (Uka), we believe the education of "And Architecture" students is a challenge to this sense of limits.

As educators, the challenge is obviously not just in deciding what precedents to use, but how we can create the environment through which students are able to examine their own understanding and potential. In line with Mezirow's model of Transformative Learning (2024), we try to encourage a safe and trusting space for dialogue and encourage students to link their learning to their real-life contexts and experiences. We celebrate mistakes. We encourage the risks and create opportunities for peers to do the same. We bring in recent graduates to help students see the value in what they are doing within and on the fringes of the architecture profession. We take time to explain how their work will be assessed, so they can see how the tasks we are setting them are just as valid a way of addressing the module criteria than the typical analysis processes they have engaged with previously.

To conclude, rather than using precedents to validate predetermined design outcomes, this chapter and the atelier advocate for methodological precedents that *challenge* and *expand* the design process. This reframing values plurality, difference and individual ambition, supporting a more inclusive and critically engaged architectural practice. We believe that architecture is messy, relational and non-linear. It is our duty as educators to immerse our students into this reality, rather than in the controlled, filtered and picturesque world of building precedents.

References

Ahmed, S. (2006) *Queer Phenomenology: Orientations, Objects, Others*. Duke University Press.

Applin, J. (2012) *Yayoi Kusama: Infinity Mirror Room – Phalli's Field*. MIT Press.

Bourdieu, P. (1992) 'Thinking about Limits'. *Theory, Culture & Society*. 9(1), 37–49. https://doi.org/10.1177/026327692009001003

Boys, J. (2014) *Doing Disability Differently*. Routledge.

Butler, J. (1990) *Gender Trouble: Feminism and the Subversion of Identity*. Routledge.

Clark, R.H. and Pause, M. (1985) *Precedents in Architecture: Analytical Diagrams, Formative Ideas and Partis*. First Edition. Van Nostrand Reinhold.

Deleuze, G. (1994) *Difference and Repetition*. Continuum.

Evans, R. (1997) *Translations Between Drawing and Building and Other Essays*. Architectural Association.

Freire, P. (2005) *Pedagogy of the Oppressed*. Continuum International.

hooks, b. (1994) *Teaching to Transgress*. Routledge.

Jeffers, O. (2007). *The Incredible Book Eating Boy*. Philomel Books.

Lakmaier, N. (2012) *One Morning in May*. Available at: https://www.noemilakmaier.co.uk/html/omim.html (Accessed: 18 December 2025).

McRuer, R. (2006) *Crip Theory: Cultural Signs of Queerness and Disability*. New York University Press.

Mezirow, J. (2024) 'Transformative Learning'. In K. Aubrey and A. Riley (eds.), *Understanding and Using Challenging Educational Theories*. Sage Publications, pp. 319–340.

Museum of Modern Art (2019) *Julie Becker: I Must Create a Masterpiece to Pay the Rent*. Available at: https://www.moma.org/calendar/exhibitions/5085 (Accessed: 18 December 2025).

Ruedi, K. (1998) 'Curriculum Vitae: The Architect's Cultural Capital: Educational Practices and Financial Investments'. In J. Hill (ed.), *Occupying Architecture: Between the Architect and the User*. Routledge, pp. 23–37.

White, S. (2017) 'The Greater Part: How Intuition Forms Better Worlds'. In B. Lord (ed.), *Spinoza's Philosophy of Ratio*. Edinburgh University Press, pp. 125–140.

Whitechapel Gallery (2022) *Zadie Xa: House Gods, Animal Guides and Five Ways 2 Forgiveness*. Available at: https://www.whitechapelgallery.org/exhibitions/zadie-xa-house-gods-animal-guides-and-five-ways-2-forgiveness/ (Accessed: 18 December 2025).

4

SNORKELLING IN SOIL

Architectural Care for the Ground

Julia Udall, Rachel Schwartz-Narbonne, Jonathan Orlek and Mel Lacey

Soil Communities and Care-Ful Architectural Praxis

The base of an architectural section is usually a dark, uniform solid block. Here, the ground carries little interest to designers beyond basic topographic considerations. It is the carefully designed and rendered spaces that sit above that are the focus of our attention. In contrast to this, we argue that architecture students should sensitise themselves to different understandings and relationships with soil as a living thing that is impacted by the choices of humans living above it.

Snorkelling in Soil is a co-produced community science project bridging architecture and environmental science, where science undergraduates guided architecture students to conduct a scientific research project on the impacts of soil pollution on soil bacteria's antibiotic resistance. It was embedded in a Master of Architecture (MArch) Design Studio, "Co-Dreaming Climates". Across the course of the two semesters, students are invited to develop a lab for a climate activist, researcher or artist that will support collective reimagining of lives, and livelihoods. We sought to enhance the architecture students' subject knowledge and soil-science literacy in ways that lead to a more ecologically sensitive approach to their project development. *Snorkelling in Soil* brought together designers and environmental scientists to explore practically how architects can respond to these issues and take ecological responsibility and, more broadly, to decolonise environmental knowledge by changing the context of its construction to one in collaboration with the human and more-than-human communities. In addition to valuing the new scientific knowledge, this project valued the scientific process as a method

DOI: 10.4324/9781003647720-6

for dialogue between communities, applying feminist architectural practices in environmental science.

Snorkelling alludes to the wonder of when, for the first time, you place your head below the seemingly opaque surface of the sea, and your perspective shifts – the uniform surface of water becomes teeming with life. Through this collaboration we wished to seed similar joy and shifts of perception in relation to the ground. That you cannot literally snorkel in soil might, we think, allude to a need for new pedagogical approaches for imagining, forming and caring with soil communities.

In introducing the question of soil care, we understood it as a fundamental challenge to the logics of architectural practice and education, across multiple dimensions. Rather than conceive of soil as an additional concern to "add in" to their education and professional knowledge, we instead consider it to be "a disruptive intervention [that] is an involvement in the mattering of worlds" (Puig de La Bellacasa, 2017, p. 203). In parallel with this, soil research has shifted from a chemico-physical approach that conceptualises it as an inert substance that can be utilised as resource, to a transdisciplinary and ecological approach which conceives of soil as a living dynamic ecosystem, at the heart of the planets' space of liveability. This shift brings into sharp relief the politics of "[…] deciding what constitutes a soil or what constitutes soils' needs […] what it means to be responsible for soils, and to the societal distribution of this responsibility" (Krzywoszynska, 2023, p. 395). This necessarily requires collaboration and the convening of transdisciplinary, and multispecies soil communities to attend to such matters of care.

In her recent paper "Taking Soil Care Seriously" Anna Krzywoszynska (2023, p. 405) argues that "[…] care is both sparked into being and propelled by attentiveness, which is both an individual and collective practice". Therefore, we envisage that through engaging in soil science through this framing and practice, we can "spark-into-being" the motivational and affective dimensions required for transformation. We envisioned that through working with their hands in the field and the laboratory and participating in the stages of growing microbes from the soil, students would be sensitised to different understandings and relationships with the ground as a living thing which is impacted by the choices of humans living above it.

Soil is a mixture of the living, the not-currently living, and the never-living. The living includes the microscopic communities of bacteria, archaea and fungi, the vertebrates and invertebrates and plant parts. As these die, their biomaterials are degraded in the soil, forming organic materials such as humus. Soil also contains the mineral components sand, silt and clay formed from the breakdown of the underlying rock, and the air and water found in the pores between solid particles of soil. A "healthy" soil has a balance of these components (Ashman and Puri, 2013, pp. 26–45).

When considering architecture as "building on", not "removing from" the soil, it can act against the interests of the soil, upsetting the balance of its components and disturbing the communities within it. The "empty spaces" of air within soil are lost when an area is built upon or compressed. Without these pore spaces, there is nothing to absorb rainwater, increasing the flood risk for those downstream. Pollution from heavy metals, such as is found in industrial or post-industrial sites, can induce antibiotic resistance in the soil bacteria (Pal et al., 2017, pp. 261–313).

Yet we cannot understand soil care purely as a technical question. As Sekulić, Tomić and Sattler point out in "Digging Up the Past: Soil as Archive" (Sekulić et al., 2020, pp. 16–23); "The soil itself is both an ecofact and an artefact and it transcends the divide between nature and culture: it is both things at the same time. It is a past, but it is also present". Any approach to engage with the ecologies of soil must work with it as a complex, entangled natureculture. As Jacobs and Wiens suggest:

> Soil cannot be isolated and thinking with it requires specificity situated in ecological, social, and political relations. Soil becomes a pedagogical challenge to unmake and de-design for design practices predicated on creation as accumulation and extraction.
>
> *(2022, pp. 168–174)*

So then, the question is posed, how do we learn to care? Puig de la Bellacasa (2017, p. 204) characterises care in relation to soil as being "actual practices and relational arrangements in messy material constraints rather than moral dispositions". Care for soil therefore requires us to actively engage in socio-material situations. Locating Snorkelling in Soil within a design studio was intended to invite speculations about how it may alter practices of propositional design research, in relation to specific interconnected sites in their complexity and contingency.

Teaching with Dirt

"Dirt" is a controversial word for soil scientists, as it indicates dead matter, and therefore is not scientifically appropriate as a term for considering soil-as-living. However, as Alex McBratney points out the familiarity of this word (particularly in the US context) could be something that enables the subject to open to a wider audience (McBratney and Raza, 2020). For feminist architectural writer, practitioner and pedagogue Jennifer Bloomer, "dirty" has further power. She used "dirty drawings" and "full-scale demonstrative construction" to connect and integrate processes of architecture with those of the female body (Bloomer, 1992, pp. 7–29). As Jane Rendell (2018) writes, "Through her dirty drawings and her incorporation of parts of the female anatomy – breasts, milk, fluids, blood, hatching, udders – into architecture, Bloomer generated a critique of the sterility of the architectural drawing process". Inspired by Bloomer's work, Doina Petrescu (who in 1999 was invited by Bloomer to run a design studio at Iowa State University, College of Design) used full-scale constructions and "'live' constructions, performative constructions using the body" within architectural design studio teaching (Petrescu, 2023, p. 909). An example of this is an MArch design studio she ran at Sheffield School of Architecture in 2005, which involved students travelling to Dakar, Africa and setting up a building workshop to empower self-building by a network of women: "Like Jennifer's full-scale models, we made one-to-one prototype walls using tires, cans, strings, bamboo, mud, and other materials women used in their everyday life. Working one-to-one, we were working at the 'scale of life'" (Petrescu, 2023, p. 917; see also: Böhm, 2023). Soil challenges the scale(s) at which one-to-one prototyping operates.

Since Snorkelling in Soil was initiated, Marija Marić, César Reyes Nájera and David Peleman ran a design studio at the Master in Architecture Programme, University of Luxembourg, called Worlding Soils (2023), which explored mining territories in Luxembourg through attention to soil:

> Understanding the underground not only as a passive recipient of political, economic, and social processes above, but as a space of resistance, as "somewhere to (dig and) plot," the studio framed soil beyond its resourcefulness and productivity for humans, trying instead to think what could be the role of design in building soil communities.
>
> *(Bose, 2024)*

Considering the role of design as part of a soil community required students to "challenge given scales we work with in architecture, and thus the views they enable, as well as those they oversee" (Bose, 2024). As with other full-scale constructions, and 1:1 pedagogies, undertaking community science with soil (which involves getting hands dirty in fieldwork and carefully working against a tendency of soil to contaminate in a "clean" lab environment) challenges the notion of a singular designer, who makes clean, formal, heroic, interventions, but this dirty learning also expands the scale at which this operates, to include the microscopic scale of life. A sensitisation to soil is one of many architectural tools and practices which can enable designers to meet (and respond to) the worlds within and beyond that which they draw. *Snorkelling in Soil* addresses, in the words of Material Cultures, "the things that are outside the frame of drawing but are critical in understanding and acting upon the wider economic, climatic and ecological character of construction" (Material Reform, 2022, p. 12).

Soil challenges what constitutes life within an architectural "live project" (Harriss and Widder, 2014). As well as broadening the scales at work in architectural design education, processes of learning with soil challenge what constitutes "life". Taking soil "not just a habitat or medium for plants and organisms" but "a multispecies community of biota" challenges students to pay attention to new life-sustaining practices of maintenance and care (Puig de la Bellacasa, 2017, p. 189). While live projects often involve students negotiating design roles alongside/in relation to social, community-based and political dynamics, for example, by "standing in the middle between the authorities and residents" (Chiles, 2014, p. 185), learning within a soil community has the potential to extend this into more-than-human entanglements.

Architecture and Soil Ecologies

Soil is impacted by architecture through land use and urbanisation, both through the capping of soil, or when market-driven development precedes the associated requirements for infrastructures around flood, food production and green spaces. The drive to move development to timescales and logics determined by the market rather than the temporalities of land, reduces opportunities to care for land through engagement in slow remediation processes. Developments can also be driven by maximising commercial returns in relation to a bounded site defined by ownership, and in doing so not think about wider landscapes and relations to other places. At the scale of a building, soil is impacted by materials that are not biodegradable, building materials that leach into the ground, and approaches to foundation construction that do not pay attention to soil.

In the UK, adopting more holistic and robust approaches to addressing ecological issues in general, and soil in particular in architectural education and practice have been patchy (Roaf et al., 2009). Some important recent steps to address this have been led by organisations such as Architects Climate Action Network (no date), who are composed of motivated networks of pedagogues and practitioners, organising to try to shift discourses and embed new approaches in the mainstream (McAulay, 2020). Royal Institute for British Architects president Muyiwa Oki (who was in post when this SiS project was developed), has been vocal in his critique of UK government inaction in relation to agreed climate targets (Spocchia, 2023) and in the past five years RIBA has published a range of climate and ecologies guidance (Hasman, 2023), including the 2019 RIBA Sustainable Outcomes Guide, which has targets around Sustainable Land Use and Biodiversity. It states the need to:

> Leave a site in better 'regenerative' ecological condition than before development; Carry out sustainable site remediation; Create habitats that enhance biodiversity; Create productive landscapes for urban food production; Zero local pollution from the development.
>
> *(Clark and Tait, 2019, p. 8)*

While the Royal Institute for British Architecture (a professional membership body) recommends the need to engage in "consultation with a local ecologist early in the design process" (Clark and Tait, 2019, p. 35), we would argue that to engage meaningfully with such aims requires moving beyond the employment of a specialist to consult on a predefined area of engagement. Instead, we argue that this requires a fundamental shift in knowledge, practices and relationships across an architects' education and professional life (e.g., inspired by approaches such as Clément, 2015; Orff, 2020). Whilst such an aspiration is perhaps beyond the scope of a single year of architectural design studio, we were curious about the seeds that we might sow, which would not only raise the architecture students' awareness of these responsibilities, but offer the motivation, skills and capacities to care for these concerns.

Convening Conversations Around Soil

The studio project was connected to a cross-University Research Group, the Landscape Lab and the Sheffield Lakeland Partnership (SLP) that had expertise around this specific landscape through either research or custodianship, or landscape decision-making responsibilities. The SLP is a ten-year agreement between Sheffield Hallam University, the Environment Agency, Yorkshire Water, Natural England and Sheffield and Rotherham Wildlife Trust (a coalition of governmental bodies, a privatised utility company, Non-Governmental Organisations and a Higher Education Institution) (Welcome To Sheffield, no date a). This partnership enabled us to invite landscape custodians, decision-makers, community development workers and rangers to join our field visits, and open-up discussion of the landscape to plural perspectives and knowledge bases through walking together and conversing. In doing so, we adopted "[…] transdisciplinary modes of practice that open[ed] new apertures for the exploration of new systems, synergies and wholly collaborative work […] toward a more rigorous, robust and relevant engagement across the domains of ecology and design" (Reed and Lister, 2014).

Transdisciplinarity aims to "co-produce action-oriented knowledge, which has the potential to contribute to transformative change" (Lam et al., 2021, p. 243). This approach is practice and research; in it, problem-finding is a shared endeavour that seeks to integrate scientific and social forms of knowledge. For us as both researchers and teachers, we considered that it allows the development of important scientific questions that have specific relevance to the field, but also to develop the practical, cultural and situated knowledges that may enable us, and the students, to start to remediate the problems found.

By having non-scientists (architecture students) perform scientific analyses for research purposes, this project falls within what is typically described as "citizen science" – an overarching term that encompasses projects where the general public is involved in scientific research (Ballard et al., 2018;

Heigl et al., 2019). Projects range from scientist-designed projects with non-scientists performing isolated tasks to projects co-designed between scientists and community groups. The use of "citizen" is problematic in the context of "citizen science"; it is individualised (citizen, not citizens) and emphasises the legal status of the non-scientists (Ballard et al., 2018). Instead, we adopt the term "community science". This highlights our goal to bring together disparate communities of architects, scientists and more-than-human in this project.

Environmental science is too often conducted in an extractive and colonialist manner, separating humans from nature (Turnhout, 2024), treating environmental data as an asset which benefits the scientist conducting the research, and the scientific community that receives the information, over other communities (Genda et al., 2022; Odeny and Bosurgi, 2022; Stefanoudis et al., 2021). Citizen science can also perpetuate these injustices (Calyx and Finlay, 2022). For this reason, a participatory approach to community science was adopted; the research methods were co-designed to meet the needs of research scientists, undergraduate student scientists and architecture students and teachers. Involving people who did not identify as "scientists" in every step of the research, from designing research questions to conducting laboratory work and data analysis, reframed these scientific processes as accessible tools producing knowledge for the wider community. The aim was to use these tools to craft a flat(ter) structure, without the gatekeeping of the scientist as the singular expert, as part of on-going work towards "doing science differently".

The scientific basis of the soil research began with the scientists' awareness of antibiotic resistance as a global health concern (World Health Organization, no date), and our concerns that this is an underrecognised facet of the growing environmental polycrisis. While it is well-established that increases in heavy metal concentration can cause microbial responses by increasing antibiotic resistance (Pal et al., 2017), more work is needed on the extent of the issue, including studies which consider mitigating effects, such as varying soil chemistry, and measure a wide range of soil-contamination levels (Pagaling et al., 2023). This study is part of a wider community science research project focusing on South Yorkshire heavy metal contamination devised by Rachel Schwartz-Narbonne (environmental chemist) and Mel Lacey (microbiologist) and embedded in schools. The scientific research needs consisted of site selection, sample collection, soil characterisation, microbial culturing and data analysis.

In bringing together architectural pedagogical concerns arising from teaching with scientific questions about soil – both grounded in the same Sheffield landscapes – we deliberately moved beyond the conventional boundaries of architectural and scientific disciplines. This move was motivated by a conviction that, in the face of the existential challenges posed by the contemporary polycrisis, professional responsibility cannot be meaningfully defined within disciplinary limits alone. Instead, such conditions demand the cultivation of new questions, forms of knowledge, relations and skills that exceed established professional frameworks.

Architecture–science collaboration, in this sense, is not an additive exchange of expertise but a reconfiguration of how questions are posed, methods are assembled, and knowledge is produced. Responding to such conditions requires the development of new shared vocabularies, relations and skills capable of engaging complex socio-ecological realities. Trained science undergraduates led architecture students in peer-to-peer learning and teaching. Over seven months, teams of architecture and science students co-conducted fieldwork sampling soil at Langsett Reservoir in the context of a day-long architecture student field trip, then they worked in Sheffield Hallam University's scientific laboratories to measure the soil's heavy metal content, and finally cultured microbes from the soil and tested if the microbes were resistant to antibiotics. These activities highlighted different ways of knowing within the scientific realm, including sensory perceptions of soil components from soil colour (Munsell, 1975) and texture analysis by feel (DEFRA, no date), technological-based analyses such as X-ray fluorescence to measure heavy metal content, and culturing microbes which allows microscopic bacteria to be visible to the naked eye. The topic of the scientific research linked analysis of the chemical components of soil and the antibiotic resistance characteristics of the soil's microbial community; this was also considered within the wider project, as teams assessed the impact of human activities on soil microbiology.

The specificity of the soil context was chosen and introduced as an ecosocial and political matter of concern that framed the design brief and also shaped the scientific enquiry. The Co-Dreaming Climates studio worked across two sites, upstream (rural) and downstream (urban), which are connected by the River Sheaf. Upstream, where the community science was conducted, is peat moorland, of Langsett Reservoir (Langsett Landscape Lab). Langsett sits within the Dark Peak of the Peak District National Park, which is a landscape comprised of moorland and agriculture that is also a place of leisure for visitors from the surrounding cities, and in Sheffield's case, contributes to the city's self-branding as the "Outdoor City" (Welcome To Sheffield, no date b). Langsett is a freshwater reservoir with a holding capacity of 1,408 million gallons. It was built in 1904 as part of an infrastructure programme to supply the city of Sheffield with water. Whole valleys have been changed forever, including flooded valleys, displaced communities or construction of elaborate dams, spillways and reservoir lodges. Much of the landscape is used for driven grouse shoots, with heather regularly burned to produce fresh shoots for young grouse. This burning damages underlying peat soils, which are a crucial carbon sink (Rewilding Britain, no date). The Peak District peat is ombrotrophic; its nutrients are derived primarily by atmospheric deposition, and when the air is polluted by heavy metals, they are deposited on and incorporated into the peat (Rothwell et al., 2005). Given the industrial heritage of Yorkshire, some Peak District peatland sites possess high concentrations of heavy metals including lead, nickel and zinc, which can be released via erosion or dissolution during storm events (Rothwell et al., 2007).

The initial field trip, hosted at Langsett, brought together practitioners, students and researchers, including experts from the local Wildlife Trust working both at decision-making level and in community engagement, a Countryside and Recreation Advisor from the landowning water utility company, a hydrology and geography academic, and the Snorkelling in Soil architects and scientists. Each gave a short introductory talk at the start of the day, explaining their role, concerns and practices. We then walked the landscape together, each sharing our understandings and experiences, responding to students' questions and curiosity, before small groups of science and architecture students co-selected sites based on their shared learning, and engaged in soil sampling.

Field-based techniques were followed by laboratory-based chemical and microbial analysis. Students were enrolled in scientific practices of care and attention, in order to build appropriate relations. For example, when students were preparing microbial growth media and manipulating bacteria, aseptic technique was used. Aseptic technique is where a stationary Bunsen Burner is used to sterilise a small area of lab space for microbiology work, removing the risk of contamination from bacteria in the lab environment into the experiment. Care was taken throughout to ensure experiments were performed in a consistent manner, so each test was reproducible within the data set, within the laboratory and by the wider scientific community.

At five key points in the process, undergraduate science students hosted peer-to-peer focus groups with architecture students to reflect upon their learning. To reduce bias in the focus groups from unequal student/academic power dynamics, focus groups were led by trained undergraduate science student researchers who were outside of the MArch course, and no member of academic staff was present, and transcriptions were anonymised before being returned to the researchers. All members of our transdisciplinary research team engaged in analysis of the transcripts from these sessions. Emerging themes were (i) understandings of soil ecologies, (ii) design practices and (iii) professional and personal response-abilities. In the remainder of this section, we foreground the voices of the students in presenting these themes and how they evolved across the community science process.

Understandings of Soil Ecologies

One core aim in developing this collaborative project was to invite students to question how soil might matter. In the initial focus group, prior to commencing the project, soil existed only in relation to technical architectural design concerns such as foundations.

> [W]hat potential does the [soil] have to use, basically [...] more of a structural perspective of like what, what that soil can take as a weight.

While there was some consideration of the more-than-human living at the site, these were described in vague terms with very little on the interaction between humans and more-than-human actors mediated by soil. During the second focus group, conducted at the end of the Langsett Reservoir field trip, architecture students showed a development in their awareness of the interconnectivity between soil and wider ecological and material processes, facilitated by their increased scientific understanding.

> I am learning about how everything is connected here; I've never really thought about soil.

This connection is multidirectional between humans (and their buildings) and more-than-human actors, breaking down distinctions between "natural" and "manmade", and expanding their understanding into the relations between soils and trees. This understanding of the interconnectivity of soil communities with architecture and the wider environment deepened.

> [O]bviously everything that we do to the ground affects how the bacteria and that process works.

During the final focus group, architecture students had arrived at a more scientifically literate and nuanced understanding of soil and its impact at multiple scales. Soil communities were considered more holistically, with an understanding of the relationship of more-than-human actors on the soil, and on each other as well as on, or by, humans and buildings.

> [Soil] make-up can change and differ so much, soil taken down river can relate things.
>
> [My architectural scheme is] all about wildlife and invasive species, and plant life, so all that is [...] an extension of the soil itself.

This integrated understanding of soil ecologies changed the value the architecture students placed on soil and more-than-human actors in their design processes:

> It's not even just the foundations [...] but the purpose of the building and how it will last and so for tree roots and plant roots we will now look at it

> differently, that they actually might provide such important role on the site not just in terms of wind and temperature but also in terms of the flood risk and also sucking up nutrients into the plants.

Design Practices

To embed the learning beyond the project, we wished to shift practices of design research, including tools and forms of representation. In the first focus group, at the start of the first day on site, soil was expressed as a technical issue.

> I will just do a block of basically just browned-in Photoshop to represent [soil], and I never really considered what was actually in there or how the buildings were going to sit on it unless it was specific to that module, like construction and technology.

After a day in the field, conversation became speculative, altering the geographies of design and mapping practices:

> [W]e are doing mapping, I look in the generalised area, maybe at the scale of 1:5000, but it's interesting to kind of think about places that are forty-minute or hours' drive away can still impact your site […] so mapping further afield, upstream.

Reflecting on how soil could be understood as "yet another problem", one student instead suggested this new understanding could be regarded more positively,

> [T]he building could be a part of the solution. [soil] can create design ideas as well; the consistency of the soil might change what material you should use in the building or how you plan. […] If there's a piece of very rich soil that has a lot of nutrients and perfect pH for certain plants you might want to not mess with that.

During the third focus group, a more sophisticated, yet tentative approach to design is posited, requiring feedback "from the land" prior to making design decisions:

> I think the most concerning thing for me is the coniferous forests and other aspects of the landscape [implemented to improve water quality] were done with good intentions based on the current knowledge […] it turns out they do have negative effects and require expensive [work] to remedy the effects. It is concerning because potentially our knowledge right now

> might not be sufficient to understand the ramifications of what we build now and how that could affect the future. I think it is important that we collect as much data as possible and find those connections before we do anything permanent in the future. [...] It is having an intervention, studying that intervention, and then using that as a precedent

The notion of thinking about the future as interdependent is clearly present. By the final focus group, soil knowledge informed agendas, briefs, selection of materials and construction approaches. It is a more careful looking, and care towards processes and tools:

> I didn't really ever think before this that so much around climate change can be seen within soil [...] and it really, [...] it makes you think, it makes you think a lot more about what are other things that you're just doing a quick map about.

Professional and Personal Response-Abilities

This project sought to transform how students understood the role of the architect, in terms of response-abilities (Haraway, 2016, p. 2 and pp. 110–111) and agencies. Whilst Haraway does not explicitly define the term "response-ability" in *Staying with the Trouble: Making Kin in the Cthulucene*, it resonated with us, and we find it useful here. We interpret it as an entreaty to put collective work in to define who and what we should and can be responsible for, and to develop the knowledges, and capacities to be able to act well with and for those things.

In the first focus group, students had some understanding of the impact of architecture on soil health, but professional boundaries, knowledge and roles were clearly delineated, with substantial decision-making around ecologies seen to fall outside of the scope of the architect.

> "In terms of foundations and subgrade and soil, [...] I would have always thought that would be a consultant's bag [...]."; "[H]and your drawings off to a construction company or like an engineering firm, they will just make it work."

After the day sampling at Langsett Reservoir, new understandings of soil ecologies led students to identify new expertise required by architects. They suggested architects needed to engage with new types of specialist consultants; however, this was often framed as another thing to "tick off". These reflections demonstrated a widening awareness of soil, however a dynamic of "generalist architect" and "external expert consultant" remained. Students further discussed the limits of their agency as architects:

> "[Y]ou obviously can't change the land management"; "I mean you probably wouldn't have a say in it but if you, like, chose to put your building somewhere else if it wasn't appropriate ..."; "...in real life you don't usually get that say but if you could ..."

In the third focus group, there was growing awareness that architects can be teachers or advocates and introduce new ways of seeing and doing.

> I am designing something to do with rainwater, flooding with natural defences...but [I'm] trying to change people's relationship with the river [...]
>
> Thinking more long-term [a soil-science collaboration] would be helpful because when you outsource something you kind of give up responsibility and knowledge of it.

The role of the architect as a connector across specialisms and specific consultant expertise emerged in the final focus group. Students described the work they were doing to identify and understand a network within which they are entangled, which included humans and nature. This ecological approach was underpinned by the philosophy of the studio, which has implications for architectural roles and surfaces some of the ethical responsibilities of being a connector.

> So, you're instantly a connector and I think architects as a whole are the connector, they're the connector between the builder, the surveyor, the client, the whoever, the artist if it's like ..., the activists, the wildlife, you know, volunteers, you know, it's anything, you are the central component and you already knowing or having some knowledge about that is important.

Shifting Grounds: From Extractive Capitalism to Models of Care and Reciprocity

The structure of the project alongside MArch design studio work meant that students were learning, reflecting and making connections outside of the soil-science sessions. By the end of the project, some students had incorporated complex soil and ecological knowledge into their brief-writing, spatial scenarios and drawings. We observed these shifts in modes, tools, scales and temporalities for design within their portfolio work, and they had consequences for how they articulated wider professional roles and practices within architecture.

There was a recurrent student expectation that if we open soil as a matter (of care) that we, as tutors, should also tell them what the (architectural) remediation solution is. Whilst those aspects of the brief they considered to be social and aesthetic questions were spaces of exploration that could lead to a multiplicity of design responses, for such "technical" and scientific concerns the response would be a matter of fact, and certainty. This would be to mirror the initial articulations they had of the profession and a wider design team – dynamics of "external expertise", things to "tick off", displacements of responsibility – within educational contexts. Our aim was for them to become active in the figuring of this in ways that were specific to their context.

The students contributed to a wider study on antibiotic resistance in South Yorkshire soils which compared sites ranging from visibly contaminated ochre-rich soils to recently remediated soils found within schools. Within this larger dataset, increased antibiotic resistance in soil bacteria correlated with high levels of soil heavy metal pollution. The samples from Langsett Reservoir were relatively uncontaminated and had correspondingly low levels of antibiotic resistance. Through this contribution the students are enrolled in different forms of knowledge production and different ways of thinking how soil matters and for whom.

Our laboratory methods are scientifically accepted as producing replicable, rigorous results, and we kept these methods and standards when collaborating with the non-scientist community. The presence of architectural students and tutors with scientists opened our perspectives on the work we were conducting; rather than being highly specialist, with the scientist disseminating knowledge for the public to learn, it turned into a decentralised model of knowledge production, where science students taught non-scientists skills, and they performed them at the same level as the formally trained scientists.

Our intention for the scientific knowledge resulting from this study was to decontextualise it to look for universal patterns; in this case, Langsett Reservoir became a handful of data points on the low end of a graph. There is value to the wider scientific community in understanding the general behaviour of microbes. However, the communities that interact, directly or indirectly, with a space require more situated applications of knowledge. Langsett Reservoir is the source of drinking water to Sheffield and Rotherham, and for the authors of this manuscript. Our study was small-scale, and we cannot guarantee that our results would hold if a larger sample collection occurred, but it was reassuring to find minimal antibiotic-resistant bacteria or heavy metal contamination in the soil that we tested.

This scientific research does not provide a guide for what to do in other South Yorkshire sites that we measured which were heavily contaminated. The scientific method is designed around changing one variable at a time, but policy responses require multifaceted, multi-community thinking. While we do not offer a solution, we hope that the transdisciplinary approach we trialled here might provide a roadmap towards creating the interconnected thinking that is required to address the crises on our planet. This approach requires adaptability on the part of the scientists, who need to acknowledge the limitations of their field even as they teach it, and who need to be open to learning unfamiliar tools and shifting perspectives.

In convening a transdisciplinary soil community, which embedded community science within a MArch Architecture design studio, we sought to explore the relationship between soil and architecture. Thinking with soil requires an expansion of scales at which architects operate from micro to urban/macro. The scientific work emphasised this: microscopic analysis was required to determine levels of antibacterial resistance in the soil and reflecting on the results from the different soil sample locations took into consideration the proximity of roads and concentrated human activities. Whilst recognising the relationship between extraction and the material culture of architecture, we sought to expand the focus to that of the microbe.

> [...] To envision an architecture beyond extraction, beyond exhaustion, beyond depletion, we must first begin with the ground—in its soil, roots, creatures and stones—and in the human and more-than-human worlds that tend to it.
>
> *(Bhatia et al., 2024)*

The interdependencies between soil, architecture and landscape/infrastructure were considered in both the work of architecture students and the scientific experiment. Over the duration of the studio, soil moves from being understood as a resource, ground, and capacity, to being interdependent and lively. This change – the creation of an entangled soil community of which the students were a part – resulted from shifts in students' knowledge of soil, shifts in how they understood design processes, and shifts in how they envisaged their role within the architectural profession.

Our ambition is to further entwine soil and architectural design with questions of social and multispecies justice, through deepening their engagement with specific and situated histories of sites and the struggles around land and pollution. Future studios will be aligned with transdisciplinary, and trans-European research projects and networks to support this. We hope this will enable them to stay with the response-abilities that this project has engendered.

Located in their first year, this studio led to a radical shift in the way that the students worked over the MArch Architecture course, into the remainder of their studies. Whilst relatively small and experimental, we do not consider it to be outlier, whereby students revert to previous approaches, once the module has finished. Instead *Snorkelling in Soil* embedded a more ecological approach to architecture, with students developing more entangled, and careful relations with place.

References

Architects Climate Action Network. (no date). *Architects Climate Action Network*. Available at: https://www.architectscan.org/ (Accessed: 9 May 2024).

Ashman, M. and Puri, G. (2013). *Essential Soil Science: A Clear and Concise Introduction to Soil Science*. John Wiley & Sons.

Ballard, H.L., Harris, E.M. and Dixon, C.G. (2018) *Science Identity and Agency in Community and Citizen Science: Evidence & Potential*. White paper. Commissioned paper for the Committee on Designing Citizen Science to Support Science Learning. Available at: https://www.mspnet.org/library/33673.html (Accessed: 22 January 2026).

Bhatia, N., Matson, Z., Hutton, J. M. and Utting, B. (2025) 'From the Ground.' *Journal of Architectural Education*, 79(1), pp. 2–8. Available at: https://doi.org/10.1080/10464883.2025.2463288.

Bloomer, J. (1992) 'Abodes of Theory and Flesh: Tables of Bower.' *Assemblage*, 17, pp. 7–29. Available at: https://doi.org/10.2307/3171221.

Bose, S. (2024) 'Follow the Dirt: Worlding Soils in Post-Mining Minett' (3 April 2024), *KoozArch*. Available at: https://www.koozarch.com/interviews/follow-the-dirt-worlding-soils-in-post-mining-minett (Accessed: 19 January 2026).

Calyx, C., and Finlay, S.M. (2022). 'Improving a Framework for Evaluating Participatory Science.' *Evaluation*, 28(2), pp. 150–165. Available at: https://doi.org/10.1177/13563890221085996

Chiles, P. (2014). 'Live: Between Citizens and the State', in H. Harriss and L. Widder (Eds), *Architecture Live Projects*. Routledge, pp. 183–188.

Clark, G., and Tait, A. (2019). *RIBA Sustainable Outcomes Guide*. Royal Institute of British Architects. Available at: https://www.riba.org/work/insights-and-resources/sustainable-outcomes-guide/ (Accessed: 19 January 2026).

Clément, G. (2015). *The Planetary Garden and Other Writings*. University of Pennsylvania Press.

DEFRA. (no date). *DEFRA Cross Compliance: Guidance for Soil Management ENGLAND 2006 Edition (PB11162) Appendix 2- How to Texture Your Soil*. Available at: https://adlib.everysite.co.uk/adlib/defra/content.aspx?id=000HK277ZW.09MCX1JN2A4408 (Accessed: 24 May 2022, site no longer available).

Genda, P. A., Ngoteya, H. C., Caro, T., and Mulder, M. B. (2022) 'Looking Up and Down: Strong Collaboration Is Only the First Step in Tackling Parachute Science.' *Conservation Science and Practice*, 4(5), e12677. Available at: https://doi.org/10.1111/csp2.12677

Haraway, D. (2016) *Staying with the Trouble: Making Kin in the Cthulucene*. Duke University Press.

Harriss, H., and Widder, L. (2014) *Architecture Live Projects: Pedagogy into Practice*. Oxon: Routledge.

Hasman, M. (2023). *RIBA Climate Guide*. RIBA Publishing. Available at: https://doi.org/10.4324/9781003382485 (Accessed: 19 January 2026).

Heigl, F., Kieslinger, B., Paul, K. T., Uhlik, J., and Dörler, D. (2019). 'Toward an International Definition of Citizen Science.' *Proceedings of the National Academy of Sciences*, 116(17), pp. 8089–8092. Available at: https://doi.org/10.1073/pnas.1903393116

Jacobs, S., and Wiens, T. (2022) 'Breaking Ground: Sifting Soil Stories at Bos Park.' *Journal of Architectural Education*, 76(2), pp. 168–174. Available at: https://doi.org/10.1080/10464883.2022.2097537

Krzywoszynska, A. (2023) 'Taking Soil Care Seriously: A Proposition', in N. Patzel, S. Grunwald, E. C. Brevik and C. Feller (Eds), *Cultural Understanding of Soils*. Springer, pp. 395–408. Available at: https://doi.org/10.1007/978-3-031-13169-1_19.

Lam, D.P., Freund, M.E., Kny, J., Marg, O., Mbah, M., Theiler, L., Bergmann, M., Brohmann, B., Lang, D.J., and Schäfer, M. (2021) 'Transdisciplinary Research: Towards an Integrative Perspective.' *GAIA-Ecological Perspectives for Science and Society*, 30(4), pp. 243–249. Available at: https://doi.org/10.14512/gaia.30.4.7

Material Reform. (2022) *Building for a Post-Carbon Future*. MACK, p. 12.

McAulay, S. (2021) 'Beyond Zero: Sustainable Design Is Not Enough.' *RIBA Journal* (3 September). Available at: https://www.ribaj.com/intelligence/rising-stars-2020-column-scott-mcaulay-regenerative-design (Accessed: 23 October 2025).

McBratney, A., and Raza, A. (2020) *Alex McBratney in Conversation with Asad Raza – The Understory of the Understory*. 10 December. Available at: https://www.youtube.com/watch?v=guegD1QagvE (Accessed: 19 January 2026).

Munsell, A. H. (1975) *Munsell Soil Color Charts*. Munsell color.

Odeny, B., and Bosurgi, R. (2022) 'Time to End Parachute Science.' *PLoS Medicine*, 19(9), e1004099. Available at: https://doi.org/10.1371/journal.pmed.1004099

Orff, K. (2020) 'What Is Design Now? Unmaking the Landscape.' *Architectural Design*, 90(1), pp. 94–99. Available at: https://doi.org/10.1002/ad.2531

Pagaling, E., Hough, R., Avery, L., Robinson, L., Freitag, T., Coull, M., Zhou, X. et al. (2023) 'Antibiotic Resistance Patterns in Soils across the Scottish Landscape.' *Communications Earth & Environment*, 4(1), p. 403. Available at: https://doi.org/10.1038/s43247-023-01057-0

Pal, C., Asiani, K., Arya, S., Rensing, C., Stekel, D. J., Larsson, D. G. J., and Hobman, J. L. (2017) 'Metal Resistance and Its Association with Antibiotic Resistance.' *Advances in Microbial Physiology*, 70, pp. 261–313. Available at: https://doi.org/10.1016/bs.ampbs.2017.02.001

Petrescu, D. (2023) 'Learning and Teaching with the "Body": Pedagogical Hatches from Jennifer Bloomer.' *The Journal of Architecture*, 28(6), p. 909. Available at: https://doi.org/10.1080/13602365.2023.2281625.

Puig de la Bellacasa, M. (2015) 'Making Time for Soil: Technoscientific Futurity and the Pace of Care.' *Social Studies of Science*, 45(5), pp. 691–716. Available at: https://doi.org/10.1177/0306312715599851

Puig de la Bellacasa, M. (2017) *Matters of Care: Speculative Ethics in More Than Human Worlds*. Vol. 41. University of Minnesota Press.

Reed, C., and Lister, N.-M. (2014) 'Ecology and Design: Parallel Genealogies,' *Places Journal*, April 2014. Available at: https://doi.org/10.22269/140414 (Accessed: 23 October 2025).

Rendell, J. (2018) 'Only Resist: A Feminist Approach to Critical Spatial Practice.' *Architectural Review*, 19. Available at: https://www.architectural-review.com/essays/only-resist-a-feminist-approach-to-critical-spatial-practice (Accessed: 19 January 2026).

Rewilding Britain. (No Date) *20% of National Park Land Is Nature-Impoverished Grouse Moor*. Available at: https://www.rewildingbritain.org.uk/press-hub/20-per-cent-of-national-park-land-is-nature-impoverished-grouse-moor (Accessed: 14 June 2024).

Roaf, S., Crichton, D., and Nicol, F. (2009) *Adapting Buildings and Cities for Climate Change: A 21st Century Survival Guide*. Routledge.

Rothwell, J. J., Robinson, S. G., Evans, M. G., Yang, J., and Allott, T. E. H. (2005) 'Heavy Metal Release by Peat Erosion in the Peak District, Southern Pennines, UK.' *Hydrological Processes: An International Journal*, 19(15), pp. 2973–2989. Available at: https://doi.org/10.1002/hyp.5811

Rothwell, J. J., Evans, M. G., Daniels, S. M., and Allott, T. E. H. (2007) 'Baseflow and Stormflow Metal Concentrations in Streams Draining Contaminated Peat Moorlands in the Peak District National Park (UK).' *Journal of Hydrology*, 341(1–2), pp. 90–104. Available at: https://doi.org/10.1016/j.jhydrol.2007.05.004

Sekulić, D., Tomić, M., and Sattler, P. (2020) 'Digging up the Past: Soil as Archive.' *Architectural Review*, 1468, pp. 16–23. Available at: https://www.architectural-review.com/essays/digging-up-the-past-soil-as-archive (Accessed: 19 January 2026).

Spocchia, G. (2023) 'Government Has No Real Intention to Lead on Net Zero, Says Riba.' *The Architects' Journal* (21 September). Available at: https://www.architectsjournal.co.uk/news/government-has-no-real-intention-to-lead-on-net-zero-says-riba (Accessed: 23 October 2025).

Stefanoudis, P. V., Licuanan, W. Y., Morrison, T.H., Talma, S., Veitayaki, J., and Woodall, L.C. (2021) 'Turning the Tide of Parachute Science.' *Current Biology*, 31(4), pp. R184–R185. Available at: https://doi.org/10.1016/j.cub.2021.01.029

Turnhout, E. (2024) 'A Better Knowledge Is Possible: Transforming Environmental Science for Justice and Pluralism.' *Environmental Science & Policy*, 155, p. 103729.

Welcome To Sheffield. (no date a) *Sheffield Lakeland Landscape Partnership*. Available at: https://www.welcometosheffield.co.uk/content/articles/sheffield-lakeland-landscape-partnership/ (Accessed: May 6, 2026).

Welcome To Sheffield. (no date b) *Sheffield: The Outdoor City*. Available at: https://www.welcometosheffield.co.uk/content/articles/the-outdoor-city-for-all/ (Accessed: May 6, 2026).

World Health Organization. (no date) *Antimicrobial Resistance*. Available at: https://www.who.int/health-topics/antimicrobial-resistance (Accessed: 14 June 2024).

5

THE CASE FOR THE DISSERTATION

Tanya Southcott

The dissertation is a fundamental component of architectural education in the UK. Typically conceived of as a long-form piece of writing, this intensive research project is often designed to complement studio-based design work or to enable students to develop a specialisation linked to future practice within the profession. While this interpretation of the dissertation seems to support current trends in the curriculum towards professionalisation and training, it also invites discussion about how this assessment might be leveraged within more exploratory and experimental processes of education.

In this short essay, I consider the question: in what ways can the dissertation help to prepare students for the unpredictable challenges of their future both within and beyond the profession? This discussion is informed by my own reflections as a lecturer on a series of interviews I held with third-year undergraduate students across courses in architecture and interior architecture at the University of Brighton. Here, the dissertation is a 20-credit module that students take in the first semester of their final year of study. It is mostly completed through independent work supported by one-to-one tutorials and workshops. The final assessment can be a written essay (5,000 words) or a hybrid essay (2,000 words) where the main argument is made through film or graphic content. At the end of the academic year, I invited students to discuss their projects and how they chose their topic, and to explain what they learned and why they thought their work was important. While students described their research in relation to professional qualification and as a significant moment in their personal development, they also identified ways in which they used the dissertation to challenge the boundaries of the profession and their learning. The activist agenda revealed through the interviews was an unintentional outcome of the assessment that, I argue,

DOI: 10.4324/9781003647720-7

highlights the transformative potential of the dissertation and its capacity for subversion within an increasingly standardised and professionalised approach to learning.

The Dissertation within Architectural Education

How the dissertation fits within architectural education is an interesting question. In *The Dissertation: A Guide for Architecture Students*, Ian Borden and Katerina Rüedi Ray (2014, p. 2) describe this assessment as an "architecture made of words" and "a way of conceiving and producing architecture through sentences, paragraphs and considered argument". Project-based learning and teaching within the design studio is the dominant paradigm for architectural education (Hettithanthri and Hansen, 2022). Design projects are thought to simulate the best real professional action because they account for the complexities of problems professionals face in the real world as well as how professionals work in practice (see Donald Schön's influential work on "Reflective Practice" [1987, 1991]). The dissertation, by contrast, draws attention to the integrated nature of the architectural curriculum and the ways subject-based modules are used to introduce theoretical, historical, technical and professional knowledge. The QAA Benchmark Statement for Architecture (2020, p. 15) further promotes integration and synthesis by positioning the dissertation as "a specialist research study" or "other analytical and structured piece of writing" designed to support students in developing research and writing skills essential to professional practice. In this way, the dissertation complements studio-based learning by creating alternate ways for students to build disciplinary knowledge, while also honing their ability to devise, sustain and communicate considered arguments.

At the University of Brighton, the dissertation fits into a suite of modules called Architecture Criticism. The intention behind this area of study follows the practice of exposing students to various historical and theoretical contexts in which architectural design occurs while also fostering their capacity for critical thinking. This practice can be compared to the works of a number of other scholars such as Huxtable's (1990) discussion of architecture criticism, Macarthur and Stead's (2006) work around historiography and criticality in architectural discourse and Rendell et al.'s (2007) exploration of architectural critical practice. As the culmination of the Architecture Criticism modules, the dissertation creates the opportunity for students to pursue a self-directed research project through a sustained process of investigation, reflection and writing. Developing their own research interests and agenda is paramount to this process and students are free to select their own topic provided they define their work in relation to architecture or other spatial design disciplines. Students are supported in this exercise by an individual tutor who acts as a mentor and editor rather than as an expert in their field of study.

My interest in interviewing students stemmed from the desire to better understand the role of the dissertation as an extended piece of writing within a curriculum primarily driven by project-based learning and teaching. Existing scholarship on the architectural dissertation tends to take the form of "how-to" manuals (Romice and Yaneske, 2005; Borden and Ray, 2014; Laycock et al., 2016) and while this work mostly targets students, little attention has been given to the experience of this assessment from the students' perspective. The interviews were video recorded, edited and screened in the End of Year Show and displayed alongside printed copies of completed dissertations and abstracts. This was a voluntary exercise, and 13 students participated (roughly 13% of the cohort). While the opportunity to exhibit this work attracted students who were clearly invested in the assessment and proud of their outcomes, it bears noting that the dissertations discussed spanned across A, B and C grade-bands with a median mark of 67. The intention behind the installation was thus to showcase Architecture Criticism work to a wider audience, but it also created a moment of reflection for both staff and students about the real value of the work accomplished in and through this assessment.

Looking across this small sample of interviews, I can see three key ways in which the dissertation contributes to the resilience of our students in the face of an unpredictable future both within and beyond the profession. My observations are based on the ways students interpreted the task and communicated the significance of their research rather than how the task was described in the brief or the module specification. First, the dissertation invited students to contemplate their career trajectories in relation to professional qualifications but also in terms of other, alternate career opportunities. Second, the dissertation encouraged self-discovery, empowering students to develop a clear sense of self and identity through reflection. And finally, the dissertation prompted students to see the transformative potential of their research, in other words, to see themselves working within a world they could make better for themselves and others. Taken together, these points make a strong case for the dissertation as a significant moment in undergraduate architectural education where students can confront their future with criticality and confidence.

Career Trajectory

How the dissertation related to their career trajectory was important to many students. Throughout the interviews, students made direct connections between their research and future employability. They argued that the dissertation reinforced their commitment to the architectural profession by helping them define an area of specialisation and think strategically about how they wished to present themselves as graduates entering professional practice. For instance, one student explored retrofit housing in relation to the cost-of-living crisis in the UK, while another student looked at historical examples of non-hierarchical, more inclusive methods of practice. Yet another student used the dissertation to develop photography techniques in order to drive their design projects. Students also described their dissertation work as a gateway to further research either by proposing to continue working on their topic or to pursue a research degree, creating the possibility for a career in academia. In a few cases, students described how the dissertation prompted them to question their commitment to the profession. For example, one student noted that through the dissertation they identified gaps in their skillset, such as conflict management and mediation. The dissertation, thus, prompted students to imagine themselves as professionals, but it also opened them up to alternate career paths and a broader understanding of their discipline and professional practice.

As part of the teaching team on this module, I recognise that the dissertation fosters transferable skills not necessarily specific to architectural practice – skills related to research to inform design work, but also to communicate ideas in relation to the ideas of others. The module's focus on autonomy and independent learning helps to prepare students to work in professional environments by encouraging them to develop and discuss their ideas through a rigorous research process. Managing this process on their own terms also teaches them to take responsibility for their work and for the consequences of their actions. Seeded in this approach to assessment, however, is also the potential for the dissertation to work subversively and to develop a more activist agenda. Students chose topics related to architecture, but their research often propelled them to think beyond the discipline and to question the value of what they were learning. In other words, the dissertation created a space for students to challenge the traditional boundaries of the discipline while remaining firmly focused on the trajectory of their future.

Personal Journey

Another way in which the dissertation helps students prepare for the unpredictability of their future is by supporting their personal development. The freedom to choose a topic and to set their own agenda is intended to encourage students to develop a clearer sense of identity professionally, but also personally. The interviews supported this contention by drawing attention to the dissertation as a personal journey. Students described working on their research projects as a transformative and empowering process responding to my questions with comments such as "I feel like I've opened my own eyes", and "I guess I came into my own". They spoke in passionate terms, describing the pride they took in their work and the confidence they gained by developing expertise on a subject. One student described this work as "game changing" noting, "it was a daunting process at the beginning, but yeah, it was equally, if not more rewarding during". Again, they recognised that the dissertation allowed them to develop and showcase skills not recognised in other modules, for example, in critical writing. Although many students found this process challenging, they also described how it made the outcomes more meaningful.

What stands out in relation to the dissertation and students' personal development is the way the work of the assessment served as a legitimising process. Not only did the dissertation give students the opportunity to interrogate their learning, but it also prompted reflexivity and enabled them to draw on personal experiences and prior knowledge, all important skills for professional development (McCarthy, 2011). Family relations, childhood memories, experiences in school and on other degrees, as well as issues they were drawn to personally became ways into the research project and helped students to build momentum and confidence. For international students, studying in their home country offered a way to localise their learning and to establish agency and a sense of belonging. Students were able to use the dissertation to reconcile a broad range of interests (Borden and Ray, 2014), but the dissertation also gave them space to reframe or better understand the ways in which their interests were architectural. This self-awareness and the ability to situate themselves and their knowledge helped them to better engage in the evaluation process, but also to see beyond the traditional boundaries of the profession and to imagine their own pathway forward.

Transformative Potential

Finally, the dissertation helps prepare students for the unpredictability of their future by prompting critical engagement with questions about how to make the future better for themselves and others. While the interviews captured the dissertation as a vehicle for personal and professional growth and development, they also revealed an underlying commitment to understanding contemporary issues within society more deeply. Some students used the dissertation as an opportunity to address what they perceived as negative stereotypes and social inequities perpetuated by the built environment while other students used it to challenge long-held beliefs and value systems embedded in professional practice and culture. In discussing their research projects, students described the real impact their work might have for society by relating it to global issues such as social justice, climate and cost-of-living crises and colonial oppression. By encouraging students to take a position in relation to a topic, the dissertation also pushed them to think beyond their own autonomy and to better understand themselves as members of society. Given this opportunity, students used the dissertation to explore ways they might enact change within that society for the benefit of themselves and others.

The activist agenda underlying this work was an unanticipated outcome of the assessment, but also a welcome antidote to the increasing consolidation of architectural education as training in the service of practice. Writing in relation to higher education, Jan McArthur (2022, p. 87) argues for a shift in the way we conceptualise assessment that resonates here with questions about professionalisation. To meet the unpredictable challenges of the future, we must encourage students to be forward looking in the face of mutability. For McArthur, this means shifting assessment planning away from "the world of work" towards thinking in terms of the whole of society and shifting our focus away from the task itself to the value of the task for students. The potential for this approach to teaching and learning is that rather than reinforcing the status quo, higher education becomes a vehicle for transformative change in society (McArthur, 2022, p. 97).

While the design studio has traditionally been the space where students are encouraged to push against the status quo by offering alternate proposals in response to project briefs (Tafahomi and Chance, 2024, p. 519), the activist agenda that emerged through the interviews discussed in this essay suggests that the dissertation also plays a crucial role in preparing students for their future. Students in undergraduate architecture need a space to be critical of the discipline and their education now more than ever, given architectural education's increasing entanglement with the requirements of the profession and a marked movement away from exercises that elicit risk-taking, speculation and experimentation. Thinking of the dissertation as a subversive element does not compromise the design studio's claims to complexity, creativity and synthesis. Rather, the dissertation makes architectural education more meaningful for students by enabling them to situate themselves as both designers and individuals within a more expansive understanding of society and the world around them. Thus, the case for the dissertation is that it offers students more than an alternate modus operandi for learning; it also creates a space for students to hold both their future selves and the profession accountable.

Acknowledgement

This research was completed as part of my Post Graduate Certificate in Academic Practice at the University of Brighton. Thank you to my supervisor, Dr Jo-Anne Lester and course leader Dr Alison Willows. Thank you also to Simon Vincent, Technical Team Manager in the School of Architecture, Technology and Engineering who was instrumental in creating the interview videos.

References

Borden, I. and Ray, K. R. (2014) *The dissertation: a guide for architecture students*. Third Edition. Abingdon: Routledge.

Hettithanthri, U. and Hansen, P. (2022) 'Designing studio practice in the context of architectural education: a narrative literature review', *International Journal of Technology and Design Education*, 32, pp. 2343–2364.

Huxtable, A. L. (1990) 'Architecture criticism', *Proceedings of the American Philosophical Society*, 134, pp. 461–464.

Laycock, E., Watson, P. and Howarth, T. (2016) *The journey to dissertation success: for construction, property, and architecture students*. London: Routledge.

Macarthur, J. and Stead, N. (2006) 'The judge is not an operator: historiography, criticality and architectural criticism', *OASE*, 69, pp. 116–139.

McArthur, J. (2022) 'Rethinking authentic assessment: work, well-being, and society', *Higher Education*, 85, pp. 85–101.

McCarthy, J. (2011) 'Reflective writing, higher education and professional practice', *Journal for Education in the Built Environment*, 6(1), pp. 29–43.

Rendell, J., Hill, J., Dorrian, M. and Fraser, M. (2007) *Critical architecture*. Abingdon: Routledge.

Romice, O. and Yaneske, P. (2005) 'Undergraduate dissertations in a Department of Architecture', *CEBE Transactions*, 2(2), pp. 4–15.

Schön, D. (1987) *Educating the reflective practitioner*. London: Jossey-Bass Limited.

Schön, D. (1991) *The reflective practitioner: how professionals think in action*. Farnham: Ashgate Publishing.

Tafahomi, R. and Chance, S. (2024) 'Comparing the meaning of 'thesis' and 'final year project' in architecture and engineering education', *European Journal of Engineering Education*, 49(3), pp. 514–539.

The Quality Assurance Agency for UK Higher Education (2020) *Subject benchmark statement: architecture*. Third Edition. Available at: https://www.qaa.ac.uk/docs/qaa/subject-benchmark-statements/subject-benchmark-statement-architecture.pdf?sfvrsn=3cecf781_14 (Accessed: April 21, 2025).

6

(RE)MAKING THE CASE FOR STUDIO

Cith Skelcher

Introduction

For many students, the studio is no longer considered the default location of their architectural education. Whilst staff have been working at capacity, fielding relentless institutional change and an ever expanding and increasingly codified curriculum, our studio spaces have been quietly emptying. The pandemic demonstrated the potential for remote learning, and, post pandemic, some students have been reluctant to return to the studio, preferring the familiar confines of their kitchen table/bed/laptop. The increasing demands of paid work on students' time as the cost-of-living crisis bites further impacts on attendance. Outside of a teaching day, studios often sit empty and with mounting financial pressures facing the sector, the studio is becoming increasingly hard to justify to university estates departments.

The picture across the sector is mixed, but overall, access to studio space appears to be under threat. Pressures on space often translate into an increasingly professionalised idea of studio, more akin to that found in the medium to large-scale architectural practice. "Hot desking" seems the obvious solution to sharing a shrinking studio environment, where students pass through, leaving no trace. The implications of this are not only a restriction of the creative possibilities of studio to support the individual student's development, but also the erosion of a collective studio "culture" – a loss of contact within and between different cohorts, affecting attendance at student-led events and reducing opportunities for cross school conversations.

If we are to remake the case for studio, the audience that really counts is the student body. Ultimately, an energised student body holds the most power to reclaim and protect studio space provision, but before we discuss

DOI: 10.4324/9781003647720-8

the potential value of the studio, we must first address its challenges. A critical reflection of its culture, its teaching traditions and its relationship to practice are needed, given that all these are, to some extent, contributing to its current demise.

Studio on Trial

Within the context of architectural education, the studio has evolved into an almost mythical status. Describing both the physical space where students develop their designs and the social structure within which they are taught, the studio is traditionally the place where students find out if they "have what it takes" to make it as an architect.

Reyner Banham in his essay, "A Black Box: The Secret Profession of Architecture" (1990, p. 184), describes the studio as a tribal longhouse where students are socialised into the profession, absorbing by osmosis (or not) the magical formula for designing Architecture.

This patrician and protectionist method of teaching has historically supplied the profession with a reliable crop of well-trained and "socialised" employees, along with a few notable beneficiaries of exceptionalism and privilege.

Writing a few years later in *The Favored Circle* (1998, p. 3), Garry Stevens provides an in-depth critique of what he describes as the broader field of architectural privilege and pupillage that underpins the studio system and its relationship to the profession – arguably still recognisable today. It can be read in the power dynamic of the "studio master" (or tutor)/student relationship; in the competitive pitting of students and "units" against each other and in a kind of "survival of the fittest" work ethic. The impact of this negative working culture combined with stress linked to workload and the financial burden of such a long course on the well-being and mental health of architecture students has become alarmingly apparent over the past ten years. The Bartlett Report, commissioned by the Bartlett School of Architecture in 2022 following allegations of bullying, sexual misconduct and racism, detailed what it called a "culture of favouritism and fear" (Howlett Brown, p. 41), which had been allowed to develop unchecked over decades. Maryam Al-Irhayim, writing in the Architect's Journal (2022), described it as "the tip of the iceberg", and undoubtedly the resulting media coverage put student well-being at the top of the agenda in most architecture schools. However, with many of the traditional studio structures and practices within UK architectural education at least still seemingly intact, one wonders how much has really been achieved towards addressing the inequality, long hours and sleepless nights that we know can carry through into the profession.

Another legacy of the "tribal longhouse" described by Banham is a potential narrowing of academic enquiry. Banham observes a close adherence to what he describes as a kind of *pattern and repeat* exercise led by the "studio master" along with a general discouragement from pursuing "modes of design that come from outside the studio". The downward transfer of knowledge from tutor to student not only perpetuates inequality, with success often relying on the student's ability to reproduce the interests, skills and style of their tutor; but also an over-reliance on this teaching relationship, which can represent a narrowing of opportunity for exposure to new skills, methods and critical perspectives.

We also need to be wary of limiting architectural education to the prescriptions of the profession – to what Harriet Harriss, in her introduction to "Radical Pedagogies, Architectural Education and the British Tradition", called "compliance driven tropes of credentialism" (2015, p. xii). Compliance is not enough! As educators we should be empowering the designers of the future to be critical of existing systems; to question and move beyond normative practices; to pursue restless and rigorous research-led design; and to explore alternative, just and resilient futures.

In times of crisis and uncertainty, the temptation is to retreat, to defend our educational traditions and our patch of professional turf. The studio has the potential to provide us with a crucial counter space within this educational context. Through resistance, play and co-production, the studio might offer an opening up rather than a closing down of architectural inquiry and exploration.

The Studio as a Space of Resistance

Within the context of a conversation about social, spatial and material justice brought into focus by the pandemic and compounded by the cost-of-living crisis, the studio has a crucial role to play as "leveller". The pandemic revealed and "exacerbated the disproportional inequality that students face, especially those from lower financial backgrounds balancing work and studying" (Maryam Al-Irhayim, 2022). More recently, the "Student Working Lives" report, published by the Higher Education Policy Institute (Wright, Wilding, Lawler and Lowe, 2025) has evidenced the significant impact that paid work has on academic outcomes and student experience. The studio can provide equal access to creative resources and neutral ground for all to dream, think, draw and explore, where students can develop their own approach and methods as spatial practitioners.

But we must start by acknowledging that the studio, and the institution in which it sits, is not neutral. As stated by Leslie Kanes Weisman in her introduction to "Gender, Space, Architecture: An Interdisciplinary Introduction", "Be it affirmed: The built environment is largely the creation of white, masculine subjectivity. It is neither value-free nor inclusively human" (2000, p. 4). All space is political – the very act of design requires the taking and enclosure of space and the extraction of resources.

In its initial guise as "Studio Invisible Cities" (2019–2022), my postgraduate design studio was chiefly concerned with revealing and disrupting the hidden inequalities and power dynamics that shape our environment. As "Studio Feminist Ecologies" (2022–2025) it has evolved a broader preoccupation with architecture's complicity in the colonial project and its legacy of exploitative and extractive structures and processes. The framing of the studio and the projects coming out of it each year have all been exploring variations of the same question, that is, *How can we maintain an ethical position and pursue a positive reparative practice within the context of this problematic legacy?*

In the seminal work, "Teaching to Transgress – Education as the Practice of Freedom", bell hooks talks about a truly engaged pedagogy that embraces the complexity of both the personal and the political. She urges us to open our hearts and minds,

> so that we can know beyond the boundaries of what is acceptable, so that we can think and rethink, so that we can create new visions, I celebrate teaching that enables transgressions – a movement against and beyond boundaries. It is a movement that makes education the practice of freedom.
> *(hooks, 1994, p. 12)*

A truly engaged pedagogy can be transformative and hugely rewarding but pushing through the cynicism and exhaustion in these fraught times can also be challenging. Mel Dodd, writing in "Radical Pedagogies, Architectural Education and the British Tradition", offers encouragement, suggesting a tactical approach, described as "Double Agency", whereby we, "nurture a constant, knowing and wary negotiation of complicity with resistance" (2015, p. 29). Understood as "an emancipatory and transformative project for society", cultural, creative or arts-based practice can energise us by giving us the tools to "contest institutional norms and fixed hierarchies" (Dodd, 2015, p. 22).

Critical thinking, as described by Paulo Freire in "Pedagogy of the Oppressed" (2017), is the bedrock of emancipatory and transformative pedagogy. It is essential to a creativity that goes beyond the production of image and form to a real engagement with the socio-political impact of our decisions as designers. It reminds us to question first principles – to situate and critique our design decisions within the context of the many and varied challenges we face as a planetary species.

The demands and requirements of practice and accreditation bodies currently weigh heavily on architectural education and can in some ways be seen to prioritise technical and formal skills. Year-on-year students are showcasing ever more sophisticated and seductive digital image making, but as educators we must continue to pursue understanding, criticality and innovation. Architectural education must go beyond the transferral of skills, to supporting our students to develop a questioning and critical approach to practice.

Encouraging and celebrating a plurality of approaches and outputs is key to maintaining a critical and creative studio. At postgraduate level in particular, our role as teachers is to create the conditions within which students might develop their own alternative readings, approaches, methods, outputs. In short, to develop their own practice. We need to give students the tools and support to gain knowledge through experience, and to maintain the studio as a space of acceptance and equality where this can happen.

Acts of resistance represent a critical engagement with, rather than avoidance of areas of contestation, and can occur at a range of scales both within and beyond the studio. At the scale of the architecture school, taking up space and transgressing expected behaviours can provide a powerful opportunity for disruption. In 2002, "Taking Place", a group of feminist spatial practitioners, architects, artists and writers, some of whom based at the University of Sheffield, staged a three-day feminist whole school take over, a participatory event which performed, through a series of writings, objects, arguments and interventions, "a critique of the academic institution and architectural education, both in terms of programme and space" (Hoskyns and Petrescu, 2007, p. 29). As Hoskyns and Petrescu note, this event provided a moment of intensity, an exchange that seemed to slow down and stretch out time, allowing for a shift and expansion of the territory of feminist academia within the context of architectural education.

In 2020, staff and students from the Sheffield School of Architecture, including some involved in the original "Taking Place" event several years before, co-produced "The Feminist School of Architecture Teachout: Foundations Fields and Futures". Held during a period of industrial action at Foodhall, a community kitchen and DIY arts space out in the city, the event attempted to provide neutral ground to further expand critical conversations to include voices perhaps hitherto excluded from feminist academia, partly in response to the Black Lives Matter movement.

The Teachout revealed a shared desire and commitment to gather and consolidate work done to avoid "lost ground", but also to create support structures to ensure the continuation of the feminist work happening in and around the Sheffield School of Architecture over the past 25 years. The result of this conversation was the "The SSoA Feminist Library", an online archive of feminist voices, practices, projects and events, added to at regular intervals, intended to provide a platform for the growing body of projects exploring decolonial and intersectional feminist approaches coming out of the school.

These kinds of support structures can help to reinvigorate the studio as a space of resistance and creativity. But what might this creativity look like? How might the students experience it? How do we re-engage those that have "checked out"?

The Studio as a Space of Play

Learning should be fun! I had to wait until I was 40 to receive validation for this view in the pages of bell hooks, having been told emphatically in an undergraduate dissertation seminar that "play" was not a serious enough topic for an architectural thesis. I was introduced to the potential of participatory design through my first experience in practice, but it was not until I began teaching at a school with an interest in the *process* of making architecture, in understanding architecture as a *social* practice, that I began to think deeply about the importance of *how* we design.

In the absence of a culture of playful creativity, the process of design can be painful. Anxious they may not be blessed with sufficient talent and intimidated by the talent of others or feeling that they should just "know the answer", students are often reluctant to share the contents of their sketchbook, if they are using it at all. They might prefer to work from home; to work it all out in their heads or in a 3D digital model before sharing it for comment, which then becomes an incredibly stressful moment of exposure.

So how do we nurture a studio culture that actively encourages playful experimentation? Lettice Drake is a designer, facilitator, artist and activist who teaches part time at the Sheffield School of Architecture and Landscape. In conversation with Lettice, I asked her about "joy" as a key driver of her practice. What she described goes beyond following one's own interest and passions – it has a clear political resonance – it is joy found through collective effort. This approach informs the way she undertakes projects, which often sit somewhere between architecture and performance; driven by a restless, playful design process; and are always enacted in collaboration with others (Drake, 2025).

Working with Practice Architecture, which Lettice set up with two friends in 2008, projects such as Frank's Cafe, a seasonal event space on the roof of a multi-story car park in Peckham, were typical in their experimental approach and use of found or reclaimed materials. Each project was seen as an opportunity for research – to "learn through doing" – working creatively within a set of often challenging physical or financial constraints. Lettice acknowledges that this method of "on site intuitive design" was only possible through having access to large disused spaces or sites for exploration, an opportunity not open to all.

Lettice has brought this approach to her studio teaching through the meanwhile use of vacant spaces in the city, setting up interdisciplinary collaborations with local artists, crafts people and organisations.

In 2022 her postgraduate design studio, Studio in Process, explored the idea she now describes as PAM, "Party as Method", where the studio was tasked with the design and curation of a space to host a series of events within a limited budget. Rehearsing the production of space through a series of very ordinary questions such as "how do we want to address the street?", "what should people feel like on entering the space" or "how can we construct a demountable screen with this pile of materials", sets the tone for a more fluid and engaged design process that builds confidence and skills.

Whether teaching out in the city or back in the studio, Lettice advocates for a looser, more playful working environment, one perhaps more closely aligned to the artist's studio, "a place of creative possibility, where material scraps and work in progress is all around, and where people feel they have permission to experiment" (Drake, 2025). She goes further, arguing for time spent free of analysis or judgement, trusting in the process of making to suggest new ways forward. As educators we can, through light touch but well-structured briefs and workshops, and the provision of agency, even if only temporarily, over a particular allocated space, help to create the conditions for a more enjoyable, discursive and student-led studio environment – fertile ground for a range of projects to emerge.

The Studio as a Space of Co-production

In the spirit of Audre Lorde, I propose that we exorcise the myth of Banham's "black box", which still haunts the studio, and replace it with an alternative metaphor: a new box of tools, where sewing machines and teapots sit alongside laptops and scale rules, with material scraps, questions, ideas and even agreed rules and rituals for use, reassembled each year by students and staff together to facilitate resistance, play and co-production. In short, to support the studio as a space to nurture creativity for all.

I envisage this task as a reinvigoration of the "Homemaking" brief that I have given to my studio for the past six years, one that I increasingly see the value of. Underpinned by discussion of Fisher and Tronto's "Ethics of Care" (1990), it invites the students to assume a collective responsibility for their studio at the outset through co-designing a social and physical "infrastructure of care" to anchor and support them through the year.

To design a studio space that works for all, the students must first get to know each other; share something of their own lived experience, interests and working habits. "Show and Tell", the first part of the brief, invites the sharing of personal mementoes, which then find a home on a makeshift mantlepiece somewhere in the space, alongside areas for making, storage, drawing and conversation. The students need to balance individual and collective needs and negotiate differing ideas of mess and order, and of shared and solitary space.

There is a heightened awareness of the differing needs of individuals within the studio in the context of conversations about embracing neurodiversity. Social and digital structures can help provide a scaffold, with shared daily or weekly activities such as breakfast meetings, project swaps and housekeeping balanced with periods of quiet time, online Miroboards and resources providing alternative ways to participate. The students are encouraged to explore the tensions set up by competing or conflicting ideas of what a studio should be – to visualise and spatialise opportunities to accommodate both difference and common ground.

Perhaps reflective of a wider tendency towards individualisation within society coupled with the culture of competition within education, students are often reluctant to work in a group, anxious to get on with their own projects in their own time and on their own terms. But in doing this they are closing themselves off from the hugely valuable culture of support and learning that the studio can provide; from learning the social skills required to hold cross disciplinary conversations and to be agents for change in practice. Collective briefs can be followed by group tutorials, where the tutor's voice is one of several, and the students become invested in supporting each other's projects. As tutors, we can model a kind of "learning together", supporting conversations where all are encouraged to contribute, where the tutor steps back, where the students set the agenda.

In terms of what a studio should "look like", I would argue that this should remain an open question, with a range of possible answers formulated each year through creative collaboration between staff and students. While I will continue to advocate for the value of a dedicated studio space for every student, this is clearly not always possible at present given increasing financial constraints of an underfunded education sector, so we need to find creative ways of reimagining and reclaiming the space we do have to provide a rich and diverse learning environment for all, attracting students back into the studio to rebuild our studio culture.

Protecting space for situated studio work in some form is key, as well as allowing space for cross studio, cross school interactions, but other configurations should be explored. Common rooms, rotating "residencies" and pop-up workshop events as well as the use of "urban rooms" and meanwhile spaces out in the city might also have a role to play in a reimagined and reinvigorated studio experience. Although it can be hard to persuade educational institutions that the value of securing access to these kinds of spaces outweighs any real or perceived financial or health and safety risks involved, the case can be made under the banner of "civic engagement". An institution that is meaningfully embedded in the community beyond the campus is certainly a more resilient one.

At the Sheffield School of Architecture and Landscape, the creation of Live Works, project office and "urban room", has provided a powerful space for connecting the school with local communities through projects that engage the design and research expertise of staff and students on projects that have real social impact. Expansion of the studio's praxis beyond the "ivory towers" of the architecture school will always offer rich opportunities for students to explore new perspectives and to really understand design as a collective, social practice.

Studio Remade

Creativity is a practice that requires time and space to be nurtured. Part of the potential value of the studio is that it can support students to develop habits and working practices that will both enable their creativity and support their productivity as they prepare to enter practice, but crucially, through the collective dialogue and critical framework that the studio provides, it can also support them to develop their own critical position. Sitting outside of or parallel to the lecture theatre, the workshop, the office and the laptop, studio is the space where students can develop their own critical position and research-based practice, which ultimately with support can lead to students discovering authentic projects, where their methods inform distinctive, meaningful and critical outputs – other ways of doing architecture.

It is no longer enough to rehash the same repudiations of the studio's once romanticised but now widely discredited foundational myths – the architect as solitary genius; the "all-nighter"; the overt competition of the beaux arts charrette. Despite our protestations, traces of these tropes linger, pushing more and more students away, with an emptying studio proving harder to defend as a physical resource open to all.

Let us begin the urgent task of rediscovering the pedagogical value of the studio and restating its case to ensure its survival as a space of resistance, play and co-production, providing the best rehearsal for architecture as a social practice.

References

Al-Irhayim, M. (2022) 'The Bartlett Is the Tip of the Iceberg ... a Toxic Culture Is Widespread in Schools', *The Architects' Journal*. Available at: https://www.architectsjournal.co.uk/news/the-bartlett-is-the-tip-of-the-iceberg-a-toxic-culture-is-widespread-in-schools (Accessed: 5 November 2025).

Banham, R. (1999) 'A Black Box: The Secret Profession of Architecture', in Banham, M., Barker, P., Lyall, S. and Price, C. (eds.) *A Critic Writes: Selected Essays by Reyner Banham*. Berkeley: University of California Press, pp. 292–299.

Dodd, M. (2015) 'Double Agency: The Art School, Critical Practice and Architecture', in Harriss, H. and Froud, D. (eds.) *Radical Pedagogies: Architectural Education and the British Tradition*. Newcastle Upon Tyne: RIBA Publishing, pp. 21–31.

Drake, L. (2025) *Telephone Conversation with Cith Skelcher*, 15 July.

Fisher, B. and Tronto, J.C. (1990) 'Toward a Feminist Theory of Caring', in Abel, E.K. and Nelson, M.K. (eds.) *Circles of Care: Work and Identity in Women's Lives*. Albany, NY: State University of New York Press, pp. 36–54.

Freire, P. (2017) *Pedagogy of the Oppressed*. Translated by M.B. Ramos. London: Penguin Classics.

Harriss, H. (2015) 'Introduction', in Harriss, H. and Froud, D. (eds.) *Radical Pedagogies: Architectural Education and the British Tradition*. Newcastle Upon Tyne: RIBA Publishing, pp. xii–xix.

hooks, b. (1994) *Teaching to Transgress: Education as the Practice of Freedom*. New York and London: Routledge.

Hoskyns, T. and Petrescu, D. (2007) 'Taking Place and Altering It', in Petrescu, D. (ed.) *Altering Practices: Feminist Politics and Poetics of Space*. London: Routledge, pp. 15–38.

Howlett Brown (2022) *The Bartlett School of Architecture: Environmental Investigation*. 9 June. Available at: https://www.ucl.ac.uk/bartlett/sites/bartlett/files/the_bartlett_school_of_architecture_environmental_investigation_report_june_2022p_6.pdf (Accessed: 28 November 2025).

Lorde, A. (2018) *The Master's Tools Will Never Dismantle the Master's House*. London: Penguin Classics.

Sheffield Feminist Library (2025) *Sheffield Feminist Library*. Available at: https://feminist.ssoa.info (Accessed: 3 December 2025).

Stevens, G. (1998) *The Favored Circle: The Social Foundations of Architectural Distinction*. Cambridge, MA and London: MIT Press.

Weisman, L.K. (2000) 'Women's Environmental Rights: A Manifesto', in Borden, I., Penner, B. and Rendell, J. (eds.) *Gender Space Architecture: An Interdisciplinary Introduction*. London: Routledge, pp. 1–5.

Wright, A., Wilding, M., Lawler, M. and Lowe, M. (2025) *Student Working Lives*. HEPI Report no. 195. Available at: https://www.hepi.ac.uk/reports/student-working-lives/ (Accessed: 15 December 2025).

7

THE OTHER SCHOOL

Anna Gidman

The Other School

Hey, it's lovely to meet you despite the driving rain! Let's begin the tour!

A student jumps in behind us as the door closes, she is holding her model in a box for the open reviews on the top floor. The receptionist greets her and flips her name on the *Wall of Faces* as she hangs up her dripping coat. She drops her phone at reception and laughs as she rushes upstairs, a drawing tube bouncing on her back. The *Wall of Faces* register was created a while ago by a student in frustrated response to the hellish and exclusionary practice of two-factor authentication. It's handy as we know who is in the building, there is no need for us to track attendance, and, if there is a fire alarm it automatically prints a list, including who may be waiting in a refuge for assistance.

Nursery kids are chatting in multiple languages and wandering through the hall as they head to the glass house; one boy carries an obliging rabbit under his arm, another is dragging a large cardboard box. Most silent work pods are illuminated at various levels in the atrium meaning they are occupied, and below us, day two of the "Beyond Entanglement: More Than More Than" conference is underway in the lower ground galleries. The energy production monitor on the wall is low, which is usual for this time of day.

I hope you're warm enough. I forgot to say that our building is quite cold as some students decided to turn the heating off a while ago to see how well we adapt. To be honest, you do get used to it. It does make me wonder how we arrived at the point of expecting buildings to be the same temperature all year. It's not that bad even in November! If you'd like a hat we have spares at reception. You would? Great! Cornflower blue. A good hopeful choice.

DOI: 10.4324/9781003647720-9

Our café is over the bridge, next to the workshops. It was built by students a few years ago using materials gathered from the careful deconstruction of a local building. As a school we consider demolition an act of violence and fully embrace reuse as exemplified by projects such as Sala Beckett (Flores i Prats, 2016). The earth block flooring was made by students, and currently, some walls are covered in experimental biobased materials adding an interesting aroma! Staff papers, books and journals are located along this shelf to acknowledge and celebrate their work. Comments are encouraged and slow handwritten dialogues take place on the wall above.

Local (non-student) residents run the café and use our workshops. There was a recognised need for lifelong learning and general support of creativity and making in the northern community in which we are based. Two members of staff sit in the café trying to work out how to challenge students to develop and test nontoxic protection methods for timber in humid environments. All modules are led in pairs to allow ideas to surface through collaboration and conversation, and of course, it takes the pressure off. Allowing this space for critical thinking is one of the best things we've done. Staff publishing rates have soared, and module sessions are dynamic and dialogic. It also mitigates the disruptions caused by family emergencies and illness, so no mad dashes to find cover. We've also noticed an improved mood in staff since we made the change. Interestingly, Learning Objectives are given to the students to personally manage and record. We guide them through this of course, it's going well.

There is a lot of writing on the café walls, it's our living notebook. In fact, you'll see that there's a lot of writing and drawing in our school in general! Like tattoos on a body, we mark the skin of the building, layering in memory and sharing our thoughts. Over time, themes have developed in certain spaces, from deep theory to love notes. Nothing is removed. Everyone has a voice. Our building acts as a call to action whilst questioning values of ownership. Actually, here's a pivotal one, "less is more…mess is the law", inspired of course by Architecture Depends (Till, 2009), to which was added "ASSESS NO MORE!!". This led to staff-student debates and resulted in us no longer marking. Instead, at the end of modules we have group conversations with students and discuss the work. Then together we agree if they've experienced enough or need to study more before moving on. Any utterly outstanding pieces of work are celebrated at the *End of Year Festival* which is more joyous. The best essays are read out in full. Yes, in full! It's great. So much student work goes hidden otherwise don't you think?

This evening, we have an afterschool architecture club in the model workshop, and our monthly *Design Pop* in the café, where members of the public drop in with design queries which students help resolve. *Design Pops* are particularly successful for members of the public who prefer to have a discussion in a language other than English, as we have a wide mix of students from around the world.

To our right, the courtyard is packed full of delightfully tiny buildings as part of the *(Re)Home* module where more experienced students construct full size shelters with experimental materials in which other students sleep – inspired by the excellent Pods Project in Alabama (Rural Studio, 1999). All materials are from our warehouse and returned there after use. There is a joke about the returned materials becoming increasingly smaller as they are cut up each year, and that eventually everything in the warehouse will be so small that we will need to develop a *(Re)Composite* project with biobased binders. There are some very wet-looking students climbing or being hoisted out of the shelters this morning, as some roof details have failed, but they are laughing as they pile in for showers and breakfast. One shelter each year is donated to the city, and they are sometimes adopted in strange ways. The most memorable to date is *The Rizz*, a tiny love hotel on a roof top. It's internally lined with cork and sends a pink laser into the sky when it's occupied. Brilliant!

Earnest hammering starts in the empty building we also own across the courtyard. Students in our retrofit course are carefully removing all materials back to structure under the instruction of our module leads in *Make Do Mend*. This is in collaboration with our *Heritage Construction Skills* course for 16–18-year-olds, as we are concerned that retrofitting without construction team understanding of the principles of building physics will lead to a future mould epidemic amongst other things. The need to plan for "healthier as well as more efficient buildings" in retrofit is critical (Monteiro, 2023). Our self-imposed challenge is to retrofit the new building without mastics or plastics and to only use reclaimed, biobased and experimental materials. As usual, it's risk and insurance that exhaust innovation and progress!

As we literally build our school, a new unpredictable architectural typology of palimpsest, reuse, care and maintenance emerges in resistance to endless growth. We want our students to be emancipated from extractive linear economic flows, and instead, reconnect with more innate circular experiences. As you can therefore imagine, regular guests to our school for these courses include leading innovators in transitional methods such as Lionel Devlieger, Anders Lendager, Immy Kaur, Aurore Baulier, Sarah Edmonds and more (Rotor, Lendager, Civic Square, Architects Climate Action Network (ACAN), National Retrofit Hub, respectively; 2025). I feel we are finally shifting from being antibacterial, and becoming more probiotic as architects perhaps. We could do with a new word for this palimpsestuous era of care and darning … Loopism?! Hmm, let's wait and see.

We are passionate about making natural materials a first choice when specifying. To support this, we own land outside the city which we use for summer builds, and we grow timber and crops as part of a wider project supporting biobased material research and development. Currently, a group of students are experimenting with waste fibres to create binderless fibreboards for the retrofit project after being inspired by an article on material production (Vitrone et al., 2021). We are working with the British Board of Agrément to test and certify materials before installation and monitoring. One student developed a block mixing sunflower husks and lime, and the thermal resistance came out surprisingly similar to hempcrete which is exciting. He's named it suncrete! (Pound, 2025).

It will take a few years for the *Make Do Mend* building to be finished, and at that point, the space we are standing in now will turn into a larger public gallery and cinema. We are so happy with our 100-year vision for the school, inspired by Squash in Liverpool (Squash, 2024). It took staff and students a long time to develop this together. Having a robust plan helps us secure funding and supports our continued discussions. Not only did we create the 100-year plan, but we also developed our school values and created a pledge and ceremonies each year to acknowledge the turning of the seasons.

I forgot to tell you that our year begins in late January. We get a lot of visitors interested in our systemic experiment. Starting when the ground is waking aligns with growth; we become energised as the year turns. We still break in summer when it's hottest and slowly retreat in autumn for reflection and deep research before hibernating over winter. We work in four quarters and have roused interest, and dare I say it, envy among staff in other institutes, especially as the shift in timetable created a need for our own administration team in the building. You can see them up there across the atrium. They are a big part of our family, and we'd be lost without them.

Anyway, let's walk upstairs and sneak in the back of the Salon to see what's happening ...

It's quiet. Heavy curtains are drawn. It has a soothing effect on the space. The reverberation time is short. Colours are natural and light, avoiding the soporific effects of darkness. The space is circular, with sofas on a subtle rake of deep steps. Fresh cool air circulates from the floor keeping everyone alert. The space also smells good, a combination of natural fibres, timber and earth flooring. It's surprisingly grounding. Not a single electronic item is visible. Instead, students take notes which they will discuss in their *Theory and Context* lab.

A student is leading an encounter on spatial rights in the built environment. This was requested on our *Close Encounters* wall by our EDI student group *Architects Building a Living Equity* (ABLE). We stopped calling them lectures a while ago now, as that's not how we see them. The fixed power dynamic of a "lecture" can lead to failures in pedagogic interactions. With "encounters", staff encourage freedom, love and care. We welcome student interruptions, acknowledge that we are all learning, and nurture genuine uninhibited dialogue as we are willing to be open with our (lack of) knowledge. We create participatory space for students to develop a sense of agency and hope, and "experience education as the practice of freedom" (Hooks, 1994, p. 15).

[whispering] Shall we move on? Let's leave them to it and go and see the studios. We have seating outside the lecture purposely located to extend pedagogic discussions after sessions have finished...

Come along this corridor. Do you like the models? We keep the best ones every year and display them everywhere. This one's a personal favourite, despite it not looking like much. It hasn't used any deathly laser cutting, and the rammed earth blocks contain human waste. That took a risk assessment and a half! A microbiologist taught them how to autoclave the waste before use. We have a fantastic risk manager in our team which is why you might spot students wandering around with power tools or climbing scaffolding.

We have a rigorous student selection process and aim for a mix of students from different backgrounds and locations, from round the corner to round the globe. We interview every potential student in person. They spend a day with us in workshops and conversations, so we understand their potential – which can be very different to school grades. This is a mutually beneficial experience as after spending the day with us they get a sense of our school and if we are a good fit for them too. If not, we advise them of other institutions they might prefer. We also remind them that the course isn't everything. We ask them to imagine living in this part of the world ...does this place feel like it could be a future home?

Once here, we encourage them to develop their own positions and philosophy. We come together as a school every week to nurture relationships. Wednesday afternoon sessions are included in our annual pledge; everyone is welcome to participate, where we host a surprise activity in our hall; sometimes we dance, other times we simply lie on the floor. I know you're thinking this sounds like a cult, but we aren't, we're a school, and want everyone to feel safe and confident in themselves by pushing our boundaries together. It's not simply about what we want the students to know, it's bigger than that. It's about being free to play, to make mistakes, it's about being kind and brave, being rigorous and questioning everything. And we must never be too serious.

So...this one often causes a stir for the introverts, but staff have their desks in our studios; we don't have offices. It creates a more collegiate atmosphere, allows role modelling, and students also appreciate how busy the staff are. We flipped the traditional model on its head where you leave your private office for meetings. Instead, we primarily care about being together – if we need to do deep or private work, we go to one of the reading rooms, in-house library or move to a silent pod. Many part-time staff use our building for free on practice days to work on their own architectural projects which is great for the students to experience, especially when they see design team meetings in action. What else is there to tell you? Let me think ... ah yes, we have a maximum of 60 students per year, and we have three minibuses (as well as a van) which means staff can take groups somewhere easily, or students can drive themselves to visit places as part of their self-curated summer *Curiosity* module. We don't want to grow too much as a school, we have a good atmosphere right now, and great ratios. More students would give us more fees yes, but we don't believe in the corporatisation of the university. Do you know any educators who do?!

We are reflexive staff, developing short- and long-term plans so we can adapt if a discussion or project takes a turn. Project Outputs have been known to change entirely halfway through a semester when students have decided they'd prefer to know more about something different. It is only the most competent staff who can respond to and develop a module as it unfolds. Structure and planning are key, but the ability to be vulnerable and grow along with students is transformative (Reggio Emilia Approach, 2022). Having an in-house admin team also works well for spontaneous trips: we can have an idea in class on Monday and be visiting somewhere in Europe a few days later if we wish. Our support staff are exactly that, supportive. We have ideas and they enable them, instead of putting up barriers. They do all the administration, so no budget stresses, chasing students for payments or checking guest passports. It's liberating and appreciated. They often come on trips with us and attend studio discussions, because every voice matters.

Following an open round table a few years ago, we established a course for developers and clients from the region, for them to understand and respect the principles of architectural history, theory, sustainability and contextualism. It can be frustrating as an academic in an architecture school observing often misguided judgements made by those who hold financial power in our built environment. Councils across the north no longer approve any planning application without a client being certified as having taken our course. There's a *Creating Communities* session going on right now. Students with more experience are running a workshop on post occupancy evaluation, something which was never given much thought a few decades ago. There is absolute joy in seeing students educating developers don't you agree?

Here are the studios. New students experience the analogue: no laptops, tablets or phones to be seen. Staff sometimes refer to this as *The Great Recalibration!* Some find it difficult to begin with but eventually discover and appreciate the peace and clarity. For the first two quarters, students only work in black and white. They gain a deep respect for colour after this, having been denied it for so long. Their current project brief focuses on air, soil or water. It is vital for all students to grasp that without caring for these three basic elements we won't survive as a species. That hole in the wall is intentional; it shows how the building is constructed. Mind your head, this plant is huge!

Anyway, we should probably head back to reception, passing that rowdy bunch! It's a reading group – we discourage hidden labour, so reading only happens when they meet, and they simultaneously read different texts of their choice. They read to each other and discuss anything that comes up, and it can get quite lively. It sounds bizarre but was inspired by Mia Kealey who presented a paper at an Association of Architectural Educators conference, and it's been incredibly successful (Kealey, 2023). They've created a collective social space where they fathom out their interests at their own pace.

Well, here we are. Thanks for coming today. I hope it's been interesting. I can't believe we've got to the end and haven't specifically mentioned process! Education is simple yet complex and brings so many unknowns together into emergent, unique situations. We hope you sense that everyone has a voice here and that we allow the peaceful unease of sitting in liminal space. It's so important that students become comfortable with the uncomfortable, that they understand that failure is progress, and that magic lies in the slow unfolding messy and risky stories in research and design. We don't want to "lecture" best practice but instead create an environment that favours deep "encounters" and repeatedly asks "why?", a place that welcomes a shared responsibility of difference, change and care. When we began our school, we thought a lot about how to acknowledge and respond to issues that arise from operating within a patriarchy. We preferred not to flip this and work as a matriarchy, but to find balance in common space, in harmony over conquest, in what we call a gyliarchy, derived from the term "gylany" coined by Riane Eisler (1981, pp. 499–507). We consciously define a more mindful, dialogic approach to the school, where we hear all voices and admit vulnerability. Yes, the place looks chaotic, but it's their place, they leave marks, take it apart, rebuild it, and crucially they aren't graded. In giving them ownership of the space and liberating their journey they become relaxed, fearless and enjoy the moment. They want to be here. Attendance is excellent because we don't record anything to watch later, unless we need to for specific student needs – life is complex and messy, and we care about being in the present. If you aren't here, you've missed it, and there is no extra catching up to do. Sorry, I'm doing my autopilot sales pitch. I'll stop!

Well ...it sounds as though the conference is taking a break. If you've got time before you cycle back to the station, let's go down and join them. There is a fabulous exhibition on right now showing the drawings of last year's show. We leave the *End of Year Show* up for a few months, not days, to honour how long the work took to produce. The first project our new students are given is to study the show and carefully record everything with scaled hand drawings and photographs. These are then bound into a book for our records. It's a great way for students to begin, by starting at the end.

References

Architects Climate Action Network (2025) *Architects Can!*. Available at: https://architectscan.org/ (Accessed: 26 May 2025).

Civic Square (2025) *Demonstrating Neighbourhood-Scale Civic Infrastructure for Social, Ecological, Economic, and Climate Transition*. Available at: https://civicsquare.cc/ (Accessed: 26 May 2025).

Eisler, R. (1981) 'Gylany: the balanced future', *Futures*, Vol 13 (6), pp. 499–507.
Flores i Prats (2016) *Sala Beckett*. Available at: https://floresprats.com/archive/sala-beckett-project/ (Accessed: 18 December 2025).
Hooks, B. (1994) *Teaching to Transgress*. 1st edn. Routledge.
Kealey, M. (2023) 'Taking and making care within schools of architecture through careful, collective, and resistant practices of reading', *Productive Disruptive*, Cardiff, 12–15 July 2023, pp. 362–371. Available at: https://padlet.com/aae2023/productive-disruptive-puupwva4u7fy5euv/wish/mlNDZ3v6yX5yQznG (Accessed: 15 July 2023).
Lendager (2025) *Lendager Form Follows Availability*. Available at: https://lendager.com/ (Accessed: 26 May 2025).
Monteiro, C. (2023) 'Retrofit mustn't ignore the tragic health impacts of damp and mould', *Architects Journal*, 19th April.
National Retrofit Hub (2025) *Enabling the Delivery of Housing Retrofit at Scale*. Available at: https://nationalretrofithub.org.uk/ (Accessed: 26 May 2025).
Pound, J. (2025) 'The sunflower collective – community of growth and healing', *Assignment for Studio 3.2, BA Architecture*, Manchester School of Architecture. Unpublished.
Reggio Emilia Approach (2022) *Values*. Available at: https://www.reggiochildren.it/en/reggio-emilia-approach/valori-en/ (Accessed: 18 December 2025).
Rotor (2025) *Rotor Is a Cooperative Design Practice that Investigates the Organisation of the Material Environment*. Available at: https://rotordb.org/en (Accessed: 26 May 2025).
Rural Studio (1999) *Pods*. Available at: https://ruralstudio.org/project/pods/ (Accessed: 14 July 2025).
Squash (2024) *The 100 Year Street*. Available at: https://squashliverpool.co.uk/wp-content/uploads/2024/12/Squash-100-Year-Street-News-2.pdf (Accessed: 12 April 2025).
Till, J. (2009) *Architecture Depends*. Cambridge, MA: MIT.
Vitrone, F. et al. (2021) 'Binderless fiberboards for sustainable construction. Materials, production methods and applications', *Journal of Building Engineering*, Vol 44, p. 102625.

Insights

8

A HOPEFUL GLIMPSE THROUGH THE WINDOW – AN OUTSIDER'S PERSPECTIVE OF PEDAGOGY AS CREATIVE PRACTICE

Christopher Little

Introduction

This chapter is about hope – it is about the hope that the creative practitioners contributing to this collection inspire. The words of Paulo Freire here provide a fitting backdrop to my reflections on what is important in teaching and learning and what I have been privileged to see in this collection of creative and hopeful pedagogies:

> Nor yet can dialogue exist without hope. Hope is rooted in men's incompletion, from which they move out in constant search – a search which can be carried out only in communion with others. Hopelessness is a form of silence, of denying the world and fleeing from it … Hope, however, does not consist in crossing one's arms and waiting. As long as I fight, I am moved by hope: and if I fight with hope, then I can wait.
>
> *(Freire, 1996, pp. 72–73)*

As readers will have seen by now from the first seven chapters in the Discussions section, this collection collects insights from ambitious, creative and impactful educators creating learning experiences for their students that will remain with them for the rest of their professional careers and lives.

This chapter will first show the circumstances of this hopeful and creative work. It will then reflect upon my own position as an academic from outside of the Architecture discipline and as someone who labels themselves "not a creative" and the profound impact working on this collection has had on me. This chapter offers higher education architecture professionals and lecturers a reflective lens, from a position of externality, on creative pedagogical

DOI: 10.4324/9781003647720-11

practices in times of challenge. Drawing on autoethnographic insights and key educational theories – such as transformative learning, relational pedagogy and authentic assessment – it explores how architectural educators are resisting neoliberal pressures and fostering spaces of hope, care, and social justice. It will finally look towards the Insights section of this book and the remarkable practices detailed therein. However, to truly see the remarkable practice here, it is important that readers first consider the difficult circumstances facing these colleagues and their students in the UK Higher Education (HE) sector at the time of writing.

Context Matters

This book is being assembled across the 2025/2026 academic year and the picture for the HE sector in the UK at least is looking bleak. After decades of growing student numbers, underfunding and conflicting priorities, the HE sector in the UK is in a challenging position to say the least. In addition to the above, the sector is in a state of constant reaction to significant external pressures and events affecting both staff and students.

Context – Students

The sector, in the UK, is responding to a cost-of-living crisis that is pushing more students into full-time work alongside full-time studies than ever before and impacting upon studies in a myriad of ways (Pulman et al., 2024; Schofield, 2024). While teaching quality and content are still hugely important in student engagement, recent research has shown the significant impact that cost-of-living crisis is having (Jones and Bell, 2025; Lowe et al., 2025). Jones and Bell (2025) discuss the impact of the above crisis, noting key impacts upon the ability of students to engage fully while studying, while foregrounding the ways in which the pandemic also exacerbated pre-existing mental health issues for learners. A combination of this increase in poor student mental health and the financial pressures affecting their studies is a challenge to say the least for contemporary educators.

Recent research shows that 68% of students now undertake paid employment during their studies, with the average amount of time spent in paid employment now reaching 39.8 hours per week (Moss and Neves, 2025). A staggering 30% of students now report working more than 50 hours of paid employment per week – as Moss and Neves state, these demands on students' time outside of studies are "objectively excessive in their totality".

Global issues also continue to affect our learners. For students, the trauma and displacement caused by international conflicts in Gaza, Syria and Ukraine, among others, are felt acutely throughout campuses and will have untold consequences for many years to come. Recent high-court rulings are making members of the LGBTQIA+ community feel less welcome than ever in public spaces. The rise of far-right ideologies in the UK and accompanying policy shifts have made the landscape more challenging than ever for our visiting international students too. Any one of the above would be a barrier for students and their ongoing wholehearted engagement with university studies, but the combination of the above is potent and troubling.

Given the above, it is not surprising to find that research into student experience of contemporary HE reveals some concerning patterns. The consequences of this are, naturally, significant, with the National Union for Students reporting that 37% of students have reportedly considered dropping out of university due to poor mental health (NUS UK, 2025). The number of students reporting poor mental health conditions continues to grow, with 4.9% of all students reporting a mental health condition, challenge or disorder in 2022/2023 compared to 4.5% in 2020/2021. The previously noted research by Jones and Bell (2025) particularly highlights the stark increase in students reporting mental health issues since the Covid pandemic.

2023 saw the much-discussed degree awarding gap between white students and students of colour grow for the first time in almost a decade. In 2023, Advance HE reported that 83% of white undergraduate students graduated with a first-class honours degree or an upper-second class honours degree (known in the UK as a 1st or a 2:1 respectively). For students classed as Black, Asian or Minority Ethnic (BAME – Advance HE's terminology, not my own), just 72.3% of BAME students graduated with a first-class honours degree or an upper-second class honours degree. This presents an ethnicity awarding gap of 10.3%. The labels and final metric may be slightly crude, but they give some insight into the challenges affecting some students more so than others in UK HE post-pandemic.

The above trends in students' economic difficulties, student mental health and disparities in outcomes on ethnicity are all set in the context of ever-growing HE student numbers, with Advance HE (2023) reporting a 24.3% increase overall registered student numbers since 2015/2016 in the UK. Therefore, those percentages and findings discussed above are from an ever-growing population, representing more and more students often requiring acute and specialist support.

Context – Staff

For academic staff, who are also wrestling with the wake of the above, the explosion of Generative Artificial Intelligence (Gen AI hereafter) is a paradigm-shifting occurrence for considerations around assessment and integrity, prompting significant course and assessment redesign work across the university system. The sector, rightly, has placed a renewed focus on eradicating differential awarding gaps, such as the gap between white and Global

Ethnic Majority students achieving higher degree awards. Finally, as if the above was not sufficient, universities are recovering from a once-in-a-century global pandemic that has, as some argue, irreparably changed student engagement with on-campus attendance. In a stretched and under-funded HE landscape, staff are given little to no extra relief in teaching and research demands to learn about and respond to the above pressures. These additional pressures to ease the above societal issues for our students are being felt acutely by educators across the HE sector (Smith, 2022; Dickinson, 2025).

Like students, it is perhaps no surprise that research exploring staff morale is similarly worrying to the data presented regarding students above. WonkHE (Kernohan, 2025) researched the experiences of 5,000 HE staff and revealed that 75% of those surveyed would still recommend working in the HE sector. However, this research also reveals that only 31.7% feel their organisation is well-run, 33.3% feel adequately recognised for their contributions and just 44.3% are satisfied with professional development opportunities. Further analysis by McVitty (2025) revealed that within this data, just 57.8% of colleagues on academic contracts agreed that they were reasonably secure in their jobs.

So, for the HE sector, and specifically for Architecture as a discipline in HE as noted in our introductory chapter, we are producing this collection at a daunting time, but at an important moment. In *Pedagogy of the Depressed*, Schaberg talks of how the changing mental health of his students during and after the pandemic "changed the feel of the classroom, it altered the possibilities of how we could learn together" (2021, p. 2). Furthermore, Schaberg notes the hesitancy of students since Covid to engage with the world outside of the classroom: "I'm talking about the discomfort with the physical world, things like sitting on grass: many students just won't do it" (p. 43). The pedagogies in this collection continue to "fight with hope" (Freire, 1996, p. 73) against this changing dynamic, persevering with dynamic and relational pedagogical approaches and proving their worth and feeling as Schaberg notes "the thrill of learning, the rush of uncertainty at the edge of a breakthrough" (2021, p. 149).

In this collection, we see educators connecting students to the physical world, to the environment, to shores and to soil. Against this backdrop detailed above, the practices showcased in this collection take on even greater significance.

A Reflection on Our Event

My current role in HE is as a Senior Lecturer in Academic Development. While there is no uncontested definition of academic development as a discipline, the editors of the *International Journal of Academic Development* in 2021 brought together a working definition of academic development as practice which "aims to enhance the practice, theory, creativity and/or quality of teaching and learning communities in higher or post-secondary education" (discussed here by Le-May Sheffield and Serbati, 2022). My work involves project work and consultancy with colleagues across the university on curriculum design and change, and educational and pedagogic research and this is where this work was borne. I approach this work with the core principles of building trust through person-centred approaches cultivated through what McDonagh and Sanders (2025) would call intentional, consistent behaviours. This approach, centred upon trust, is noted by Pleschová et al. as particularly important right now, serving as an "anchor" in difficult circumstances for the sector (Pleschová et al., 2025).

It is through this person-first approach that I began working with my co-editor, having met while sharing our educational research in 2023. I was invited into this book project and began the process of welcoming potential contributors into the work of creating this collection. To achieve this, we hosted an event in Summer 2024 for potential contributors to come together and discuss the themes and practices that would be important to a collection regarding creative pedagogies. Our attendees, barring myself, were all creative practitioners in Architecture or Architecture-related fields.

Regardless of this outsider position (which I had clearly branded myself with), I was welcomed into all discussions. Across the day, colleagues engaged fully with all discussions and activities. In response to key readings that we posited as inspirations for discussion, we had full debates and discussions, creative installations at the venue we used, performances and contemplative tours of the city of Sheffield. Not once did I notice a single colleague checking their emails or Microsoft Teams messages. Not once did I see colleagues creating teaching resources or checking their phones. Colleagues were honest, authentic, creative and heartfelt. In short, they exemplified the kinds of student engagement in creative education that we would all wish to inspire in our learners – they showed up for the debates, discussions and to advocate for their creative pedagogical practices.

Importantly, I do not mean to imply here that I work with, or inspire (I hope), disengaged academic staff in my day-to-day work. However, often the work of helping to develop academics falls victim to the pressures mentioned in the opening section of this chapter – increasing workloads, the pace of change and competing demands often mean that staff can be distracted in academic development sessions, often needing to be in many places at once and complete many different projects simultaneously. As noted, the pressures previously discussed are immense and I note the above with no judgement on colleagues.

Here, though, I found academics working collaboratively, with complete engagement, to showcase and troubleshoot their current creative practices through what I would identify as authentic and transformative learning. Transformative Learning was pioneered by Jack Mezirow (1985, 2003) and, alongside relational pedagogy as a guiding principle, provides a suitable frame for the types of teaching and learning showcased in this collection. In short, when summarised from Mezirow's countless works on this area, transformative learning can be thought of as a process of adult learning where individuals critically examine and revise their existing assumptions, beliefs and perspectives through reflective dialogue, leading to a more inclusive, discriminating and integrative understanding of their experiences.

Kitchenham (2008) provides an in-depth overview of transformative learning and its evolution since inception. While exploring the changes to the model over the years, Kitchenham notes the centrality of critical self-reflection in all discussions of transformative learning. The importance of critical discourse, where a learner understands not just the results of certain situations, but the factors influencing them and the nuances of social situations. Naturally, such self-examination, often completed through and while completing projects, installations and assessments, can be personally challenging and uncomfortable (Mezirow, 1985, p. 85). Yet this transformative effect of learning is not easily gained, nor can it be forced. Illeris's (2015) theoretical exploration of transformative learning highlights the crucial role that educators have in creating the right conditions to "optimize or promote the probability of transformative learning" (p. 1). Illeris goes on to note the importance of project-based learning and how it provides true scope for transformative educational experiences.

During our exploratory event, another relevant educational trope that came to mind was that of relational pedagogies. The discussions on the day itself, and in the contributions across this book, clearly embody that way of being. Here, Su and Wood (2023) define this as a truly intentional practice aimed towards building connections between learners and between learners and staff with the aim of a "latter, more democratic and less hierarchical power structure in the classroom" (p. 232). Bell's (2022) study of the relationship between student satisfaction and relational pedagogies noted the key significance of providing students with opportunities to develop respectful learning relationships together. Here, I can see the ways in which standard practices of architectural education enacts the above ethos – the culture of professionalism, studio culture, the importance of ateliers and the prominence of peer-feedback mechanisms like group critiques. The prominence given to these kinds of strategies in architectural education is not the norm outside of creative disciplines in HE, in my experience.

Taking this exploration of relational pedagogies further is Gravett's recent theoretical discussions of relational pedagogies and authentic assessment:

> What is the role of trust, dialogue and care within assessment practices? What freedom do we enable for diverse learners to approach their learning in different ways?
>
> *(Gravett, 2025, p. 609)*

While Gravett warns against the dangers of terms such as "authentic assessment" becoming "encrusted" buzzwords, their discussion how assessment can either provide further meaningful opportunities for a relational approach to assessment or undermine such teaching pedagogical approaches is striking. When reading Gravett's work I was reminded of how much of architectural education assessment would, in many disciplines, be classed as highly authentic – it mirrors work-place practices and products, tackles societal issues around social justice and often intersects with the civic responsibilities of modern universities by working with local businesses and practices.

Furthermore, assessment in architecture frequently provides the space for flexibility and personalised approaches to assessment, that is, rightly, being discussed as the future of HE by excellent researchers like Firth (2025) in their *Framework for Flexible Assessment*. This framework notes the potential of optionality in assessment:

> Flexible assessment is about maintaining academic rigour while recognising diverse student strengths, lived experiences, and future goals. By aligning assessment with inclusivity and authenticity, it prepares students for the complexity of real-world professional and academic contexts.
>
> *(Firth, 2025, p. 4)*

Additionally, however, Firth's work notes how flexibility in assessment can be challenging when disciplines must navigate professional accreditation. I also, from the outside, feel that deciding to complete your studies in Architecture is quite a high-stakes decision – the courses are long compared to other HE routes, additional costs can often be high and employment outcomes appear to be potentially shrinking in the current economic climate. So, combining these thoughts, it is striking to me that Architectural education continues to deliver teaching and assessment which manages to navigate accredited body requirements and economic factors and continues to align embodied practices with concepts of flexibility and authenticity. These elements have long been a staple of the ways in which Architecture is taught, with its focus on independent projects, studios and ateliers. In my own experience of consulting with academics across several institutions over the past decade in HE, other creative disciplines such as Fashion, Design, Media and others provide similar agency and autonomy in their teaching and assessment practices. However, beyond Architecture and other creative disciplines, in my experience, this level of student choice and autonomy is often considered radical and cutting edge.

Reflecting on the above, these educational theories are present in my own teaching in quite similar ways to the strategies showcased in this book, albeit in a different discipline and type of classroom. My own practice has long advocated for honest transparency with students and confronting these moments of educational failure together (Little, 2024) and through this, a sense of engaging students as co-conspirators in the classroom. If sessions are not working, I like to be honest about this and work with students to fix the session, sharing equal responsibility. Additionally, I like to build time into my teaching practice for contemplative time where my students – academics – can reflect and problem solve during the sessions, not as "homework", conscious of the immense time pressures on the modern academic. I also like to challenge and ask provocative questions, not shying away from contestation and positionality. Flexibility and authenticity in assessment, shown by many of our contributors in this book, are paramount to me and have long been a focus of my own educational practice and research (Little, 2025). In short, I like to offer spaces of compassionate education, rooted in opportunities for self-reflection and self-discovery and I found kindred spirits in this group of creative architecture educators at our event.

Across the day, the event itself saw colleagues creating art installations, presentations and artefacts that showed their personal reflections on key texts relating to creative architectural education practice. Without expecting it – after all I felt so different from creative practitioners initially – I saw many of my own educational principles and practices echoed, or at least translated into, the creative practice discussed by colleagues at our project event. Within an hour of the event starting, and it was a whole day event, I felt at home and saw the commonalities.

The final tenet of my own personal pedagogy that I found validated at our event, and in this collection, is that of hopeful and relational pedagogy. Kevin Gannon, in his 2020 manifesto *A Radical Hope*, notes how hopeful and transformative pedagogies are rooted in student-entered practices which foreground "critical thinking, exploration, creativity, play and the construction of knowledge" (2020, p. 47). This is not always logistically easy but it is a central tenet of hopeful and transformative pedagogies – these are the things which give education its vitality. On that day in Summer 2023, I saw a whole room of creative educators discussing the ways in which they provide meaningful learning opportunities for their students, to find space for students and staff to remain creative and not purely functional, and how they really are having to fight to hold on to these practices in light of some of the pressures noted previously. To return to Gannon, he discusses committing to hopeful pedagogies as a form of advocacy:

> This advocacy – think of it as a pedagogy for a better world – will almost certainly meet some resistance.
>
> *(2020, p. 48)*

Through the activities of our exploratory day breathing life into *Pedagogy as Creative Practice* as a viable book idea, and through the contributions collected in this book, you will see how colleagues have remained steadfast, how they have "shown up" for this hopeful and creative way of learning, teaching and assessing students.

A Reflection on Our Collection

Whatever the label – transformative learning, andragogy, hopeful or relational pedagogies – these approaches and ways of being have the shared purpose of making our practices as HE educators equitable, socially just and inclusive. Some of the statistics I discussed in the opening section of this chapter highlight the growing need to make our practices more inclusive and compassionate.

As noted, this chapter is about hope. Having set a somewhat apocalyptic tone in the opening sections, the reflections on the Creative as Pedagogic Practice catalyst event in Summer 2024 show that I firmly identify the practices of our contributors as hopeful, compassionate and, in a time of competing demands and neoliberalism, somewhat punk and countercultural. Colleagues are committed to meaningful educational experiences, rooted in relational pedagogy, authentic assessment and social justice, resisting the banking model of education critically skewered by bell hooks (2014) and Freire (2001). Each of the two sections of this collection shows a gamut of creative and impactful approaches that encourage critical thinking and a critical awareness of the discipline of Architecture.

Reflections on Discussions

Our Discussions chapters all advocate for critically, socially and environmentally aware practices which encourage, and often provoke, students and staff criticality. These discussions are often offset against the very tensions, crises and stressors noted at the beginning of this chapter. They are heavily informed by critical pedagogy and written with great care and passion – a shot in the arm to recent scaremongering that both student learning and teaching could be usurped by Gen AI. Rather than succumbing to crisis, these contributions position creative pedagogies as solutions to the challenges facing architectural education. This is perhaps most starkly shown in the contrast between the bookends of this Discussions section. Here, Miles' critical history of the sector offers numerous critical provocations and questions for us to consider which challenge the neoliberal direction of architectural education. These questions and fears are counteracted by Gidman's reimagining of the Other School – a place where care is paramount – care for students as whole beings, care for teaching staff and researchers, care for the communities we serve and care for the discipline of architecture itself.

This sense of overt care is a recurring theme across the Discussions section. Udall et al. work from the ground up – literally – instilling care and responsibility toward the soil in which architecture is rooted. This practice transforms students' perspectives and their relationship with their surroundings. The need to not only fight for the studio as a radical space, but to ensure that it delivers this space in a way which is just, equitable and compassionate is clear across Skelcher's essay on studio culture. Citing the findings of the Bartlett report, Skelcher reminds us that studios can only remain thriving spaces of "looseness" (I love that term) if the inherent inequalities and inequities, and accompanying power dynamics, are challenged and reimagined with compassionate pedagogical practices. Building on this emphasis on studio culture, the AND Atelier collective demonstrates the powerful use of precedents, reminding us that when we encourage students to think differently, we create spaces for their lived experiences and interests to come alive. We see these same experiences mirrored in the ways in which Southcott shows how the dissertation, a traditional long-form essay, can be a space for personal growth, development and reimagining.

Another striking commonality across our first section is an unshakeable commitment to social justice and education as a vehicle for societal change. Miles highlights the myriad forces working against socially just and engaged education whilst reiterating the need for such practices, now more than ever. This rallying call is answered in our chapters. First, Kasia Nawratek explores her practice based on vertical and horizontal axes, rooted in environmental and societal sustainability. Here, Kasia prompts us to consider how incorporating edgelands and a volumetric understanding of landscapes can enhance architectural practice. The AND atelier practice, demonstrated in Chapter 3, shows that encouraging the application of tangential or unrelated precedents from outside of architecture opens student work to more socially just and civically connected practice. Most strikingly for me, they create spaces where students can truly engage their own positionality in relation to these concepts of place, power and culture. Udall et al.'s work on soil continues this theme and delivers a practice which forever changes students' relationship to the ground beneath their feet – a change that will stay with students – future architects and creatives – for the rest of their careers. Southcott's discussion of the dissertation shows another practice of encouraging student awareness in their own potential, as one student commented "I feel like I've opened my own eyes". Continuing this thread, Skelcher's assertion that "all space is political" reiterates the responsibility that the studio must ensure creativity is facilitated in relation to socio-cultural forces and in a way that acknowledges and challenges inequalities. Finally, this commitment to socially just practices is ever-present in Gidman's reimagined school of architecture – a contribution which imagines the answers to the "what if"s present in the other contributions present in *Discussions*.

Returning to discussions of transformative learning, particularly noteworthy here is the Kitchenham's (2008) discussion of the "disorienting dilemma" as a pivotal point in student processes of engaging in transformative learning. Here, Kitchenham notes how Mezirow's thinking around transformational education was heavily influenced by Freire's discussions of critical consciousness and conscientisation (Freire, 1973). Here, we can see in these explorations of key practices in architectural education – the dissertation, the studio, in edgelands and polyphony, the soil itself, amongst other topics in *Discussions* – a concerted effort by educators to ensure their practice encourages this critical consciousness in their learners. Furthermore, not all dilemmas can be solved but the process of navigating unsolvable problems is the learning: "the learner encounters a problem or anomaly that cannot be resolved through present meaning schemes or through learning new meaning schemes; the resolution comes through a redefinition of the problem" (Kitchenham, 2008, p. 112). In our *Discussions* chapters, we clearly see authors offering "disorienting dilemmas" not only to their students through their creative practice, but also to readers and fellow architecture academics and creatives. The social justice focus of these contributions chimes with Gannon's thoughts on hopeful, transformative pedagogies:

> When we adopt a student-centered philosophy, the possibilities for a truly transformative pedagogy open before us ... transformative pedagogical is *radical*...it asks us to engage in root-level, fundamental changes to the not only our own designing and teaching, but our institutional structures as well.
>
> *(Gannon, 2020, p. 43)*

Together, these contributions affirm creative education as a radical, hopeful and socially engaged practice – one that challenges existing structures and imagines new possibilities.

Reflections on Insights

Relational pedagogies, transformative learning and authentic assessment underline the importance of creating learning experiences that matter to students – assessments that challenge them and shift their frames of reference (Gravett, 2025). Additionally, these opportunities must provide opportunities for peer-to-peer learning, with projects providing spaces for different competencies and abilities to excel. These opportunities depend on practices that nurture relationships between learners and educators. Education can only be transformative if it provides this and I have felt inspired by the collections in the *Insights* section, the ways in which they "show up" for their students and the ways in which they provide individual and team-based teaching and assessment which facilitates growth in diverse student groups within architecture. The contributions in *Insights* bring together creative pedagogies grouped around overlapping areas of critical dialogue and ecological responsibility through iterative design.

The role of dialogic pedagogies is clear across the *Insights* contributions. Vinall notes, in their chapter on the Foundation studio how dialogue facilitates "points of connection" and this rings true across all contributions in this latter half of our collection. Dialogue plays a crucial role in the important, yet sensitive, processes of unfolding "academic armour" noted by Ray and

Bushnell-Wye. This is mirrored in the dialogue-dependent student explorations of feminist architecture discussed by Crompton, where dialogue facilitates students' understanding of self, of architecture and of community.

This theme continues in the ways in which Wei and Bradshaw's "Grand Day Out" module encourages students to understand and reject precedents, and to negotiate roles in their design and building of sandcastles and support structures. Here dialogue creates space for serendipitous disruption, challenge and affirmation. Vinall notes how their Foundation Year studio brings together students from different architectural pathways, with group-based discussions central to students understanding their differences and commonalities. Finally, Miller's "manifesto for making" highlights the crucial role of developmental discussion in understanding physical materials while advocating for making to take a more prominent place in architectural education than it currently occupies. Here, in studio and workshop spaces, dialogic practice is not merely conversational; it is iterative and reflective, enabling participants to challenge preconceptions and co-construct meaning.

Dialogue not only shapes learning relationships but also connects students to the ethical and ecological dimensions of design. Intrinsically present in these dialogue-centred pedagogies is an inherent respect for local communities and environments and community is invoked not only as a social construct but also as an ecological and ethical commitment. Indeed, the iterative inquiry that dialogic approaches bring leads students to a deeper understanding of their local communities, and the very physical fabric of their locales. The process of facilitating these contributions into our book has inspired me to think about the ways in which my own role – teaching university teachers – could benefit from bringing in community and location into its language and practices more. Miller's manifesto stresses the learning to be gained from seeing the "rough edges" of materials, and this sense of unexpected learning and physicality is present across many of our *Insights* chapters. Many of the contributions highlight ecological reuse and repurposing of existing materials too – from Crompton's reimagining of a 1960s building through a feminist lens, to the careful ways in which students prepare model materials for reuse after the sandcastles have been washed away in Wei and Bradshaw's work. By weaving care and time into iterative and dialogic processes, the texts suggest a way of working that responds to society while staying deeply connected to ecological concerns.

The common philosophical approach here, for me, is that of iterative development. As Crompton notes, these cycles of making, testing and refining often lead to student projects being "sketched out and marked up again and again (and again)". Crucially though, our *Insights* show that this isn't about repeating the same thing for the sake of it, it is about letting ideas evolve through constant adjustment. This approach values flexibility and sees mistakes as part of the journey, not something to avoid. By working iteratively, staff and learners can explore possibilities, respond to change and discover unexpected solutions along the way.

Earlier, this chapter noted how Illeris (2015), in their discussion of transformative learning, noted the crucial importance of project-based learning. Individual projects, such as dissertations or model making, provide space to experiment and understand and critically reflect upon the process. Group projects, such as building sandcastles or working on enhancing community buildings through a feminist lens, provide students with space to maximise the benefits of learning opportunities and to have their frames of reference forever changed by learning from others.

Several of our *Insights* chapters showcase not only the successes of their students and their own educational practices, but also the crucial role of failure, of providing havens for safe failure. This is a crucial element of transformative and relational learning, and its importance is excellently described by Gannon:

> We have to carefully cultivate the spaces in which risk-taking and the encounters with failure likely to ensue can be experienced in ways that prompt both reflection and metacognitive action. This, in turn, will create a learning environment marked by mutual respect, trust, and the understanding that at its best, learning is a collective enterprise.
>
> *(2020, pp. 138–139)*

This space to fail is also partnered by space to collaborate and disagree in a mature and professional manner. Here, educators have the key role of creating safe spaces where learners can critically reflect, "formulate personal standpoints and also to express uncertainty and doubt" (Illeris, 2015, p. 49).

Concluding Thoughts

While the opening of this chapter presented a bleak outlook for HE, or certainly a difficult context within which our contributors practice – there is hope. This collection has shown the benefits of engaged, meaningful creative educational practice. Jones and Bell's (2025) recent research on the challenges students are facing post-Covid, noted a range of pressures affecting students, discussed earlier in this chapter. The authors also note that potential of engaged and committed academic staff, providing spaces for connection, belonging and relational practice. Indeed, they recommend that educators "make greater efforts to build strong, trust-based relationships (staff-student and student-student) as these appear to be key to diminishing loneliness and reducing barriers to student engagement" (Jones and Bell, 2025, p. 16). I feel that as we reflect upon the positions of authors in the Discussions section of this book and look towards the more applied examples found in the *Insights* section, this book offers hope for creative educators. Here, we see engaged and informed educators wrestling with the challenges noted above, and with more discipline-specific challenges, such as professional body requirements. What is most striking however, is that our contributors are not looking towards efficiencies in their examples of practice, or in their recommendations – here, colleagues are showing the value of iterative and contemplative educational practice – they are willing to wait and provide supportive and appropriately challenging spaces for their students to navigate these stormy waters. Returning to the opening of this chapter and the thoughts of Freire which I foregrounded: "Hope, however, does not consist in crossing one's arms and awaiting … if I fight with hope, then I can wait" (Freire, 1996, p. 73). The practice contained within this collection does fight with hope, and that is hugely needed in today's challenging, ever-shifting HE landscape.

References

Advance HE. (2023). *Equality in Higher Education: Statistical Reports 2023*. Available at: https://www.advance-he.ac.uk/knowledge-hub/equality-higher-education-statistical-reports-2023 (Accessed 20 November 2025).

Dickinson, J. (2025). *Universities Should Face the Consequences for Misleading Students over the Cost of Living*. WonkHE. Available at: https://wonkhe.com/blogs/universities-should-face-the-consequences-for-misleading-students-over-the-cost-of-living/

Firth, M. (2025). *Framework for Flexible Assessment: A National Model for Inclusive, Future-Ready Assessment Design*. University of Manchester. Available at: https://www.qaa.ac.uk/membership/benefits-of-qaa-membership/collaborative-enhancement-projects/assessment/optionality-in-assessment# (Accessed 13 November 2025).

Freire, P. (1973). *Education for Critical Consciousness*. New York: Continuum.

Freire, P. (1996). *Pedagogy of the Oppressed*. London: Continuum.

Hooks, B. (2014). *Teaching to Transgress*. Routledge.

Jones, C. and Bell, H. (2025). They are being 'squeezed left, right and centre': English Higher Education students under pressure following Covid-19. *Journal of University Teaching and Learning Practice*, 21(6). https://doi.org/10.53761/b96chc12.

Kernohan, D. (2025). *Exploring the Motivation and Satisfaction of Higher Education Staff*. WonkHE. 29th September. Available at: https://wonkhe.com/blogs/exploring-the-motivation-and-satisfaction-of-higher-education-staff/ (Accessed 5 November 2025).

Le-May Sheffield, S. and Serbati, A. (2022). Our academic development stories: exploring identities, complexities, and experiences. *International Journal for Academic Development*, 27(4), pp. 301–305. https://doi.org/10.1080/1360144X.2022.2154138.

Little, C. (2024). Confronting failure as self-care: critical honesty as a springboard for positive change in teaching and learning. In N. Lemon (Ed.), *Prioritising Wellbeing and Self-Care in Higher Education* (pp. 71–81). London: Routledge.

Lowe, T., Naughton, C., Struetzel, T., Adams, R., Walker, J., Kynaston, P., and Mackey, C. (2025). Why are students not attending in-person classes post-COVID-19? An explorative study in student engagement. *Active Learning in Higher Education*. https://doi.org/10.1177/14697874251366213.

McDonagh, L. and Sanders, E. C. (2025). 'You almost feel like you've got a friend, somebody who's backing you up': exploring the building blocks of trust within a relational pedagogy approach to academic development. *International Journal for Academic Development*, 30(1), pp. 40–52. https://doi.org/10.1080/1360144X.2024.2443214.

McVitty, D. (2025). *The WonkHE HE Staff Survey – How Good Is Work in Higher Education?* WonkHE. 29th September. Available at: https://wonkhe.com/blogs/the-wonkhe-he-staff-survey-how-good-is-work-in-higher-education/ (Accessed 5 November 2025).

Mezirow, J. (1985). A critical theory of self-directed learning. In S. Brookfield (Ed.), *Self-directed Learning: From Theory to Practice* (New Directions for Continuing Education, 25) (pp. 17–30). San Francisco, CA: Jossey-Bass.

Mezirow, J. (2003). Transformative learning as discourse. *Journal of Transformative Education*, 1(1), pp. 58–63.

Moss, A. C. and Neves, J. (2025). *The Risks of Eroding Work and Study Conditions for Students*. Advance HE. Available at: https://www.advance-he.ac.uk/news-and-views/risks-eroding-work-and-study-conditions-students (Accessed 5 November 2025)

NUS UK. (2025). *BREAKING: Student Foodbank Use has Doubled since 2022*. National Union of Students. June 12, 2024. Available at: https://www.nus.org.uk/cost-of-living-survey-2024 (Accessed 5 November 2025).

Pleschová, G. *et al.* (2025). Trust-building as inherent to academic development practice. *International Journal for Academic Development*, 30(1), pp. 1–13. https://doi.org/10.1080/1360144X.2025.2454704.

Pulman, A., Fenge, L. A., Mazarura, P., and Sanis, N. (2024). Struggling with studying and earning – realities of the UK's cost-of-living crisis on students on social work programmes. *Research in Post-Compulsory Education*, 29(4), pp. 681–701. https://doi.org/10.1080/13596748.2024.2403825.

Schaberg, C. (2021). *Pedagogy of the Depressed*. New York: Bloomsbury Publishing.

Schofield, C. (2024). The impact of the cost-of-living crisis on online student engagement and future study plans. *Research in Post-Compulsory Education*, 29(3), pp. 502–519. https://doi.org/10.1080/13596748.2024.2371643.

Smith, R. (2022). *The Cost of Living Crisis: What Does It Mean for Further and Adult Education?* Association of Colleges. Available at: https://www.aoc.co.uk/news-campaigns-parliament/news-views/aoc-blogs/the-cost-of-living-crisis-what-does-it-mean-for-further-and-adult-education-rob-smith

9

A GRAND DAY OUT

Wei Shan Chia and Matthew Bradshaw

Year One of the architecture course at the University of Sheffield School of Architecture and Landscape focuses on the collective and the joyful, embracing the unexpected but grounded in physical realities. The year is the beginning of an architectural education for a cohort, more than a quarter of whom are dual students, studying landscape or structural engineering alongside architecture, with their single honours colleagues. This mixed group is introduced to collaborative ways of thinking and making through a teaching approach that over the years has developed an enduring, collegiate and distinctly Sheffield studio culture. We see Year One as a testing ground, a supportive safe place to take risks, to enjoy success and to learn from failure if it happens.

This will be illustrated in this piece through an examination of the fifth and final design project in the Year One programme, which was designed and developed by the Year One leadership team comprising the authors with Laura Mark. This project is in many ways the embodiment of this risk-taking safe space, displaying, as we will see, some characteristics of the "risky learning spaces" advocated by Gullberg and Rødne (2023, p. 104) – start by doing, work in teams, work off site, and have fun (2023, pp. 105–109). This is a guided project, with tutors offering light-touch advice, encouragement, and words of warning as necessary, and is subject to summative assessment worth 25% of the semester two design module. That assessment takes the form of a day at the coast building, testing, discussing and dismantling, which gives the project its title, "Life's a Beach".

The studio projects that precede Life's a Beach in the Year One curriculum include two group working projects where students are carefully introduced

DOI: 10.4324/9781003647720-12

to key concepts, such as context and appropriateness, and core skills, such as surveying, modelmaking and architectural drawing conventions. These are followed by two individual building design projects of increasing complexity, which comprise the bulk of the credits awarded for the year. Life's a Beach marks a return to group working for the end of the year, but rather than going back to the safe introductory environment of those early group projects, this one has a purpose, structure and ambition that concludes the year in a more challenging and sometimes spectacular fashion.

In this final project, students are tasked with building a sandcastle and protective beach tent structure to be erected at a Northern English seaside town. Working with a limited amount of timber and fabric, they are encouraged to assume roles within the project, mirroring those in practice. They are asked to experiment and design using practical, empirical and haptic methods to iteratively test the possibilities of their materials (Figure 9.1).

At the end of the two weeks, each of the tents is tested for stability, deconstructed and packed into a van. Then, on the last studio day, we all drive to the beach where the sand structures are sculpted, and the shelters are reconstructed above them. As the tide returns, students rejoice and despair in the reclamation of their sandcastles by the sea, before packing everything back into the vehicle at the end of the day, ready for sorting for reuse and recycling within local community organisations.

Figure 9.1 Students rescuing their beach tent from the incoming waves on Cleethorpes beach.

Structure

Within the Year One curriculum, we look to encourage experimentation through a range of techniques and media, but constraints on space and resources mean that it is often difficult to find opportunities for large-scale making. This project was born from discussions at the end of the Covid pandemic, with a cohort of students that had experienced significant isolation and disruption to their education, and funding was granted by the School of Architecture for a project that would encourage large-scale interaction within the student cohort.

The project moves quickly, the students have four studio days to design and construct their beach tent and design their sandcastle. The emphasis is to complete the work during studio hours, whilst everyone is together.

Reveal

The project begins, as all Sheffield Year One architecture projects do, with a collective year forum, where logistics and essential information are covered. In these briefings, students are always introduced to precedents relevant to the project being undertaken. In Life's a Beach we focus on the use of precedent to introduce ways of working with materials and to raise the ambition for what a beach tent or sandcastle might be. The precedents offered do not include any examples of previous students' structures or sand sculptures. This is a frequent point of debate amongst the teaching team, but we have found in other design projects that, consciously or unconsciously, some precedents can become disproportionately influential on final designs. In this project, we have found that the engagement with the limited palette of materials the students are given, gives rise to consistent responses in how basic connections are made, but that leaving a gap where previous students' work would have been, not showing a pre-determined outcome, has allowed each new year creative freedom. As a result, a variety of forms and expressions have flourished, and no two structures have been the same over the years the project has been running.

Gathering/Regrouping

The project regroups the students in studio for the third time in the year, re-mixing the cohorts into groups of 20–25 students. For the most part, it is a student-led project, with tutors acting as facilitators. The students gather to assign themselves various pre-determined roles, such as project manager, sourcing and pricing materials, reporter, health and safety officer, etc. in a structure that reflects the division of responsibilities of a project team in practice. It gives an opportunity for our dual honours cohorts, Architecture and Landscape, and Structural Engineering and Architecture, to explore their distinct skillsets and act as consultants and specialists in their field.

As we approach the end of the year, we often assume that the year group, having spent over 20 weeks together, nine to five, for at least two days a week, would already know each other well. However, year on year, we are reminded of the small gestures that can change the dynamics in an inclusive studio community, and that often in the increasingly vast intakes, it takes a little time and luck to find your future collaborators. The open and experimental approach that this project encourages gives space for serendipitous meetings of minds. On arrival in Year One, students naturally cluster with those with whom they have shared lived experiences. The working environment in Life's a Beach, coupled with the collegiate studio ethos, provides another and distinct opportunity to bridge across existing associations and create new creative connections, to establish co-working collaborations that over the years have proved enduring throughout the undergraduate degree and beyond.

Bend/Break

The cohort is typically academically high achieving, and whilst there is a diversity in home and international students, students have become accustomed to increasingly structured and scaffolded methods of learning in schools. This project challenges these structures, asking students to work with an open-ended methodology, embracing unknown outcomes and providing a space to take risks, embracing the idea that education itself is inherently risky and that this is to be celebrated rather than designed out (Biesta, 2013).

Students are encouraged to design through making, to engage with their haptic senses and to develop through experimenting at 1:1 scale. Often architectural education prioritises visual analytical and experimental tools – orthographic drawing, sketching, photographing. Here, we suggest that students design through tactile means, determining texture through touch and understanding the flexibility and fragility of a material via testing through movements of the body (Paterson, 2007).

This is an opportunity for students to play, to start to define their own interests and motivations whilst rooted in the reality of a physical material, exploring how delicate timber laths become more structural under tension and bending, how taut kite fabric pulses and hums in the wind, and how the direction of grain in a timber stud affects how it will respond to the saw and the chisel. The principles of unconstrained play as a means for open-ended development and expression for young children, advocated by Friedrich Froebel (Froebel and Hailmann, 1912, p. 303), can also be seen as essential in a higher education setting.

We have found that, for almost all the students, working with actual construction materials is a new skill and language to be learnt. This project's focus on hands-on sensory experiencing of materials as a means to understanding their potential for design and construction is a thread that can be seen, for example, in Peter Zumthor's approach to architectural education:

"to experience architecture in a concrete way means to touch, see, hear, and smell it. To discover and consciously work with these qualities – these are the themes of our teaching" (1999, p. 58). Various Sheffield Year One making projects have explored this strand over the years, but after the hands-off detachment of Covid teaching, we saw Life's a Beach as a much-needed opportunity to re-engage powerfully with a sensory making process. It is also a chance to take joy from simplicity – it's just a tent and a sandcastle, made from a couple of materials. At a stage of the year where students may feel overwhelmed by accrued information, the limited palette allows a certain freedom. Additionally, as very few students have prior experience of building and forming space for real, the playing field is levelled, and everyone is free to speak up, inviting contributions from those who may otherwise feel intimidated.

Life's a Beach is in some ways a very modest project, using limited resources over a short space of time (these are, we think, some of its strengths). However, the hands-on play-centred methodology it embodies can also be seen in more expansive programmes in current architectural higher education, such as the "Making is Thinking" programme at NTNU, the Norwegian University of Science and Technology. In Life's a Beach, it is the role of the studio tutor to offer students advice, but also to allow them to make "errors", echoing the pedagogical approaches of both Froebel and Making is Thinking – "mistakes are acknowledged as a necessary and productive condition for the creative processes" (Rødne and Hokstad, 2022, p. 1). This can be challenging and counterintuitive to a traditional, hierarchical model of architectural education, but in this foundational first year, we aim to engender a studio culture that "balances risk with trust, confidence and belonging" (Rødne and Hokstad, 2022, p. 3) in order to give students the space to develop their own voice, outlook and language.

Studio/Culture

We have mentioned this Sheffield *studio culture* before. These behaviours and attitudes are encouraged and engendered by peers and tutors are bound up with the physical spaces of the studios in the Arts Tower in Sheffield, and how their use changes with activities from day to day. In common with the pressures on space and resources prevalent in UK universities at present, the Year One and Year Two cohorts share the same studios, working on different days, each year leaving traces for the other, like ghostly flatmates. This necessary versatility perhaps erodes the traditional ideal of what studio in an architecture school might be (Corazzo, 2019, p. 1250). However, the studio spaces during Life's a Beach exhibit all six of the themes that Corazzo identifies in current academic discourse around studios – making, bridging, meaning, enabling, backgrounding and disciplining (pp. 1255–1256). Of these, most apparent in this project is of course making, whilst bridging – the connection of academic and professional contexts – such as through the design team roles conferred on students is also strongly felt.

However, it is also worth considering the great importance of the *enabling* qualities, or otherwise, of the physical studio space here. This project revolves around large-scale making and space in our building is tight. This is constraining (the converse of enabling) on how making activities are carried out and how the studio is inhabited by those who are not at any given time participating in that making. Often this starts to disrupt and dissolve the expected allocation of studio space as satellites from each group find their own corners in which to progress their investigations, to find their own informal learning spaces within the building. This intensity of use alongside a re-mixing of the students contributes to the overall inclusivity of the studio community and can be instrumental in making those personal working connections we mentioned above.

The boundaries of the studio are further disrupted as students travel (with some tutor encouragement) to sandpits in community playgrounds around the city to test proposed sand-shaping methodologies, and on one occasion the whole year decamped to a nearby park to develop their tent structures in the sun. The variety of spaces, of learning environments, and the level of control the students have over their own hands-on activities in Life's a Beach, at times blurs the project from formal learning into a more informal and particularly non-formal, learning experience for the students (Cantürk Akyildiz and Özgüven, 2024, p.194), and can be seen to foreshadow the influential Live Projects, which follow in later years of the Sheffield architecture programme (for an introduction, see Butterworth and Care, 2014). This challenge to the formal studio environment is completed on the last grand day out on the beach, where the material parameters of the "studio" change with the weather and tides, and ice cream is constantly available.

Don't Bend or Break

While granting the cohort their wonderful new freedom to make, test, and refine or destroy, the project also must recognise the necessary realities of the haptic making process – saws are sharp, hammers will find thumbs, the wind can gust strongly enough to give flight to an unsecured tent, and the North Sea is definitely cold and wet with deceptive tides ready to catch out unwary builders. It is imperative that the students are briefed to work safely in the studio and on the beach, but much more than this, a culture of creative safety is encouraged within the project groups. Students are encouraged to work and think in ways that maintain the freedom of the design process whilst designing-out hazards that could harm the students and other users of the beach. Examples of this include developing production lines for connections,

Figure 9.2 A completed structure, made from flexible timber laths and kite nylon, on the beach ready for review by students and staff.

prefabrication of key components that can fold away to fit in the van and fabrication of specialist tools or jigs for cutting wood or carving sand.

The parallels with construction industry good practice are evident, but beyond this, the project aims to explicitly reject the still all-too-common view of health and safety as a boring but necessary add-on to design. Instead, from the beginning, students are introduced to the notion that safe working should be part of the creative process, and, subversively, something that might actually be fun (Figure 9.2).

Mould

Students working on the sandcastles face very different challenges from those constructing the tents. As a medium, there is a similarity to casting, of constructing additive volumes whilst imagining negative spaces. However, it differs in that there is an element of plasticity to the material, once cast, it is possible, perhaps desirable, to cut away, to smooth, to shape. Students are encouraged to create their own tools to make these forms, experimenting with bending and fixing thin sheet materials, creating moulds with the vacuum former, appropriating and adapting plastering tools and utilising found objects.

The students need to work quickly, and on a large scale, the sandcastles must have a minimum footprint of 8 m^2 and measure at least 800 mm tall. There is a need to be agile, to accept the unpredictability of their working material, the bed of black clay lying just below the sandy surface or the mosaic of seashells littering their site and adapt their designs and methods accordingly.

Join/Connect

Richard Sennett describes

> the desire to do a job well for its own sake... the craftsman often faces conflicting objective standards of excellence; the desire to do something well for its own sake can be impaired by competitive pressure, by frustration, or by obsession.
>
> *(2008, p. 9)*

In many ways, whilst a 1:1 making project might initially suggest a focus on craft, the opposite is true. Students have produced well-crafted projects, but this is often a happy by-product, rather than the singular intent of the project.

Sennett describes an "engaged material consciousness" (2008, p. 120) as a way of becoming particularly interested in the things that we can change. In this project the metamorphosis or iterative process is not something that happens slowly, passed down through generations, but is immediate, intuitive and rough. It invites discussion, but more so, a choreography, as students lift and lever the timbers, temporarily testing permutations and discovering the limitations.

On day one of the project, students are encouraged to immediately interact with their materials. Sketching is discouraged, and no individual controls the paper and pencil – experiments are made and evaluated quickly by all. At times, a determination by some students to design as fully as possible on paper or 3D computer models before engaging haptically has served to demonstrate shortcomings of these design methods, as the realities of wood and tenon saw, nut and bolt, prove uncooperative in practice.

In future years of education, the visual and particularly the drawn naturally dominate. This brief interlude suggests the start of a tactile understanding of the materials that are drawn, how they can be handled, along which axis they are strongest. It provides one of hopefully many physical references for Juhani Pallasmaa's description of embodied imagination, as a tool for design (1996, p. 13).

Construct/Reconstruct

Over the course of the first two weeks, students assemble, deconstruct and reassemble their structures. Within their groups, students negotiate, aligning and developing designs for the sandcastles and the beach tents. The process is animated and often loud, but disagreements about design are rare, perhaps because the physical design process is open and accessible for all to see and alter.

At the end of the two weeks, the tents and sandcastle designs are checked by tutors for suitability and stability. It is made clear from the outset of the project that a fabrication that is hazardous, or is too big for the van, cannot be taken to the beach. Several projects have failed this assessment over the years, and in all cases very hasty modifications were undertaken to rectify the defects sufficiently for the group to travel to the seaside. Sometimes this resulted in projects disappointingly compromised by inelegant bracing, accompanied by some recrimination and regret. At others, an exciting new design direction was opened in the last hours of making, resulting in a jubilant, if frenetic conclusion.

Once approved, the tents are demounted and all loaded into a single transit van, along with all the equipment needed for the build day. There is often joy in this moment, careful numbering and labelling of pieces, the counting of equipment, the process becomes performative, a rite of passage.

Digging

Faced with the English seaside, and the vast, flat horizon, there is often an initial collective pause amongst the students. For those who have not been before, they often remark that even after reading maps, researching the history and looking at pictures, the sense of place has not been fully described, the changing of the tides, the undocumented and dynamic nature of the land emerging from the water between high and low tide, is temporal and difficult to capture. There is often a reluctance to walk out to meet the sea, even if the tide is retreating, many preferring to stay close to the high tide line, but once gently encouraged, students start to survey the site, to look closely to understand the micro-topography of the sand and to find and agree on a place to site their sandcastles and start digging.

Ebb and Flow

The students are encouraged to site their projects so that they can be reviewed as the tide meets their sandcastles. At the moment when the sea starts to reclaim the sand, there is a flurry of activity, tents are rescued and moved to shore whilst others look on, trying to predict when the towers of sand will finally collapse. This point of finality, a definitive conclusion to the project, is a point that is difficult to achieve in their other designs as feedback always suggests "one more thing" that could be considered, however, here on the beach, this end feels like a point of celebration.

Circularity

Of course, the project is not actually finished at this point, and there is "one more thing" before the project is complete. It is a stipulation of the brief that, where possible, all the materials must be either reused or recycled. Upon returning to Sheffield, the van is unloaded, and the workshop turns into a processing unit, cleaning tools, removing staples from timber, sorting materials into piles. Partnerships with local community organisations have seen the timber used for Forest Schools, mobility steps and local playgrounds, with fabrics being taken to a community scrap craft shop. Where possible, tools are saved for the following years' students, and the black box of miscellaneous cordage and fixtures grows more eclectic each year, a collective memory box for the next cohort to decipher and reimagine.

As we write, Life's a Beach is about to begin its fourth outing. Each year, small refinements have been made to some aspects of the project, including the project timetable, the detailed specification of the materials, and this year, a move from Cleethorpes to further north up the coast. As much as we conceal previous years' designs from each new cohort, the project has built up some public momentum through social media and promotion at open days, as well as, crucially, discussions between year groups in the studios. The details of each previous beach structure might not stick in the minds of each incoming cohort, but we hope the potential to participate in something explorative, risky, unexpected and fun very much does, and is instrumental in helping students establish for themselves the open and pluralistic approach for which the school has become known.

References

Biesta, G. (2016) *The Beautiful Risk of Education*. London: Routledge.

Butterworth, C. and Care, L. (2014) 'A Live Currency: Introducing The SSoA Live Projects Handbook', *Charrette*, 1(1), pp. 72–81.

Cantürk Akyildiz, E. and Özgüven, Y. (2024) 'Out-of-School Activities in Architectural Education: MUISCARCH International Architecture Students Congress', *International Journal of Art & Design Education*, 43(2), pp. 190–204.

Corazzo, J. (2019) 'Materialising the Studio. A Systematic Review of the Role of the Material Space of the Studio in Art, Design and Architecture Education', *The Design Journal*, 22(1), pp. 1249–1265.

Froebel, F. and Hailmann, W.N. (1912) *The Education of Man*. New York; London: D. Appleton.

Gullberg, J.S. and Rødne, G. (2023) 'August. Risk, Trust and Big Beautiful Mistakes*: Keys to Innovation in Architectural Education', *Annual Conference of the European Association for Architectural Education*. Politecnico di Torino (Italy), 30 August–1 September, pp. 102–111.

Pallasmaa, J. (1996) *The Eyes of the Skin*. Chichester: Wiley.

Paterson, M. (2007) *The Senses of Touch: Haptics, Affects, and Technologies*. Oxford; New York: Berg.
Rødne, G. and Hokstad, L.M. (2022) '"Making Is Thinking": From Design Fixation to Provocative Competence', *ARENA Journal of Architectural Research*, 7(1), p. 2.
Sennett, R. (2008) *The Craftsman*. London: Penguin.
Zumthor, P. (1999) *Thinking Architecture*. Basel; Boston, MA; Berlin: Birkhäuser.

10

THE FOUNDATION STUDIO

Space, Practice and Belonging in Architecture and Design Education

Rob Vinall

Introduction

This chapter explores how creative pedagogies and situated learning environments can support and enhance the student experience through enabling a sense of belonging and community in first-year architecture and design study.

I write from my previous experience designing and leading the Architecture and Design Integrated Foundation Year at the University of Brighton. The foundation year brings together students from the Architecture, Interior Architecture and Product Design undergraduate pathways as one cohort. Developed as a shared space, the curriculum places specific value on experimentation, risk-taking and play. Projects and design briefs take a shared disciplinary approach to design, encouraging students to explore ideas of function, identity and narrative through drawing, making and collaboration.

The foundation year is made up of around 75 students from a wide range of backgrounds, and varying levels of ability and confidence, many coming from non-traditional routes and often having limited experience of creative education, particularly in drawing and making.

The majority start their learning in Architecture, with the option to move to another discipline after the foundation year.

The transition into both higher education and the subject area as taught in this context can therefore feel unfamiliar, even intimidating. In response, the curriculum design prioritises process, reflection and self-expression as essential ways to build confidence, establish identity, and cultivate a strong sense of belonging. This is not only achieved through curriculum design, but also through the physical pedagogical space. The studio becomes a site, where

DOI: 10.4324/9781003647720-13

students can take ownership of their learning and begin to feel part of a creative community (Doorley and Witthoft, 2012).

Group work, critique, and conversation are central to the curriculum. These shared experiences and opportunities for collective enquiry are designed to help students recognise themselves, and each other, as participants in a collaborative, creative practice. A key aim of the early stages of the foundation year is to enable students to start developing a design language, to explore what authorship might mean and to feel confident contributing their ideas within a group context.

Drawing on Monk and colleagues' exploration of Open-Space Learning, the curriculum frames play and experimentation not as distractions from learning, but as essential conditions for it, allowing students to "work through experiment and play to make creative progress", where failure becomes part of the process and not a deviation from it (Monk, James and Heron, 2011, p. 3). This chapter uses a single project brief as a lens through which to explore how themes of experimentation, process and pedagogic space can enable a sense of belonging – unpacked through the analysis of the pedagogic space, the brief, the experimental workshops and the reviews that take place.

The Pedagogic Space

Crucial to the analysis is the concept of pedagogic space and how the physical studio environment can enable learning, belonging and identity in design education. In this context, studio refers to the physical setting in which teaching and learning activities take place, including lectures, seminars, briefings and practical workshops. The Foundation had a dedicated space, accessible to students throughout the week, providing an environment for working, experimenting and informal interaction.

Subsequently, the foundation year was not defined by the curriculum alone, but also the environment that supported and sustained it. The shared studio, equipped with residential desks and open access to materials, was more than just a room; it *became* a pedagogical space. As Burke and Grosvenor (2008, p. 161) explain, the studio is shaped by the spatial experiences of students – learning and teaching are embedded in its physical and social form. For example, the use of designated desks may seem minor, but its symbolism was significant. In a transitional year like foundation, where many were still finding their footing, this small act of spatial permanence can be profoundly grounding.

Over time, students began to inhabit the studio not just physically, but also socially and creatively. The space became a live archive of process, filled with pinned drawings, models, notes, informal seating, posters, mess – and even a model railway. As Doorley and Witthoft (2012, p. 21) suggest, space becomes meaningful when individuals can claim it, shape it through use and leave visible traces of their presence and participation.

Studio teaching and learning activities were structured around three key contact days and regular practical workshops. This continuity supported a culture of informal exchange, peer learning and collaborative making. As Newton (2012) argues, learning is not only shaped by social interaction but is also fundamentally spatial, with teaching and learning practices embedded within and influenced by the environments in which they occur. Within this framework, the foundation studio was more than a setting. It functioned as a critical pedagogical space where students could return, contribute and take part in a shared culture of practice.

The Brief

Form/Structure/Function is a two-week project designed to introduce students to collaborative design practice through drawing, making, experimentation and critical reflection. Set in the fifth week of the first semester, it supports the development of studio culture by encouraging group identity, creative risk-taking and personal authorship. Kolb (1984) emphasises the importance of practice-based, collaborative learning, arguing that learning happens through doing, reflecting and adapting. When this is shared in a group setting, it promotes a culture where students learn not only from tutors, but also from each other. The brief was intentionally shaped in response to the physical spatial context of the studio, creating conditions for experimentation, group dynamics and collaboration at a pivotal time in the academic year.

Students were asked in groups of four to design and make a functional wearable structure in response to a given activity, exploring 1:1 construction techniques and form as key themes, whilst also considering how material, narrative and use can be expressive. From initial drawings, students constructed forms that explored a functional purpose, using simple materials to explore detail, movement and the body in relation to the built environment. The brief also investigated the narrative potential of objects and structures, considering how physical properties and use can tell a story.

The project began with a full-day studio session combining theoretical framing, task briefing and student group formation. Drawing influence from Wassily Kandinsky's teaching workshops (Poling, 1986) and the practice of Rebecca Horn (Curiger, 1983), students are invited to consider the human body as a site for abstraction, design and communication.

Whilst teaching at the Bauhaus (1922–1933), Kandinsky developed a series of classes for the foundational course that approached drawing as a rigorous, staged investigation into form and structure. His Analytical Drawing classes were structured in stages, each building in complexity to examine spatial relationships of form, composition and structural understanding (Poling, 1986). Through abstraction, students investigated the relationships between physical objects, observing and drawing out structural tensions, constructive elements and principles such as equilibrium, weight, balance and contrast, with the aim of distilling forms to their essential components and understanding how these principles operate within a composition.

This brief borrows this pedagogical approach from the Analytical Drawing class, using layered drawing to unpack complexity before gradually building it up again. The method removes the pressure of the blank page and frames drawing as a way of thinking and as an iterative process that can act as a catalyst for making. It provides a foundation for students to interpret the process in their own way, embedding a sense of identity in the work while generating outcomes that reveal structural possibilities for translation into physical form. Ultimately, it seeks to support students in making their own connections through analysis, interpretation and the synthesis of ideas (Lindsay and Vergo, 1982).

While Kandinsky's method concentrates on the anatomy and process of drawing, Rebecca Horn's work offers a more personal lens, exploring how influence and identity can be embedded within the physical piece. Her practice engages with personal experience, emotion and involvement in the object (Curiger, 1983).

The brief draws influence from Horn's body sculptures. These works explore limitation, extension and appendage as ways of communicating and examining the body. They consider identity, performative qualities, and the context of spatial relationships. These worn machines take on a human quality, extending action beyond the body, mimicking behaviour and inviting emotional connection. Horn describes these objects as "like actors", shifting character in response to the body (*Rebecca Horn* Exhibition, 2001).

There is a particular interest in how students can communicate or interpret identity within their work. By engaging with Horn's approach, the brief invited them to consider how materials, function and use might act as carriers of identity. This pedagogical framing created space for individual interpretation, encouraging students to explore these concepts in ways that reflected their own perspectives and creative voice. By drawing on these themes and approaches, the aim of the brief is to encourage individual, exploratory processes that combine drawing practice with personal expression through making and communication.

Each group is given a randomly assigned function, for example, "to provide a specific view" or "to keep out of reach". They are then asked to interpret this through designing and building a full-scale structure or object, with material constraints (e.g., bamboo, binding and found fabric). Throughout the week, students share roles, explore ideas and problem-solve together toward a physical outcome. This culminates in a celebratory review at the end of the first week that encourages reflective dialogue and group learning.

In week two, the focus shifts from the group to the individual. Students are asked to individually produce scaled technical drawings and visual responses that communicate their own interpretation of body, function and form.

This individual phase allows students to express their voice and develop design confidence. As with the first week, the second ends on a celebratory review session, this time open to the rest of the design school who are invited to participate in viewing and discussing the outcomes.

By engaging in a shared process of experimentation, students begin to take ownership – not just of the outcome, but of their ideas, their learning and their growing sense of identity as designers. As Ryan and Deci note, "Support for autonomy allows individuals to actively transform values into their own... [it] facilitates deep, holistic processing...and enables integration of meaning with one's goals and values" (Ryan and Deci, 2000, p. 73).

The intention behind the project was to create an environment where students could begin to navigate the complexity of working with others whilst simultaneously learning to articulate their own ideas with confidence. Many arrive unfamiliar with studio culture, unsure how to position themselves within it, or how to respond to open-ended briefs. The physical space of the studio as a shared and consistent space, supports this transition by offering both a sense of place and a stage for practice. This project therefore aims to ease that shift, not by simplifying it, but by providing structure, support and challenge through shared experience within a dedicated pedagogical space.

Furthermore, the group element of this project was essential. I wanted students to start with negotiation, communication and material play, not as isolated activities, but as points of connection. Through building together, students begin to understand design as a process of exchange. Collaborative learning has been shown to support both independent thinking and social interdependence, qualities that should be nurtured from the outset to strengthen the studio group dynamics (Yang, 2015).

Equally, the individual phase was designed to allow space for personal interpretation. Once the group work is complete, students are invited to reflect on what was made and reframe it in their own visual language. For some, this is the first moment they feel able to express something entirely their own. It is an opportunity to take initiative and make choices.

This acknowledgement of a student's prior knowledge and experience influenced their engagement in the learning environment. As Munger (1996) notes, overlooking this can create friction, particularly when a student's relevant experience is downplayed to fit a default tutor–student role, or that of "the new student". The result can be a breakdown in their relationship with the space, the tutor and their own confidence. In the context of the foundation year, it is important to establish this sense of volition early on, as Ryan and Deci (2000) argue that supporting autonomy fosters deeper engagement and allows individuals to align their learning with their own goals and values.

The Experimental Workshops

Whilst this chapter focuses on a specific brief, experimental drawing workshops are an integral part of how the foundation pedagogical aims are achieved. Experimental drawing workshops are a weekly fixture throughout the first semester that support every design brief. Each Monday begins with these sessions, intentionally embedded into the curriculum as a consistent structure. Running for three hours during the morning session, they establish a rhythm that prioritises observation, interpretation and confidence-building through collective drawing. In relation to this brief, the workshops offer a valuable space for students to explore ideas, test visual language and develop shared studio practices that support both individual growth and group dynamics.

In this instance, drawing is introduced not as a skill to master, but as an opportunity to engage in observing the world, unpacking the brief and participating in collective practice. The sessions begin with short, focused exercises, such as blind drawing (drawing without looking at the page to develop observation), continuous line (drawing without lifting the pencil to build confidence) and movement drawing (capturing the energy and motion of a subject through expressive marks). The exercises then combine or introduce new drawing techniques to develop more open and layered responses. The workshops are designed to shift attention away from perfection and toward process, encouraging students to relax, draw more freely and focus less on outcomes. As Mills and Payne (2024, p. 51) note, drawing in this way allows students to care more about the process than the end product, which Thurlow and Ford (2017) reinforce as supporting a more open and experimental approach to learning.

The pedagogical approach to these weekly sessions, developed in connection with this brief, draws from the previously mentioned teaching practices of Kandinsky where the foundational elements of line, form, tone and space were used to help students explore the relationships within composition and perception. His method of analytical drawing, rooted in abstraction and relational thinking, positioned drawing as a tool for constructing meaning. Kandinsky's teaching was practice-based, ensuring that students engaged directly with the course material rather than relying solely on lectures to understand the fundamental elements and principles of art and design (Poling, 1986). This approach aligns with Kolb's view that learning is best understood as a process grounded in experience, rather than as the attainment of fixed outcomes (Kolb, 1984).

This allows for drawing to become a way of observing the world and communicating personal interpretation. These experimental sessions continue in that spirit. By breaking down visual language into elemental parts, students are given time and space to experiment, testing how different components interact and gradually learning how to bring them together with intention. These drawings (Figure 10.1) were produced during the initial experimental

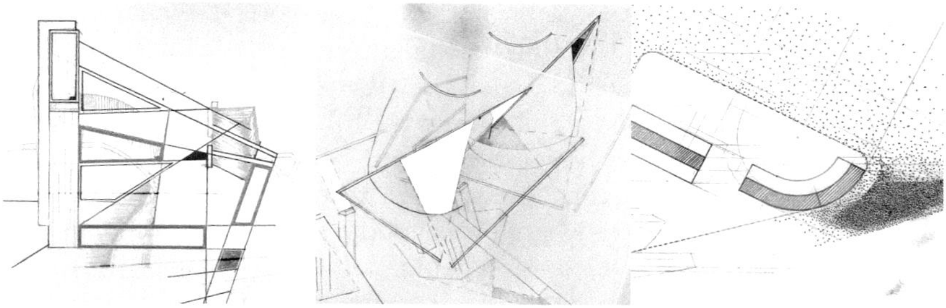

Figure 10.1 Selection of outcomes from experimental drawing workshops (Students: Will Allin, Erica Tyler, David Loja).

workshops, where students began by observing a set of still life objects and exploring their geometric qualities. Through layered analytical drawing, they developed these forms through abstraction, examining potential structural relationships. The outcome is a drawing shaped by process, but with a clear spatial quality, functioning almost like a plan or elevation with the potential to inform three-dimensional work. They also begin to reveal a developing aesthetic, a capacity for self-reflection and an emerging individual process.

As their understanding of structure and form deepens, so too does their ability to compose. Though the drawings remain abstract, they reflect growing confidence in mark-making, in decision-making, and in the ability to construct meaning through form. In this way, students begin to develop their own visual language, developed through experience and enquiry.

Crucially, these workshops were collective. Students work side by side in the shared studio space, building trust and growing confidence in their creative process. Collaborative drawing encourages play and experimentation, allowing students to take risks, work more freely, and let go of the need for perfection (Mills and Payne, 2024). This practice aligns with the brief's emphasis on testing ideas through process, while the shared act of making helps to create a sense of community and shared experience among peers.

This is not simply preparatory work, it is an active, pedagogical space where identity, belonging and autonomy begin to emerge. The sharing of knowledge within a community fosters unique and valuable connections that deepen understanding (Wenger, McDermott and Snyder, 2002). Arguably, we are engaging in drawing for its own sake – a shared, open-ended act that values process over product and presence over perfection.

The Reviews

The reviews that close each week of the *Form/Structure/Function* project are not designed as assessments, but as shared moments of critique and reflection – and in many ways, pure celebration. These are opportunities to pause, take stock, and speak about process; what worked, what didn't, and how decisions were made. In doing so, students begin to develop a language for design that is both verbal and visual. They learn to describe, comment and evolve their thinking in a space that values contribution.

Reviews take place throughout the afternoon once groups have completed their work during the morning, allowing them to set up in a space on campus that best reflects the nature of what they've made. This more flexible, informal ending keeps the energy of the session going, rather than closing it down with a strict timetable. During the set-up, each group writes a short description of their piece, how it developed and three key reflections: what worked, what they'd improve and how they might explore themes and skills covered in their future practice. We then move through the pieces as a full cohort, with each group taking the floor in turn. It becomes an ensemble approach; collaborative, responsive and based on trust and shared responsibility for experimentation (Monk, James and Heron, 2011). Every group offers structured feedback to another and the process continues until everyone has been seen and heard.

These reviews are intentionally celebratory, promoting a culture of community, affirmation and mutual encouragement. They often incorporate moments of humour, expressive appreciation and collective recognition, serving not only as feedback but as a performative gesture of support. In this context, applause and laughter function as pedagogical tools that affirm presence, value risk-taking and cultivate a sense of belonging within the studio environment. This atmosphere plays a crucial role in shaping group identity, helping students feel part of something collective rather than isolated.

Celebration in this context is not about performance for performance's sake, but about creating an environment of support, ease and mutual recognition. Students are invited to speak about their work informally, sometimes performatively, with many choosing to embody or interact with their final pieces as a way of exploring function, programme and meaning through physical engagement (Figure 10.2). This approach echoes Horn's emphasis on the relationship between object and body, and how meaning can be communicated through movement and interaction (Curiger, 1983, p. 40). In practice, students claim the space as part of the work, using it as a stage for experimentation and belonging (Monk, James and Heron, 2011; Doorley and Witthoft, 2012), allowing for informality and improvisation. The final review space is also opened to the wider school community, turning the event into a moment of visibility and connection that aims to build student confidence and a sense of wider belonging.

These regular events are central to building a sense of community. Mills and Payne's (2024) study highlights how creating together in a shared environment, combined with open discussion, can foster a strong sense of community by giving students space to exchange ideas, debate and inspire one another. Here, critique becomes a shared process, an exchange among students, tutors and ideas.

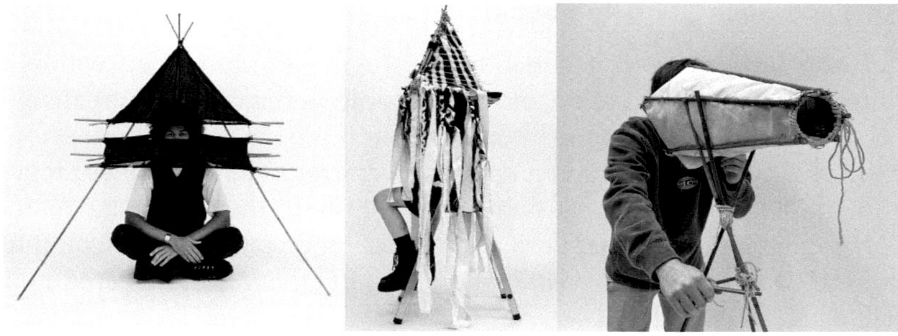

Figure 10.2 Three completed student projects exploring form, structure and function through photography (Students: Bailey Borg-Thomas, Izzy Wrigley, Oliver Twine).

This model of shared feedback supports the wider aims of the foundation year as an important transitional experience. Gorgorio, Planas and Vilella (2002) suggest that transition should be understood not just as a phase of change, but as an active experience of transformation. Students are not simply preparing for something in the future; they are already in the process of becoming. Becoming a learner, a peer, a participant in the studio. Reviews are part of that process, helping students locate themselves within the group and within their own practice.

These moments allow students to test language and build authorship, without the pressure of finality. The aim is to create space for identity to emerge, supported through dialogue. As O'Donnell, Kean and Stevens (2016) emphasise, creating regular opportunities for discourse between students and staff is essential to helping learners feel part of an academic community. What often begins as nervous presenting slowly develops into confident speaking, framed by the notion that ideas grow stronger when shared.

Student-led reviewing plays a crucial role. It can encourage autonomy and trust and affirm that their views matter. It also challenges the perceived notion that knowledge only comes from tutors, recognising that students bring their own experiences and perspectives which can shape and enrich the discussion.

Through the accumulation of these events, students begin to recognise the value of reviewing others as well as receiving feedback themselves. Yang (2015) notes that engaging in peer review can enhance students' own work, as they begin to see the process as a tool for development rather than judgement. As this awareness grows, the review evolves from a conversation into something more embedded. The physical setting of the studio as an open, consistent, and collectively held space, enables this shift, grounding the review as both a spatial and social practice. Within this shift, the review acts as a moment of anchoring, both individually and collectively.

Space, Experimentation and Belonging

The ownership and open accessibility of the studio, combined with a curriculum that values exploration and play, enable students to take creative risks within a structure that supports continuity, routine and shared presence. As Burke and Grosvenor (2008) argue, space is never neutral; it plays an active role in shaping how students come to understand themselves as learners. The physicality of a personal desk and the presence of visible, ongoing work contribute to a sense of co-ownership and participation in a shared culture of making.

The foundation studio therefore becomes more than a site of instruction; it is a pedagogical space in which knowledge is collectively formed, social interaction is embedded in practice and identity formation is tied to routine presence and visibility (Tinto, 1993; Boud and Garrick, 1999). Through playful, spatial and collaborative engagement, the studio fosters a learning culture where belonging is not an abstract concept but an outcome of shared, lived experience, framed by the unique temporal and social context of the foundational year.

Specific to this cohort, playful and experimental modes of learning lower the stakes of formal assessment and foster a process-oriented approach to creativity and personal discovery. Rather than prioritising final outcomes, students are encouraged to reflect, adapt and iterate. This approach aligns with Gauntlett's (2011) view of creativity as a social and embodied practice, and with Monk, James and Heron's (2011) concept of openness as essential to creative learning. Within this context, critique and celebration are not oppositional, but part of a shared process in which students learn to express their ideas and build confidence through dialogue. When pedagogy explores both process and pedagogic space, what emerges is not only learning, but also a meaningful sense of belonging.

References

Burke, C. and Grosvenor, I. (2008) *School*. London: Reaktion Books.

Curiger, B. (1983). 'The Anatomy of Sensitivity', in Stooss, T. (ed.), *Katalog: Rebecca Horn*. Zurich: Kunsthaus Zurich, pp. 23–63.

Doorley, S. and Witthoft, S. (2012) *Make Space: How to Set the Stage for Creative Collaboration*. Hoboken, NJ: Wiley.

Gauntlett, D. (2011) *Making Is Connecting: The Social Power of Creativity, from DIY and Knitting to YouTube and Web 2.0*. Cambridge: Polity Press.

Horn, R. (2001) *Rebecca Horn Exhibition Catalogue*. Dublin: Irish Museum of Modern Art.

Kolb, D.A. (1984) *Experiential Learning: Experience as the Source of Learning and Development*. Englewood Cliffs, NJ: Prentice Hall.

Lindsay, K.C. and Vergo, P. (eds) (1982) *Complete Writings on Art: Volume 2*. New York: G.K. Hall & Co.

Mills, H. and Payne, J. (2024) Collaborative drawing as a tool for creating a sense of community within NTU's Architecture students. *Student Engagement in Higher Education Journal*, *5*(2), 43–56.
Monk, N., James, S. and Heron, J. (2011) *Open-Space Learning: A Study in Transdisciplinary Pedagogy*. London: Bloomsbury Academic.
Munger, R.H. (1996) *Asymmetries of Knowledge: What Tutor-Student Interactions Tell Us about Expertise*. Paper presented at the 47th Annual Meeting of the Conference on College Composition and Communication, Milwaukee, WI, March 27–30.
Newton, D. (2012) *Teaching for Understanding*. London: Routledge.
O'Donnell, V.L., Kean, M. and Stevens, G. (2016) *Student transitions in higher education: concepts, theories and practices*. York: Higher Education Academy. Poling, C.V. (1986) *Kandinsky's Teaching at the Bauhaus – Color Theory and Analytical Drawing*. New York: Rizzoli International Publications.
Ryan, R.M. and Deci, E.L. (2000) Self-determination theory and the facilitation of intrinsic motivation, social development, and well-being. *American Psychologist*, 55(1), 68–78.
Thurlow, L. and Ford, P. (2017) *Where Have All the Ideas Gone? An Anatomy of Sketch Inhibition among Student Designers*. Design Management Academy Conference 2017: Research Perspectives on Creative Intersections, Hong Kong, 7–9 June, pp. 1703–1719. Available at: https://www.designresearchsociety.org/articles/design-management-academy-2017-conferee-proceedings-available-online (Accessed 13 April 2026).
Tinto, V. (1993) *Leaving College: Rethinking the Causes and Cures of Student Attrition* (2nd ed.). Chicago: University of Chicago Press.
Wenger, E., McDermott, R.A. and Snyder, W. (2002) *Cultivating Communities of Practice*. Boston, MA: Harvard Business School Press.
Yang, M. (2015) *Promoting Self-Sustained Learning in Higher Education: The ISEE Framework*. Teaching in Higher Education, 20(6), 601–613.

11

UNFOLDING – A FIRST-YEAR INTRODUCTION TO CONCEPTUAL THINKING AND REFLECTIVE PRACTICE AT LIVERPOOL SCHOOL OF ARCHITECTURE

Lucretia Ray and Luke Bushnell-Wye

Context and Ambition

The conceit that architecture is new for all first-year undergraduate students is a well-worn trope within architectural education. Like many such notions, this idea has a firm basis in fact: notwithstanding a few exceptions, the reality is that architecture is not a subject taught in further education. As a consequence, the complex processes, theoretical constructs and procedural models that are vital for the successful interpretation of architectural spaces – intangible subtleties that become foundational to the qualified architect – are often startingly opaque to the first-year undergraduate. These are skills that must be taught, learned and their application understood.

Skill-building is an essential part of the first-year teaching programme at the Liverpool School of Architecture (LSA), integrated into the course through a semester-long module dedicated to the teaching of four courses of distinct content that may be interpreted by students as being standalone, but are designed to be woven together to create the bedrock of architectural understanding; complementing and supporting their design teaching. Across a two-week timetable, students are instructed in the four "strands" of Sketching, Model-making, Orthographic drawing and Conceptual Thinking and Reflective Practice (Theory).

By removing the teaching of skills from their design module, the pressure on students to be immediately good at everything is reduced, as is the tacit implication that each design project has a sequential time and place for sketching, orthographic drawing and model-making. Instead, competencies are developed and practised as they would be required in a live project

DOI: 10.4324/9781003647720-14

(Fung 2017, p. 6) and in turn, skill-gaps identified in design modules can be improved upon the next time that strand is taught; both competencies and skill-gaps are continuously reemphasised and reinforced through a spiral curriculum (Murray 2016, p. 1). As a result, students learn freely without feeling they must immediately move on to the next task or risk stalling in their design project.

At the centre of this method of delivery is the breathing space afforded to students to feel comfortable making mistakes as part of their learning process. Architecture is not a profession that either requires or rewards the ability to solve a creative problem at the first attempt, and yet this is the academic mindset with which many enter university. Undergraduate students arrive with academic armour; focussed on attainment and achievement. It is understandable then that the student may look to continue this approach that has served them well, providing them with a comfort zone that can hinder objectivity. They find it hard to see themselves anew as "novice" (Dreyfus and Dreyfus 2004, p. 251). From the Royal Institute of British Architects' (RIBA) Code of Professional Conduct (2021, p. 3) critical reflection is a key attribute for any architect, and any hesitance from students to learn from, improve or even engage with perceived "failures" could greatly hinder them towards becoming an "advanced beginner" (Dreyfus and Dreyfus 2004, p. 251). At this early stage in their education however, students don't always possess the language, self-awareness, openness or even willingness to critically explore their own ideas or the motivations of others.

Course Structure

The Theory strand, then, is aimed squarely at developing these abilities, or "habits of mind", identified by Costa and Kallick (2000, cited in Murray 2016, p. 3). As part of their introduction to Architecture, students are led through a seminar course that helps them explore what influences their identity and how this shapes their interpretations of the world around them. Seminars on subjects such as Experience, Desire, Memory, Identity, Participation, Aurality, Ritual, Liminality and Perception, to name a few, enable students to develop powers of introspection, consideration, creativity and reflection.

The first semester prompts students to start thinking about the way they process information and how that might be different to the person sitting next to them, asking students to consider the building blocks of understanding that shape the cognitive "function machine" that forms their identity: inputs come in, we process them and we create different outputs accordingly. In the second semester we move to a more outwardly facing focus, asking students to consider how the function machine, with which they should all now be more familiar, actively processes external and sensory inputs. The course leans heavily into elements of philosophy and phenomenology but avoids labelling them as such to avoid students dismissing them as abstractions that are irrelevant to their studies.

The basis of the Theory course was conceived by our former colleague, Dr Niall O'Hare, and originated online, by necessity, in a pandemic teaching landscape. Its format translated well to in-person teaching and remains much the same. Each session follows a common pattern, combining both seminar and lecture-based teaching. It is delivered to around 50 students seated in groups of a maximum of five and begins with an introduction to the topic that shows how it sits within the context of the whole course. The image-based lecture is interspersed with short reading and response sessions. Students are provided with the texts and the sources and asked to read them in silence.

These texts are not always explicitly architectural in nature and range from descriptions of favourite rooms by novelist Banana Yoshimoto, memoirs on landscape from naturalist J. Drew Lanham, and reflections on experience by poet Elizabeth Acevedo, all the way to more "traditional" sources of architectural writing such as Jun'ichirō Tanizaki, Italo Calvino or Peter Zumthor. All are chosen for their relevance to the subject at hand and how much space there is for interpretation and extrapolation.

Following the reading, a pair of questions based on the subject matter of the text are introduced and students are asked to discuss them within their small groups. The participants are encouraged to use their different interpretations to help fuel discussion in a collaborative and interactive way, establishing the idea that the conversation's open-ended, exploratory nature can provide opportunities for self-discovery and reflection (Adams 2006, p. 249).

When debates slow down, the students' attention is brought back to the leader of the session, who asks for volunteers to share their responses to the questions from their group. After a reasonable number of views have been shared the session moves back to another series of slides, followed by a second reading. In the first semester this process then repeats for a third time but is eschewed in the second in favour of more time spent on the other two readings and a description of additional tasks that are to be completed as part of the final assessment.

Every session ends with a period of personal reflection, in which students are asked to critically reflect on what they have talked about during the session by journalling their thoughts silently. Their reflections aren't formally submitted, and it is stressed that students aren't going to be marked on their content. After a few minutes, students are asked to draw their thoughts to a close, the session is summarised, some suggestions for further exploration are made, and the session ends.

Provocation, Discussion and Response

Through trial and error, we have discovered that groups of five students are ideal, as this number facilitates discussion without any student feeling excluded. Some students are naturally braver than others when it comes to participation, and the limited size of the discussion groups allows these students to pursue a role of "active listening". As one student observed,

> I rarely spoke … but I found it just as engaging to listen to other people's point of views and opinions that may differ from mine – it opened my mind to new ideas that I would not have thought of by myself.

By extension, students are reminded that they are not forced to put their hand up during the response section to share their opinions. In practise, this sometimes means more confident students contribute more readily, nonetheless the feedback tends to reflect a range of opinions and views from the class.

It is sometimes startling to see the responses of some students upon hearing the contrasting views of their classmates, a reaction we get a glimpse of in their reflections and assessment submissions: compare the likes of

> Today I heard more of other people's ideas and how they viewed the course. Everyone has their own way of deconstructing the question to pick apart and analyse... This talk makes me want to find my own style within the course.

with "What's funny to me is that [student] told me I wouldn't enjoy the session. But I DID".

The diversity of the students is a strength it would be foolish to overlook, and they are often told that their colleagues are their greatest resource whilst studying at LSA. A proverb, attributed to the Greek philosopher Zeno of Citium (Laertius tr. Yonge 1853, p. 268) although now in common usage, is presented at the start of the year: "We have two ears and one mouth so that we can listen twice as much as we speak". This is introduced to encourage students not to speak less, but to engage deliberately with the act of listening and taking on alternative views, an aspect of the course reinforced not just by these feedback sessions but by the texts themselves – taken as they are from a wide range of sources and voices in the pursuit of diversity.

There is an element of trust given that students are talking about the subject at hand, which encourages the idea of self-driven learning. The levels of engagement and reflection we find when reading their submissions reinforce the notion that this trust is well-placed in the majority of students. On a practical level, it also means that the direction of the discussion is led by the students through their "exploratory talk" (Skidmore and Murakami 2016, p. 135). Depending on the topics raised, the session leader may choose to introduce contrary viewpoints or illustrate alternative readings of the same question, but the responses from the students themselves drive the content. Consequently, no two classes have ever been the same, even when utilising the same source material.

The questions asked after the texts are personal by design, prompting the students to share their own opinion and get more challenging as students "warm up" over the course of the session. Compare the complexity of "What happens to your experience of architecture once access to some or any of your senses is denied?" to "To what extent do you think taste is subjective?"; both delivered in the same session. Session leaders are unconcerned if discussions go "off-topic" in any way: the question "To what extent do you think taste is subjective?" in particular has delivered several memorable discussions among the wider group about the nature of taste including a heartfelt monologue about "warm-light vs cold-light" within the context of Christmas decorations.

Other questions have included: "Do you consider yourself to be a designer of buildings or a designer of spaces?", "Does place dictate identity to a people, or do we shape our land to suit us and our needs?", and even "Who do you think you are?" – provocative in its simplicity.

At the end of each session, a series of slides are devoted to the idea of further reading. Labelled as "Open Mind", these mirror the lecture slides in that they suggest books, video games, art, projects, music or films to draw inspiration or connections from, and are based on the topic of the session or its periphery. The breadth is intentionally diverse, with the hope that students will start to form their own opinions and generate a personal path of discovery.

Reflection and Self-Discovery

Where the course really comes to life is in the reflection the students undertake. During this personal, quiet period, they are encouraged to reflect on the topic we have just discussed, and to write down the points that have struck them the most. For some, these are revelations, for others, they are quieter suggestions to think on a topic that they previously hadn't considered. For the vast majority, this time to sit and be studiously alone with their thoughts, in a supportive environment, leads to some surprising insights and the sound of a seminar room that had previously been full of chatter suddenly falling quiet with cognition is inspiring.

Students aren't given a word count and are free to be as radical or otherwise as they want to be. Encouraging self-learning, they are asked only to be honest with themselves and to find their thoughts (Wiggins and McTighe 2011, p. 103). The in-session reflections are not marked, and students are able to write with the promise that nobody will be reading it and judging them on these personal journallings.

This reflection encourages students to slow down, to recognise that they have had thoughts, and to think about what they were. Crucially, they are afforded time in a bespoke environment to explore these thoughts and expand their critical analyses, rather than being expected to attain them automatically. As Graham (2022) describes it in his review of Easterling's book "Medium Design", "What architectural theory offers us, in its better moments, is language ... shorthands that help us gesture toward ways of seeing differently". This is time and space that students are so rarely afforded during their studies and was introduced as a result of student feedback on the course which expressed a need for it. We see its value firsthand as the students' language becomes more confident when describing their own work, developing a self-assuredness that goes hand-in-hand with progress in the wider course. What if all students had this opportunity at the end of every lecture? How much more critically aware might students be?

Creation and Curation

Rather than being assessed on these private thoughts, the students are tasked with creating physical booklets or objects that summarise and represent their reflections in a new way. These physical hand-ins are intended to give the students a different piece of work to engage with when their minds are otherwise consumed with thoughts of essays, design portfolios and revision. We encourage creative submissions, outside-the-box thinking and students are intentionally not given a strict submission format to avoid stifling the way they want to explore their processes.

In the first semester, this submission must include a "found image" – a cultural item from outside the course that the student should present as exemplifying one or some of the themes explored within it – but is otherwise asked to simply be a broader reflection of the course as a whole. In the second semester, the submission also includes a series of tasks that students are asked to do between sessions. With some element of choice as to which task they engage with, these tasks are intended deliberately to be something different to the rest of the course, and range from creative writing scenarios set in their design project, mapping the aural environment they are in, creating a game that can only be played in a specific location, drawing a Louis Hellman-style "Archi-Tête", or even collaboratively drawing an imagined section in the manner of the Surrealists' "Exquisite Corpse".

This act of making is intended to be cathartic; the process affords students further time to curate and to critically reflect, forcing them to consider what to include as a representation of themselves and their thoughts – as opposed to an essay where the implied purpose is to make a successful argument. Instead, students think about what they have learnt about their own thought processes, their choices, their outputs and how these can go on to influence others.

Many students gratefully seize the opportunity to create something different, and some really push the boat out in the creative ways they find to represent their thoughts; from cabinets of curiosity to pop-up books, delightfully illustrated brochures and even viewfinders.

Marking these pieces at the end of each semester is always a privilege.

Academic Unfolding

The setting of the Theory course pre-supposes that architecture is a humanity or social science even more than it is art or science. Architects primarily act as communicators who are tasked with making the intangible tangible and are thrust into human situations with other people's opinions and wants on a daily basis. It is critical therefore that students learn how to approach the everyday reality created by humans when emotional or logical responses are attempted.

Similarly, the impact of architecture is not reserved solely for those who are trained in the subject, and asking students to acknowledge this is a key learning objective. Even as we teach students how to see architecture from the professional's perspective, it is paramount to continue to remind them of the outsider's position they themselves entered the degree with, the role of empathy and its importance in design is critical, as Juhani Pallasmaa has argued in an interview with Crosbie (2021). Ironically, the most successful way of doing this has often proved to be by including anecdotes from professional practice in the talk. It is the seed placed in the centre of the teaching experience for every student from the inception of their architectural studies, whilst simultaneously introducing subversive, creative, or surprising ways of thinking in the "push-and-pull dance of making things happen in conflicted situations" (Graham 2022).

The Theory course unapologetically and unambiguously presents alternative voices and challenging concepts to the students; the aim being to introduce pieces of grit into the shell of their creative endeavours, such that they may make pearls. We seek to stretch and strengthen students' resilience to contrary and conflicting opinions and tackle any presumption on their part that an undergraduate degree requires the same academic armour as further education. And yet, these are not inherently revolutionary ideas; perhaps the most radical aspect of the course is our suggestion that it should in fact not be radical at all, but an in-built approach to the way architecture is taught across all schools.

Admittedly, it is an approach that not all students are able to fully comprehend or engage with at the time. For the benefit of this minority group, who may struggle with objectively examining concepts at this point in their development, we make sure to present the course as laying academic foundations and the start of a journey rather than a self-contained "unit". Instead of singling anyone out, we encourage everyone to participate in the group discussions and take notes for future reference, provide notes and lists of sources at the end of the course, and present anecdotal accounts of times that course leaders have referred to decades-old sources and ideas for inspiration on subsequent occasions they became relevant.

For the students that do grasp the approach however, it has a tremendous effect, and the moment of breakthrough can often be spotted by other teachers in students' attitudes to their design projects. This act of "unfolding" is ultimately a journey of self-discovery. There isn't and could never be a quantum of knowledge that we expect them to gain on this course. It should be about exploration rather than achievement and this is the true beauty of being a student, acquiring an "education that is designed for the whole person... – [preparing] students for a lifetime of success in a rapidly changing, complex, and uncertain world" (Formation by design project progress report, 2014–2015: Designing the future(s) of the university, cited by Murray 2016, p. 4).

References

Adams, P. (2006) 'Exploring Social Constructivism: Theories and Practicalities', *Education 3–13*, 34(3), pp. 243–257. Available at: https://doi.org/10.1080/03004270600898893

Crosbie, M. (2021) *Juhani Pallasmaa: "Architecture Is a Verb"*. Available at: https://commonedge.org/juhani-pallasmaa-architecture-is-a-verb/ (Accessed: 28 October 2025).

Dreyfus, H. L. and Dreyfus, S. E. (2004) 'The Ethical Implications of the Five-Stage Skill-Acquisition Model', *Bulletin of Science, Technology & Society*, 24(3), pp. 251–264. Available at: https://doi.org/10.1177/0270467604265023

Fung, D. (2017) *Connected Curriculum for Higher Education*. UCL Press.

Graham, J. (2022) 'Review of *Medium Design: Knowing How to Work on the World*, by Keller Easterling', *Journal of Architectural Education Online*. Available at: https://www.jaeonline.org/issue-article/medium-design/ (Accessed: 5 August 2025).

Laertius, D. and Yonge, C. D. (1853) *The Lives and Opinions of Eminent Philosophers*. Henry G. Bohn. Available at: https://openresearchlibrary.org/content/6f72d724-c07f-4e05-87e2-ab1207b14277 (Accessed: 6 August 2025).

Murray, J. W. (2016) 'Skills Development, Habits of Mind, and the Spiral Curriculum: A Dialectical Approach to Undergraduate General Education Curriculum Mapping', *Cogent Education*, 3(1). Available at: https://doi.org/10.1080/2331186X.2016.1156807

RIBA (2021) *RIBA: Code of Professional Conduct*. RIBA.

Skidmore, D. and Murakami, K. (eds) (2016) *Dialogic Pedagogy: The Importance of Dialogue in Teaching and Learning*. 1st edn. Channel View Publications.

Wiggins, G. and McTighe, J. (2011) *The Understanding by Design Guide to Creating High-Quality Units*. Association for Supervision & Curriculum Development.

12

REALISING FEMINIST ARCHITECTURE

Identifying "Ah Ha" Moments

Emily Crompton

Introduction

There comes a point in each academic year where theoretical positioning gives way to the practical act of design. Students are knee deep in tracing paper, hunched over laptops and swearing at the limits of their chosen drawing package. This is my favourite part of the year, when I am most animated; whole hours are given over to discussing the significance of the entrance location or a particular toilet design, and the implications of certain spatial sequences are sketched out and marked up and drawn again and again (and again). And while designing, always asking, why that might be feminist (or not).

Feminist pedagogy is emphasised through dialogue, care and critical reflection. In architectural education application focuses on ethics and relational design learning. Through a reflection on two micro teaching events, this chapter will discuss the spatial consequences of feminist architectural design decisions, illustrated by two student-led projects and their applications. By interrogating small conversations, I aim to highlight the importance of inter-personal relationships in the classroom and to discuss the power of realisation – that "Ah Ha" moment – in teaching feminist architects-to-be. These two teaching moments use spatial issues as a lens to consider what feminist architecture might constitute, as well as reflecting on the implications of adopting an explicitly feminist approach in architectural education. I want to suggest that there is no single way of being a feminist architect. Rather, there are conditions and approaches that can be employed to establish a feminist design process. Feminist architecture, much like feminist pedagogy, is relational, iterative and always questioning.

DOI: 10.4324/9781003647720-15

Feminist Pedagogy and Architectural Education

Feminist pedagogy is a relational, dialogic and situated approach to teaching that emphasises care, reflection and critical engagement with knowledge. It challenges hierarchical and authoritarian models of education, privileging collaboration, mutual learning and attentiveness to the diverse experiences of students (Noddings, 1984). In architectural design education, where hierarchy, rigid authorship and normative practices often dominate, a feminist pedagogical approach foregrounds the relational and ethical dimensions of learning. bell hooks positions the classroom as a space of liberation, where students and teachers co-construct knowledge and question taken-for-granted norms (2007, p. 12). Paulo Freire's principles of dialogical education and critical consciousness (1970) align closely with this, offering methods for reflecting on power, authority and social structures – linking effectively with Vygotsky's Zone of Proximal Development (1978) by situating learning within guided, socially mediated interactions. In the context of architecture, Jane Rendell frames "critical spatial practice" as design that engages ethically and empathetically with space, users and social relations (2010). This is the theoretical framework underpinning my practice of feminist teaching in architecture. It is grounded in dialogue, reflective practice, relationality and creates conditions for student-designers to critically interrogate both the social and spatial norms embedded in architectural design while fostering care, attentiveness and ethical responsibility in their emerging professional practice.

Situating the Feminist Educator-Architect

The feminist research and teaching collective PRAXXIS was initially developed by a group of academics and educators led by Helen Iball (previously Aston) with input from myself, Sarah Renshaw and Kathryn Timmins. This was formed from teaching and pedagogical practices that Helen had been developing for over 20 years, influenced by a studio group taught in Master of Architecture called Manchester School of Architecture projects (MSAp), led by Helen Iball and Stefan White. Helen formalised PRAXXIS in the 2018/2019 academic year with me, Sarah and Kathryn. PRAXXIS was one of six ateliers delivering design curriculum teaching for students across three cohorts, including final year BA (Hons) Architecture course and both years of a two-year Master of Architecture course. This was one of my first teaching posts and was influential in developing my own teaching style. The creation and reflections on some of the early teaching practices are detailed in a *Journal of Architectural Education* paper titled *PRAXXIS: Always Personal, Always Political, Always Pedagogical* which was published in 2020 (Aston, Crompton, Renshaw and Timmins, 2020). Over the last eight years, the studio has had input from a range of educators, architects and academics. These include, in alphabetical order of surname: Victoria Adegoke, Jakleen Al-Dalal'a, Azreen Azlan, Rachel Carter Jones, Debapriya Chakrabarti, Tommy Harrison, Rhiannon Hodgeon, Roxanne Kanda, Carma Masson, Elly Mead, Jess Mulvey, Rachel Newton, Abigail Patel, Youcao Ren, Amber Roberts, Kate Stott, Hannah Thatcher, Katherine Valentine and many more visitors and guests. The studio is now known as PRAXIS. The change of name came from a desire of staff in 2024 to consolidate an intersectional approach to feminism, and to distance us from the chromosome inspired XX in the original title. This change indicates the shifting nature of feminist theory and activism even in the last decade, as well as the reflexive practice of the teaching staff who work in PRAXIS.

The pedagogical practices of the group reflect each individual's theoretical positioning which informs a collective effort in trying to understand what feminist architecture is now, and what it might be in the future. Reflecting on my own pedagogy has allowed consolidation of my practice as a feminist architect and educator. I can only define my own theoretical approach to teaching Feminist Architecture, rather than attempt to give a "PRAXIS" perspective – which is multi-facetted and voiced, ever-changing and evolving.

As a feminist teacher-architect I draw from several learning frameworks and feminist theories, and I employ a range of techniques. Intersectionality is vital to my teaching, and it is connected to the identity of the individual and collective power of people, especially those from marginalised groups. I often draw on my own intersectional identity as a bisexual woman with a bipolar disorder diagnosis, with a keen eye to my own privileges as a white, educated, middle-class architect and academic. The starting point of being open, honest and vulnerable about my own identity allows an engaged and creative pedagogy which prioritises lived experience and invites reciprocity from students (hooks, 1994, p. 21). This can simply be the moment I "come out" to students as bisexual, giving space for them to readjust their preconceived image of the Architect. Drawing on Paulo Freire's and bell hooks' writings, I subscribe to the notion that education can either reproduce systems of dominance or become a "practice of freedom" (Freire, 1970, pp. 53–54), and in the latter enable one to become fully human – critical and self-determined (hooks, 1994, pp. 13–23). The shared transformation of student and teacher or facilitator and participant is essential to my approach as an architectural educator and researcher, which means the architecture tutorial for me is more about co-creating a community of learners through dialogue and reflection than about transmitting knowledge. My own practice research on co-designing a new LGBT+ Centre with a charity and young LGBT+ groups has led to an investigation of Queer(ing) Architecture. This has strengthened my intersectional approach in the studio as an educator. Both feminist architectural pedagogy and queer theory question how norms are *spatialised* – who spaces are designed for, whose bodies and needs are centred, and how the act of design can disrupt exclusionary practices.

A Queer Feminist Architectural Pedagogy?

Marinucci argues that feminism is queer, because both feminism and queerness challenge the same hierarchies of normality (2016, pp. 139–148). A queer-feminist approach uses uncertainty, curiosity and embodied learning, with students questioning how they know what they know and to remain open to multiple ways of envisioning knowledge. In this chapter I aim to explore how small, everyday teaching moments – tutorials, conversations, "Ah Ha" realisations – can instil feminist values within architectural education. In "Living a Feminist Life", Sara Ahmed talks about the "feminist snap" (2017, pp. 188–192) and "clicking moments" (2017, pp. 29–30), as the moment when you suddenly see what is wrong in a situation you once accepted. This is an embodied realisation: anger, clarity, refusal; and those moments change how we understand the world. In looking for "Ah Ha" moments in my teaching and learning as well as in my students, I attempt to locate the conditions for a "feminist snap" in architectural pedagogy. These "Ah Ha" moments also resonate with Rob Shields' reading of Henri Lefebvre's notion of the *moment*, which describes fleeting instances that break through the monotony of the everyday and reveal a wider totality of possibilities. Moments, in Lefebvre's sense, are ephemeral but revelatory, uncovering potentialities that challenge routine experience and normative structures (Shields, 1999, p. 58). Queer-feminist pedagogy amplifies these moments by emphasising the contingency and fluidity of knowledge, encouraging students (and staff) to interrogate assumptions, disrupt hierarchies and experiment with alternative spatial, social and intellectual possibilities. What follows is a reflection on two teaching moments, and the tutorial is presented as a place where intense conversations can take place and lead to realisations for both students and staff – those "oh, yeah" moments! The following descriptions are my own recollections and do not include the students' experiences of these conversations and so only reflect my own experience as an educator-architect.

The Pedagogical Context: PRAXXIS and the Hulme Library Project

In PRAXXIS we were explicitly feminist in our teaching and did a lot of groundwork and theory-based learning in the first term. Students in the examples used in this chapter are enrolled on a two-year Master's course which must meet professional criteria as set out by the Architects Registration Board (ARB). The students in their first year have often returned to education following one or two years working in architectural practices. I find these students the most interesting in this context, as they have already been "indoctrinated" into the lexicon of architectural language and have learned and gained experience of the constraints of real-world design approaches.

This project began in the second semester. We carefully organised the students into mixed groups (ensuring a broad mix of personalities and skills). The students were presented with a brief, setting out the requirements for the design project's use and location. The brief's proposed use was a community-use building and the location was an existing 1960s public library in Hulme (an urban neighbourhood close to the university). Students were given a list of types of spaces they had to incorporate in their proposals, for example, a gathering space, childcare provision, working space, outdoor space. The student groups were then tasked with analysing the neighbourhood to generate their own more specific brief and specific uses from the information gathered. They could potentially identify a theme from what they found to be important to the area. The only other constraints were that the end-users of the space were to be local residents and that the façade of the existing building had to be retained.

Having all completed an undergraduate degree in Architecture, they were familiar with key architectural ideas – about use, materials, thresholds, light, views etc. – and importantly they have preconceived ideas about how buildings "should" work. This helped us utilise Vygotsky's concept of the "zone of proximal development" (1978) – we were not trying to ask students to reinvent architecture, but to be more inclusive, more thoughtful and take account of a multitude of needs and desires; to "add on" to what they already know. Through this project we were keen for them to develop an internal questioning of the status quo in design terms. Working in groups assisted the discussion or debate of the suitability of spaces. Open questions and speaking from personal experiences were key to this process.

Case Study 1: Designing the Nursery, Beyond the Binary of Childcare and Work

The first group's theme was all about food and their proposals included a communal kitchen and eating parlour, spaces for cooking classes and workshops, a co-workspace for new parents and a nursery. Their design built up to the retained façade and created a courtyard space behind the main building to be used as outdoor public space. They separated the nursery from the main restaurant with an entrance space. The nursery was provided its own entrance round the side.

The tutorial and design example are centred around the idea behind the relationship between nursery and workspace. The students were interested in exploring the idea of returning to work after having children. Their premise was a co-work setting with rentable space in the same building as a nursery – to reduce commuting time to childcare provision. They also investigated the affordability and discussed ways of reducing this issue by giving parents an option to be involved in the care provision at the nursery.

The original design idea proposed was to place the workspace right next to the nursery – the students felt this would be good for new parents – they could check in on their children, and the children would be able to see their parents. The first drawn idea was simple – a window: it allows visual connection between children and parents. Neither the students nor I had children – but having spent a lot of time observing my sister and her children both around nursery age, I understood there was also a need to have separate time, as well as encouraging independence in the children. I used my sister's experience of being happy to have some time back for herself; as well as the children finding it hard to be separated from caregivers in our discussions. The complexity of parenting and having children came into sharp focus – the "Ah Ha" moment being that in order for parents to get any work done, there had to be some moments away from caregiving, and the design of the nursery could enable this while maintaining some opportunity for contact or visual connection. Students diagrammed and discussed different options (Figure 12.1).

Continuing their idea of some parents may want to assist in the care provision they proposed a "Third Door", creating an environment where children, parents and staff could mix throughout the day, directly linked to the workspace – which then led to lots of discussion about the obscuring of glass! The other option discussed was creating a nursery which was double height, and placing window high up – overlooking the space, but above the children's line of sight to allow for reassurance for the parents, but can also be separated from work and not distracting to the children.

Rather than discussing the merits of the design here – I am interested in the conversation and implications of differing designs. The student's final design used the double height space and incorporated an internal window overlooking it. But the resulting drawing is not the point. The conversation required a range of options and the social consequences of those to be assessed by the students. The aim of conversations in the tutorial was to question the students'

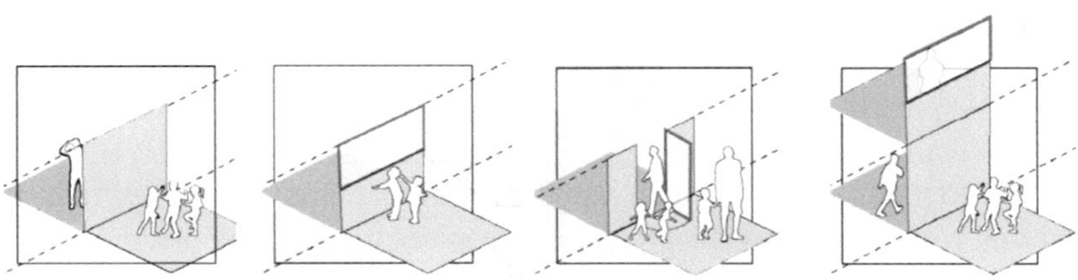

Figure 12.1 Diagrams of nursery by students Chloe Cann and Karolina Dudek.

preconceived ideas behind the provision of a nursery linked to a workspace. Facilitating the students to imagine how new parents would feel at this point in their lives was key to this discussion and centred around their own imagination as well as some anecdotal experience from my own life. The tone was light and kind, the students also felt strongly that children may well be in their own future and were interested in how a transition from looking after children to going back to work could be handled with sensitivity within their building.

In this example the student–teacher discussion enabled a questioning of the spatial separation of work and nursery. The range of spatial options explored allowed for a rigorous conversation that dismantled the assumed binaries of private/public and open/closed, producing a richer and more nuanced design outcome. This action can be understood as a queering of the "traditional" design process as well as challenging the preconceptions of the student-designers. Rather than the users of an already-designed space appropriating it for their own (queer) uses (Halberstam, 2005; Ahmed, 2006), the student-designer was invited to "queer" their own process and professional practice. As Katarina Bonnevier (2007, pp. 13–28) argues, queering architecture involves rethinking authorship, domesticity and the heteronormative logics embedded in design traditions – precisely the kind of methodological shift enacted here.

Case Study 2: Reimagining the Gym

The next group's project with the same brief and site looked at what the building could offer to minority groups, and marginalised members of society. It included offices, a shop, an eatery for people without access to affordable food, a nursery for working parents and a gym. In the plan they created a central public space dividing the programme into two sections with the façade acting as a protective barrier.

This group's tutorial and design example is centred around the idea of the building supporting people in living healthy lives. Students identified a gym as a suitable use. While they discussed disability and older users, they wanted to design a gym for all body types and chose to call this a gym for the self-conscious. I was surprised as the plan they had drawn had a standard changing room layout. There were two changing rooms (presumably one for men and one for women) with an open layout, benches and communal showers.

I asked them about their own experiences of changing rooms in gyms or at school. The dynamics of the group were important, as the self-elected leader of the group was male (and not a regular gym goer). He was challenged by the women in his group talking of their own experiences at school and in public gyms, some feeling uncomfortable and others not minding who saw them when changing. This debate helped develop a respectful peer-learning environment. It allowed them to assess their drawing in a different way, to stand back and appraise the idea from someone else's point of view. The "Ah Ha" moment here was allowing themselves to reinvent the changing room free from what they knew and experienced. The students instead started to imagine the ideal changing room, and we discussed the merits and downfalls of gender-neutral toilets or changing rooms and their suitability for this context. The students described the imagined users and considered the kindest changing room for those not comfortable with their appearance. Their final design included separate cubicles for everything, giving everyone privacy at every stage of the changing room journey.

Following the discussion (and some analysis of areas of the building which would overheat in summer) louvres were added to the façade. The justification given in portfolio (their final submission) added to the narrative of creating privacy for users of the gym and followed through from conversations about how this gym's structure and fabric – its architecture – could reflect the central theoretical idea of a gym for the self-conscious.

This example supports a feminist pedagogy that resists fixed categories – with teacher encouraging student-designers to see users of space not as "types" but as fluid, diverse and varied. Feminist teaching inherently embraces queer perspectives as within both: who gets to belong and whose experiences are assumed normal are questioned (Ahmed, 2017, pp. 29–30). This discussion on changing rooms is particularly pertinent in the current landscape of gender and space. In the UK in 2025 debate rages in national media about the definition of what a woman is, and which spaces trans individuals should be able to access. I believe this is something that is almost impossible to legislate, as how people use space is so queer that it resists any rigid rules or regulations. Space is constantly negotiated, first by those designing it and then by those using it. And rather than being for or against any potential policy, it is the discussion and debate I find endlessly interesting.

The Tutorial as a (Queer) Feminist Space

In both moments of realisation, the conversations were geared around confronting the student-designers' preconceptions – and rather than the tutor providing a solution, the conversation and reflection enabled investigation of the spatial consequences of particular attitudes. These conversations could only take place once the students had taken that leap into drawing. Laying the proposal out in front of student and teacher prompted that challenging discussion to take place. This allowed for re-appraisal and re-drawing, questioning and review. Each idea raised was then tested against theoretical users, as well as real-life friends, or relatives' experiences, as well as theoretical users to help challenge ingrained norms. When student-designers disrupt binaries, such as work/nursery they are engaging in a process that goes beyond the functional rearrangement of walls or furniture. They are actively participating in altering the social relations that the space can facilitate – reshaping how activities, roles and social interactions are organised and experienced within a space. In this sense, the designers do not only change a layout; they alter the social relations and potential embedded in that space, influencing who can occupy it, in what ways and under what norms. This aligns with Rob Shields' interpretation of Henri Lefebvre's concept of the production of space, which asserts that space is never neutral or fixed, but is always socially constructed and imbued with power dynamics (Shields, 1999, p. 191). Spaces, Lefebvre argues, are produced through social practices, and therefore designers inherently participate in shaping social relations, hierarchies and possibilities (Lefebvre, 1991, pp. 38-39; Stanek, 2011, p. 131). Through the conversations social complexity was discussed, rather than accepting abstract equality.

The tutorials became queer-feminist spaces, where uncertainty and conversation were productive – where knowledge, or in this case design ideas, could be co-created through relations. Tutorials centred around lived experiences, anecdote and storytelling. The nature of the group work allowed me as teacher to enter the tutorial as more of an equal, interested in understanding the impact of certain layouts or orientations. Students were able to draw it differently having shared experiences which advanced their architectural responses to embrace a feminist approach as well as reflecting these ideas in the building's design.

Conclusion: Realising Feminist Architecture

The title of this chapter now feels somewhat contradictory, a concept that might be impossible to achieve. Many of my students often ask me, what is Feminist Architecture? They want to know what it looks like, for me to point at a building, or present a precedent from a book. I have also had my own realisations in writing this chapter; I have realised that my feminism (expressed in teaching, designing and living) is intertwined with my queer identity. My own "Ah Ha" moment is that I believe that Feminist Architecture is queer – it resists the discipline's desire for neat answers and permanent built forms. A (queer) feminist architecture is perhaps one which is inseparable from its design process, so specific to its locational, social, political and economic context. And only now, can I appreciate that realising feminist architecture may be a life's work – constantly adapting and questioning. I hinted at being interested in how to identify what tangible; spatial proposals are feminist in my introduction (why does it look like that?) I have come to understand from teaching a Feminist Architecture that it is only in the interrogation, in understanding the implications of decisions that we can attempt to realise the impact on users of the spaces we design.

> If we become feminists because of the inequality and injustice in the world because of what the world is not, then what kind of world are we building?
>
> *(Ahmed, 2017, p. 2)*

Ahmed frames feminism as an ethic of hope and persistence. Despite exhaustion from being in a profession which continues to be an inhospitable place to be a woman (Royal Institute of British Architects, 2025); we keep doing the work. There is a hope in caring, pushing and questioning. This moves us towards designing a future we want to live in, not just fitting into and accepting the one presented to us. Feminist architecture can be framed as a practice of continually questioning, working towards repeated progression, in knowing the "answer" won't be the same in several years' time; and in that it chimes with the hopefulness of architects' practice of making space, reflective of society in all its beautiful intersections. I may never be able to satisfy students asking me to point at a building and say "that is feminist architecture", but my own "Ah Ha" moment is realising that my pedagogy is centred on the transformation of those involved, and it can only happen through ongoing critical dialogue, not prescriptive rules. In conclusion, designing and teaching feminist architecture is all in the questioning. There is no right way, and as attitudes and society change and develop so must its architectural language. I hope that the students I constantly question carry this sensibility into their own practice to enable them to keep realising their own feminist architectures.

References

Ahmed, S. (2006) *Queer phenomenology: Orientations, objects, others*. Durham, NC: Duke University Press.

Ahmed, S. (2017) *Living a feminist life*. Durham, NC: Duke University Press.

Aston, H., Crompton, E., Renshaw, S. and Timmins, K. (2020) Praxxis, *Journal of Architectural Education*, 74:2, 280–287, DOI: 10.1080/10464883.2020.1790938

Bonnevier, K. (2007) *Behind straight curtains: Towards a queer feminist theory of architecture*. Stockholm: Axl Books.

Freire, P. (1970) *Pedagogy of the oppressed*. New York: Continuum.

Halberstam, J. (2005) *In a queer time and place: Transgender bodies, subcultural lives*. New York: New York University Press

hooks, b. (1994) *Teaching to transgress: Education as the practice of freedom*. New York: Routledge.

Lefebvre, H. (1991). The production of space. Oxford: Blackwell.

Marinucci, M. (2016) *Feminism is queer: The intimate connection between queer and feminist theory*. 2nd edn. London: Zed Books.

Noddings, N. (1984) *Caring: A feminine approach to ethics and moral education*. Berkeley: University of California Press.

Rendell, J. (2010) *Site-writing: The architecture of art criticism*. London: IB Tauris.
Royal Institute of British Architects (RIBA). (2025) *Build it together: Progress and planning towards gender equity in the architecture profession*. Available at: https://www.riba.org/campaigns/policies/build-it-together-gender-equity-in-architecture/ (Accessed: 27 November 2025).
Shields, R. (1999) *Lefebvre, love and struggle: Spatial dialectics*. New York: Routledge.
Stanek, Ł. (2011) *Henri Lefebvre on space: Architecture, urban research, and the production of theory*. Minneapolis: University of Minnesota Press.
Vygotsky, L.S. (1978) *Mind in society: The development of higher psychological processes*. Cambridge, MA: Harvard University Press.

13

THE MAKING MANIFESTO

Reclaim the Joy of Practical Skills in Architectural Education

Scott Miller, Kasia Nawratek and Christopher Little

Who and Why

The intention of this book is to capture a wide range of voices involved in architectural education, including those traditionally excluded from academic discourse. The inclusion of technical staff widens the discussion and better reflects the community of practice within architectural pedagogy. What follows is Scott Miller's manifesto, edited by the book's editors for clarity. Its central claim and original voice remain Scott's: physical making should be brought back into the core of architectural education.

Scott is a technical manager at the Manchester School of Architecture's B.15 Modelmaking Workshop. Since 1970, this workshop has offered model-making facilities, along with expert advice and guidance, to students in Architecture, Planning and Landscape. It provides resources for creating scale development and presentation models to support student projects. Here, Miller's position as a technical workshop manager at the B.15 Modelmaking Workshop at the University of Manchester, allows him a unique insight into architectural education, a view from its very centre and yet removed from the main pedagogical space – both spatially and figurately.

With the changes to course accreditation in the UK on the horizon (Architects Registration Board, ARB, 2025) and as digital tools become increasingly central to studio work and visual refinement often takes focus, there is a timely opportunity to re-centre the discipline around its tactile, thoughtful foundations. This manifesto offers a hopeful and constructive call for renewed emphasis on physical making – not as a nostalgic return to a bygone era, but as a forward-looking, essential part of design education that recognises and retains the value of the learning tools used before, adapting them to respond to new design challenges.

DOI: 10.4324/9781003647720-16

In recent decades, powerful software has dramatically expanded the ways students can think about and explore design. Programs such as Rhino, Grasshopper and BIM platforms allow learners to map complex building elements, test structures virtually and generate forms that would once have seemed impossible. Yet while these tools have unlocked extraordinary creative potential, they can also, at times, overshadow the tactile processes through which students explore space, scale and materiality. Many incoming students find practical tasks challenging, which in the UK context, that can be partly explained by the marginalisation of creative subjects in favour of more academic pathways over the past decade. Further Education data shows a 57% drop in creative subject enrolments in England (Creative PEC, 2024) and while this data is specific to England, the experience of workshop staff is that many new students arrive with similarly low creative confidence. What they gain in speed and visual refinement is often balanced by a reduced capacity to work patiently, intuitively and experimentally through design problems (Creative PEC, 2024).

At its most powerful, making is not simply about producing a representation of a building – it is about cultivating curiosity, resilience, decision-making and discovery. In architectural education, such transformative moments often emerge through hands-on engagement: when a joint splinters, a plaster cast bubbles or a model collapses under its own weight. Architecture is not built in pixels; it is built in brick, timber, stone, concrete, glass and steel, and increasingly in sustainable alternatives such as bamboo, earth, hemp and recycled composites.

When students encounter material resistance, they are challenged to think creatively and adapt quickly. In doing so, they develop not only technical skills and architectural knowledge, but also self-awareness as designers, patience and inventive capacity. Making becomes a space where theoretical knowledge and embodied experience intersect, fostering both cognitive and emotional growth (Taylor, 2000, pp. 4–5). To reclaim the joy of making is not to reject digital tools; it is to place them in dialogue with embodied practice, ensuring that technology amplifies imagination rather than replacing it.

As Taylor (2000) emphasises, transformative learning occurs when learners encounter experiences that challenge assumptions, prompt reflection and enable personal growth. The following student case studies show the power of inquiry through making and exactly this transformative potential.

Case Study 1: Laura-Elena Popa – Tangible and Immediate Feedback

Laura-Elena Popa, currently in the second year of her Master of Architecture course, exemplifies the transformative power of physical modelmaking. She reflects,

> This creative process makes you immediately aware of properties such as span, load, resistance, and the way different elements fit, bend, or resist assembly.
> (Email to Scott Miller, 28th September 2025)

Unlike purely digital models, physical making grounds design decisions in material behaviour and real-world feasibility. When materials resist or fail, students must adapt, exploring alternatives and discovering opportunities that are impossible to predict digitally. Developing this approach demands confidence and a willingness to embrace uncertainty. Laura notes that she rarely begins a model "knowing exactly where it will end up ...the model itself becomes an active participant in the design process" (Email to Scott Miller, 28 September 2025). Each cut, fold, or weld provides immediate, tangible feedback, guiding subsequent steps and shaping the evolving design.

Her undergraduate work in the "Some Kind of Nature" atelier illustrates this process. The project, which sought to create structures benefiting multiple lifeforms, progressed through numerous test models and scales, each revealing insights into structural, spatial and experiential considerations. By remaining open to exploration and responsive to findings, Laura developed a nuanced and adaptable design, ultimately recognised by practising architects and B.15 Modelmaking Workshop professionals in her selection for the B.15 Modelmaking Award (B.15 Modelmaking Workshop, 2023) (Figure 13.1).

Figure 13.1 Laura Popa presents models to Stanton Williams representatives judging the B.15 Modelmaking Awards 2023 at the Manchester School of Architecture degree show.

Case Study 2: Esraa Rehan – Making as Inclusive Architectural Pedagogy

Esraa Rehan, a student with thoracic outlet syndrome that limits prolonged computer-based work, described physical making as her primary design method, allowing her to think through resistance, tactility and imperfection in ways digital tools could not. She noted that a breakthrough emerged when a rough, improvised model unexpectedly captured the spatial atmosphere of a project, reframing what might otherwise be seen as error into evidence of embodied authorship and inventive problem-solving (Email to Scott Miller, 15 October 2025).

The iterative modelmaking process acted not as a representational add-on during the design process but as a core method of spatial inquiry. This process was shaped by bodily constraint, material engagement and iterative testing, ensuring that ideas were both conceptually rigorous and materially feasible (Email to Scott Miller, 15 October 2025).

By embedding making within both studio and workshop culture, educators can better accommodate diverse bodily capacities and modes of thinking. Esraa's experience demonstrates that hands-on exploration is not simply a supplement to digital design, but a legitimate and rigorous method of inquiry. Recognising physical making as a core design practice reframes experimentation and iteration as forms of knowledge production, rather than preliminary or corrective steps, underscoring the importance of inclusive pedagogies within architectural education. Esraa's work illustrates the positive impact of inclusive pedagogical practices in making (Figure 13.2).

Figure 13.2 Mixed media models by Esraa Rehan.

Case Study 3: Wei Feng – Gravity Matters

Wei Feng describes digital modelling as "shaping clay in zero gravity" (Email to Scott Miller, 24 September 2025). Physical modelmaking reintroduces gravity, weight and structural limitations, requiring designs to negotiate tangible conditions. Early in his studies, while constructing a 1:50 façade bay, Medium-Density Fibreboard he used snapped under pressure, offering a tactile lesson in material limits. Switching to High-Density Fibreboard demonstrated that material choice must respond to function, structural load and assembly conditions.

Later, Wei encountered irregular joints in a complex timber structure that could not be cut by hand. This challenge prompted him to use 3D printing, a more precise and adaptable method for complex geometries. Each obstacle became an iterative, hands-on experiment, reinforcing the interplay between digital and physical workflows.

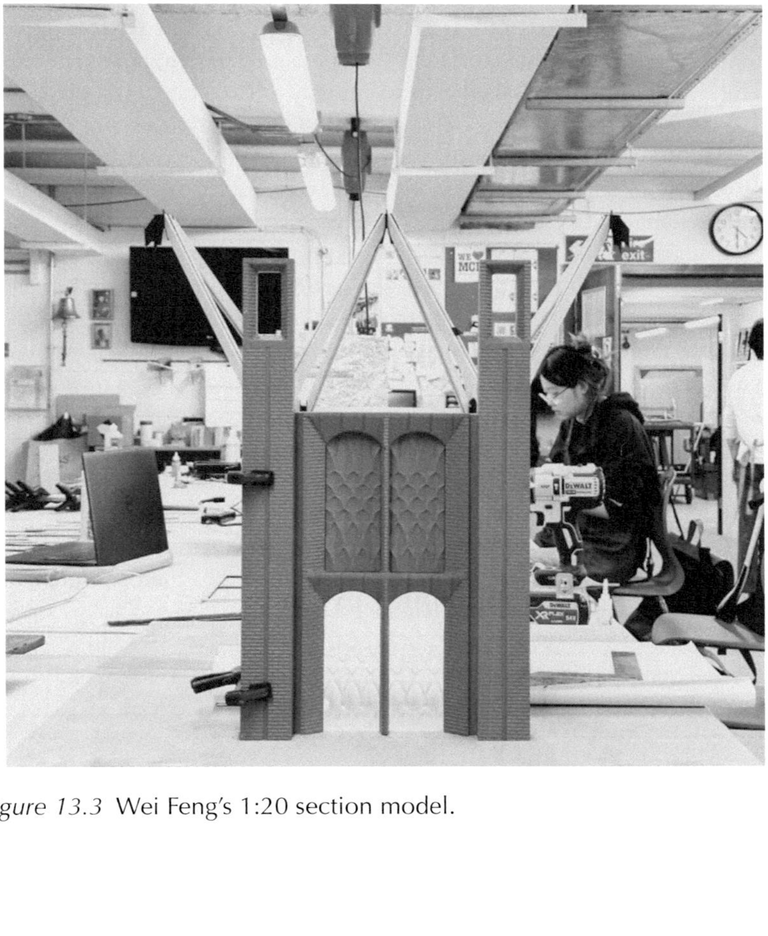

Figure 13.3 Wei Feng's 1:20 section model.

> What I value most is that technicians teach in a way entirely different from academic tutorials – it is much closer to real-world practice. They often asked me why I wanted to do something a certain way, whether another approach might be more effective, and how material properties would affect the outcome. This kind of guidance not only improved my modelmaking but also pushed me to re-evaluate my design from a fresh perspective.
>
> (Email to Scott Miller, 24 September 2025)

Wei also emphasised documenting process: "Rather than chasing spectacular final images, I focus on how the process itself shapes the design" (Email to Scott Miller, 24 September 2025) (Figure 13.3).

Case Study 4: Alina Iskrytska – Painful Prototyping

During her undergraduate studies in Ukraine, and later amid the restrictions of the pandemic, Alina relied almost entirely on digital tools, producing quick, improvised physical models in early design stages. "This often resulted in a beautiful envelope rather than actual architecture," she recalls (Email to Scott Miller, 26 September 2025). Without access to full workshop facilities, her ideas remained insufficiently tested in material form.

Her approach shifted dramatically during her master's degree when she regained access to a fully equipped workshop. Physical prototypes became essential at every stage, enabling her to evaluate scale, structure, assembly and spatial effects with growing confidence. A pivotal moment occurred during a 1:1 furniture project: although the digital model appeared flawless, the full-scale prototype revealed sharp edges and discomfort that the screen had concealed. "Some elements protruded from the surface, making our furniture uncomfortable or even painful", she explains (Email to Scott Miller, 26 September 2025). The prototype prompted a complete redesign of her project.

In the process, the workshop became an extension of her studio, a collaborative space where technicians and tutors contributed to the conceptual and technical evolution of her work. "I knew I didn't need to have a fully resolved design to come to the workshop", she explains. "I could bring intentions, questions, and half-formed ideas" (Email to Scott Miller, 26 September 2025).

The Manifesto for Making

This manifesto doesn't argue for making because it is traditional, but because it is truthful. It exposes uncertainty, demands patience and resists shortcuts. Long after software evolves and tools change, architecture will remain a discipline learned through bodies, resistance and the imperfect act of making. Only through work that is material and experienced can architectural ideas be tested beyond appearance and brought into genuine understanding.

This manifesto posits eight recommendations calling on educators, institutions and students alike to embrace making as a central pillar of architectural education. It champions process over product, curiosity over mere refinement and the tactile wisdom that emerges when head, hand and heart work together.

Manifesto for Making

1 Value the Process, Not Just the Product
2 Teach Through Making
3 Embrace Technology as a Partner, not a Substitute
4 Celebrate Mistakes as Pathways to Discovery
5 Integrate the Design Studio with the Workshop
6 Use Makerspaces as Springboards, Not Shortcuts
7 Recognise Technical Staff as Essential Educators
8 Celebrate Making!

The importance of each of these steps is explored below.

1 Value the Process, Not Just the Product

In a world saturated with polished renderings and photorealistic walkthroughs it is tempting to equate design quality with visual presentation. Yet architectural education has the potential to resist this trend and celebrate the nuanced value of process. A sketch, a rough model, or even a prototype that doesn't achieve a perfect finish can often reveal far more about a student's thinking than a flawless final image ever could. These artefacts capture experimentation, decision-making and learning in progress, offering a lens into the evolving design mindset rather than merely showcasing technical skill.

In the workshop, we often hear students ask whether there is a faster or more efficient way to reach the same outcome and interpret the brief as a need to produce a singular artefact as the objective. In these moments, it becomes clear that the learning is being mistaken for the finish, rather than the thinking required to get there.

There is also a profoundly instructive psychological dimension to prioritising process. A broken cast, for example, is not merely a failure but a moment of revelation, teaching students more about curing time, material properties and formwork techniques than a perfect cast could ever convey. However, when outputs are framed as "final products" or the result of a singular task, it becomes challenging to instil this mindset.

If assessment remains focused solely on outcomes, students may fear failure and avoid risk-taking. Discussions on continuous assessment emphasise keeping students engaged throughout the design process instead of concentrating solely on final submissions (Pitt and Quinlan, 2021, pp. 32–35). Formative assessment and feedback strategies further demonstrate that regular reflection and opportunities for improvement reinforce the idea that assessment can be an active, ongoing component of the learning journey (Pitt and Quinlan, 2021, pp. 55–60). The processes of iteratively developing physical prototypes and models, in dialogue with design studio and workshop staff, can become an active assessment journey, offering development beyond summative end-products.

Treating making as a method of thinking is to acknowledge that architecture is a conversation rather than a conclusion. Every sketch, model or experiment is a question posed in physical form, inviting exploration, reflection and engagement with complexity. Hill et al.'s (2023, pp. 76–79) research emphasises that relational, supportive and mutually understanding feedback can significantly enhance students' sense of belonging, allowing them to navigate uncertainty and develop intellectual flexibility, curiosity and resilience. These qualities extend far beyond studio practice, equipping students as adaptable, reflective lifelong learners.

The rough edges of a foam model, the glue stains on a cardboard prototype or the patchwork of taped-together fragments tell a story of iterative development. They embody the journey of exploration, documenting trials, errors and discoveries along the way. Such evidence is not of imperfection, but of growth – moments where creativity, insight and critical thinking intersect. When process is foregrounded, students begin to experience making not as a performance staged for a final review, but as a daily practice of inquiry, reflection and adaptation.

2 Teach Through Making

Architecture is inherently physical, spatial and experiential. It cannot be fully understood through images or words alone. Similarly, learning through making provides an embodied, immersive and deeply engaging form of study. When a student picks up a knife to cut foam, folds paper into a structure or cuts a piece of timber, they are not simply acquiring technical skills, they are internalising spatial, material and structural relationships, translating abstract concepts into lived experience.

Making can also provide a more inclusive and empowering entry point into architectural education, particularly for students less confident with academic writing, presentation or polished digital outputs. Inclusivity emerges when educators actively address barriers that some students encounter in workshops, including gendered assumptions about tool use, varying levels of prior hands-on experience or uncertainty about accessing technical spaces. Clear guidance, supportive induction and an explicitly welcoming culture enable students to communicate ideas more intuitively, learn at their own pace and build confidence. I have seen students who struggle to articulate ideas verbally or through digital work suddenly gain clarity and confidence once materials are placed in their hands. Making gives permission to think slowly, physically and without needing the "right" words.

This inclusivity also reflects the diverse demographics of contemporary UK higher education cohorts. For example, recent data from Advance HE and HESA/Jisc notes that approximately 35% of students classed as studying "architecture, building and planning" are first-generation entrants, with parents who have no experience of higher education, highlighting widening participation trends (Advance HE and HESA, 2025). Cohorts further include international students and varied ethnic and cultural backgrounds, each bringing distinctive learning preferences, experiences and familiarity with hands-on making practices. These differences shape patterns of progression and confidence in practical learning: some students arrive with extensive hands-on experience from previous projects or work contexts, while others require additional support to navigate unfamiliar tools, workshops or cultural norms.

3 Embrace Technology as a Partner, Not a Substitute

Digital tools now allow designers to explore geometries and forms that were once impossible. These technologies, however, do not replace material engagement; they complement it. When integrated thoughtfully, digital tools act as collaborators in creative exploration, enabling designers to investigate forms, structural performance and spatial relationships while remaining grounded in the realities of fabrication and construction (Jabi, 2006). In this sense, technology can expand imagination without disconnecting designers from the tangible world.

When studying Art and Design in 2005, my lecturers often talked of an imminent "digital takeover" with many assuming that hands-on making would diminish, and that those who resisted digital workflows would become professionally irrelevant. While such concerns were understandable, the perspective was incomplete. Traditional craft-based methods, developed and refined over centuries, remain effective, reliable and deeply connected to human experience and material reality. These methods offer insights into scale, structural behaviour and material performance that cannot be fully replicated in digital environments alone. The challenge for contemporary education, therefore, is not to choose between hand and machine, but to teach students how to integrate them (Guerra, 2025).

Developing criticality is central to architectural education. A student producing a parametric façade without considering structural implications or material feasibility may generate a visually compelling but impractical design. On the other hand, alternating between hand-built prototypes and digital simulations enables students to leverage the strengths of both approaches. Digital workflows offer repeatability, rapid iteration and allow for testing complex scenarios. Physical models introduce resistance, unpredictability and tactile feedback that reveal subtle challenges in construction, scale, or assembly. Iteratively moving between these modes fosters critical thinking, reflective learning and experimental habits that neither method alone can fully develop (Ioannou, 2018; Guerra, 2025).

The danger is not technology itself, but the assumption that it can make decisions on our behalf. When software begins to replace judgement rather than support it, authorship quietly slips away. A balanced approach also emphasises the value of feedback loops. When students see how a digitally simulated structure performs physically, they learn to adapt and refine their ideas. Mistakes or unexpected outcomes – whether a joint that fails or a simulation that produces unrealistic stress distributions – become valuable learning moments. Educators play a key role in guiding these interactions, encouraging reflection, questioning assumptions and helping students make informed decisions about which tool is most appropriate for each stage of the design process. This guidance ensures that technology enhances creativity rather than constrains it.

4 Celebrate Mistakes as Pathways to Discovery

I've observed that students beginning their higher education journey often perceive mistakes as failures to be avoided. Yet in design, error is not just inevitable – it is invaluable. It is through trial and error that innovation blossoms and through setbacks that resilience is cultivated. Architectural education must therefore reframe mistakes not as obstacles, but as fertile opportunities for discovery. Consider the failed cast that leaves air bubbles or uneven edges. At first glance, it may seem flawed. Yet those irregularities can suggest intriguing new textures or inspire inventive rethinking of formwork techniques. Similarly, a misaligned joint in a timber structure may reveal unexpected patterns of load transfer, opening pathways to fresh ideas for structural expression. The act of salvaging, adapting, or reimagining these "failures" is often where true creativity flourishes.

I have watched students instinctively try to hide these moments, sanding away evidence of struggle as if uncertainty were something to be embarrassed by. And yet, these traces often hold the most value, because mistakes are the fingerprints of experimentation that evolve into embodied knowledge. They demonstrate that a student has boldly stepped into the unknown, tested limits and engaged with uncertainty. By celebrating mistakes, architectural education nurtures designers who are not intimidated by complexity, but who embrace it as an invitation to explore and innovate.

Research by Hill et al. (2023) demonstrates that moving assessment away from strictly summative, grade-focused models toward compassionate, relational approaches fosters recognition, engagement and confidence. For example, pass/fail grading enabled some students to experiment freely and embrace risk, promoting creativity and exploration in ways conventional grading cannot (Hill et al., 2023, p. 14). By emphasising iterative development and dialogue, educators can create conditions in which students are empowered to experiment, take risks and – most importantly – see mistakes not as failures but as intrinsic parts of discovery.

5 Integrate the Design Studio with the Workshop

For making to be fully celebrated within architectural education, it must be intentionally woven into the structure of project briefs and the everyday environments in which students work. When making is positioned as central rather than supplementary, it becomes a catalyst for imagination, reflection and deep engagement. Yet treating physical making as a decorative end-stage gesture, an add-on, once design decisions have already been made digitally can still be observed in architectural education. This separation of design decisions and making, limits the potential of experimentation and reinforces the misconception that intellectual development happens in the studio while the workshop simply produces outcomes.

Embedding process can begin with the project brief itself. If briefs clearly communicate that iterative physical models are required – not as proof of final intent but as evidence of exploration – students understand from the outset that making is integral to their learning. This might include expectations for multiple forms of physical testing: massing studies, material prototypes, tectonic explorations and scale-specific investigations that accompany drawings and digital models. When assessment criteria explicitly recognise curiosity, risk-taking and iterative refinement, students gain permission to test ideas early and often. Journals, process logs and annotated photographs can further reinforce this culture, encouraging students to document both successful and unsuccessful experiments. Such records not only provide insight into design development but also establish the value of process over polished final images.

If process is not explicitly valued in the brief, students will understandably optimise for what is most visible, fastest and safest. This is not a failure of motivation, but a rational response to what the institution signals it truly rewards. Similarly, if making activity is always postponed until the end, it is silently understood as optional. What is optional is rarely taken seriously.

The integration of studio and workshop spaces is crucial to sustaining this culture. When students can move fluidly between sketching, digital modelling and hands-on experimentation, the design process becomes more intuitive and energising. Tutorials held in the workshop normalise the presence of tools, materials and technical expertise, reinforcing the idea that making is not a discrete task but a natural extension of conceptual development. When tutors join students in the workshop, they experience how ideas shift when confronted with material realities; when technicians participate in early conversations, they offer insights into fabrication, material behaviour and practical feasibility that can redirect or enrich design concepts before they become fixed.

Unfortunately, many architecture schools continue to maintain a structural and cultural division between studio and workshop environments. The physical distance between studio desks and workshop benches becomes symbolic of a pedagogical gulf: ideas are generated separately from the places where they could be interrogated, tested or transformed. A more integrated model could allow all staff groups to operate as partners. Workshops located close to studio spaces – physically, organisationally and socially – could encourage spontaneous discussion and iterative movement between thinking and doing. Cross-staff collaboration in brief-writing could ensure that material exploration was not only supported but embedded into the structure of a project.

While many studios do include elements of making, there is a danger that sometimes studios are considered the space for conceptual development, while workshops are positioned as spaces for testing ideas developed in the studio. But when these spaces are integrated – when tutorials or reviews occur within workshops, when tutors observe students experimenting first-hand alongside them – the boundary between thinking and doing dissolves, and making becomes as essential to inquiry as sketching, diagramming or written reflection. In such integrated settings, the act of making can become not an auxiliary task but a central vehicle for exploration, supporting a seamless interplay between imagination, analysis and practical insight.

6 Use Makerspaces as Springboards, Not Shortcuts

Makerspaces offer access to laser cutters, 3D printers and CNC routers – tools that democratise fabrication. Yet these technologies can unintentionally promote a mindset in which polished outputs matter more than meaningful engagement. When students rely solely on the latest digital tools, they may miss the richer understanding that comes from wrestling directly with materials and processes.

We often observe that students mistake digital fabrication for the entire act of making, rather than one component of a process of experimentation. A 3D printed model produced overnight can be impressive, but it rarely offers the tactile familiarity or spatial awareness gained through cutting, assembling and refining objects by hand. Physical interaction with materials cultivates an intuitive sense of scale, structure and material behaviour that no machine can fully replicate. There is also a hesitation to work manually, as students often use complex digital workflows to achieve simple tasks, because manual work seems risky. It's a symptom of lost confidence.

To harness the full potential of makerspaces, educators can present them as catalysts for exploration rather than efficient substitutes. A 3D-printed element might serve as the basis for a hand-modified prototype; a CNC-milled form can be tested, adapted or challenged through low-tech iterations. When digital and manual approaches are allowed to inform one another, making becomes an evolving inquiry instead of a linear production task.

7 Recognise Technical Staff as Essential Educators

Technical staff are often the quietly outstanding contributors to architectural education. They maintain workshops, ensure safety and keep machines running, yet their role is far richer than this. They are educators, offering a depth of material knowledge and practical wisdom that students cannot find in textbooks or software tutorials.

The Technician Commitment recognises their essential contributions to UK higher education, describing them as a highly skilled workforce whose expertise supports teaching, research and institutional activity (Technician Commitment, 2024). When technicians are integrated into the teaching process, students gain access to invaluable mentorship. A technician can show not only how to operate a machine, but also how to think about materials, tolerances and feasibility. They model an attitude of care and craft that encourages students to approach making with confidence and respect.

Institutions should therefore celebrate technicians as collaborating partners, not service providers. If involved in developing and delivering student briefs, tutorials and reviews, they can broaden the scope of education, further grounding abstract ideas in material reality. This integration could also foster a culture of mutual respect, where design and making are not seen as separate activities, but iterations of the same creative activity. Therefore, technical staff should be formally recognised as tutors, in full acknowledgement of their unique and crucial role in architectural education.

8 Celebrate Making!

When making is fully embraced, it can elevate the culture of the architecture school with energy and optimism. Models should not be hidden away until final review but displayed proudly in studios and corridors, celebrating process at all stages. Workshops should be placed at the heart of the school's building, signalling their importance and, crucially, showcasing not only "final" pieces but also tests and iterations that spark discovery.

Photographs of models, videos of fabrication and narratives of trial and improvement can all emphasise the richness of making. When students see their peers experimenting boldly, they are encouraged to do the same. In my own role I have for over a decade aimed to encourage and promote student work with practice recognition through our annual B.15 modelmaking awards (Mecanoo, 2017). The voice of practice strengthens and affirms the value of these activities for students. Exhibitions such as the recently opened "Civic Vision" by Foster + Partners aim to demonstrate that "models are far more than an architectural marketing gimmick; they are a critical tool in the design process" (Burke, 2025).

Faculty, too, must model this culture of celebrating process. When tutors bring their own prototypes to tutorials, when reviewers engage with rough models, they signal that making matters. Over time, these practices shape a collective ethos where exploration, curiosity and material engagement are not peripheral but central to architectural education.

Final Thought

This manifesto reaffirms the central role of making within architectural education as a means of cultivating deep, embodied understanding. It argues for a renewed equilibrium between digital innovation and material practice, recognising that both are essential to the development of critical, reflective designers. Making is not positioned as a nostalgic return to craft, but as a dynamic mode of inquiry through which knowledge is generated, tested and refined.

To make is to engage directly with complexity, to think through materials, to negotiate resistance and to learn through iteration. These encounters foster intellectual resilience, curiosity and adaptability, qualities that extend beyond the workshop into all aspects of design thinking. By integrating physical making with digital tools, architectural education can nurture practitioners who are both technically adept and materially literate designers who understand that technology achieves its fullest potential when informed by human judgement and sensory experience.

References

Advance HE and HESA/Jisc (2025) *Equality in Higher Education: Statistical Report 2024*. Advance HE. Available at: https://www.advance-he.ac.uk/knowledge-hub/equality-higher-education-statistical-report-2024 (Accessed: 8 January 2026).

Architects Registration Board (ARB) (2025) *ARB Advances Education Reforms with Plans to Transform Professional Practical Experience*. 29 May. Available at: https://

arb.org.uk/arb-advances-education-reforms-with-plans-to-transform-professional-practical-experience/ (Accessed: 5 November 2025).

B.15 Modelmaking Workshop (2023) *B.15 Modelmaking Awards Sponsored by Stanton Williams – Winners!* [online]. B.15 Modelmaking Workshop. Available at: https://b15.humanities.manchester.ac.uk/?p=5869 (Accessed: 5 November 2025).

Burke, K. (2025) 'Tiny Beautiful Things: Architectural Exhibition Showcases the Enduring Role of Scale Models', *The Guardian* [online] 31 Oct. Available at: https://www.theguardian.com/artanddesign/2025/oct/31/tiny-beautiful-things-architectural-exhibition-showcases-the-enduring-role-of-scale-models (Accessed: 1 November 2025).

Creative PEC (2024) *Creative Further Education in the Four Nations: A State of the Nation report*. London: Creative Industries Policy & Evidence Centre. Available at: https://pec.ac.uk/state_of_the_nation/creative-further-education/ (Accessed: 3 November 2025).

Feng, W. (2025) *Email to Scott Miller*, 24th September.

Guerra, A. (2025) 'Craft-Based Methodologies in Human–Computer Interaction: Exploring Interdisciplinary Design Approaches', *Multimodal Technologies and Interaction*, 9(2), p. 13. https://doi.org/10.3390/mti9020013.

Hill, V., Broadhead, S., Bunting, L., da Costa, L., Currant, N., Greated, M., Hughes, P., Mantho, R., Salines, E. and Stevens, T. (2023) *Belonging through Assessment: Pipelines of Compassion*. Quality Assurance Agency for Higher Education (QAA). Available at: https://www.qaa.ac.uk/membership/benefits-of-qaa-membership/collaborative-enhancement-projects/assessment/belonging-through-assessment-pipelines-of-compassion (Accessed: 8 December 2025).

Ioannou, O. (2018) 'Opening Up Design Studio Education using Blended and Networked Formats', *International Journal of Educational Technology in Higher Education*, 15, Article 47. https://doi.org/10.1186/s41239-018-0129-7.

Iskrytska, A. (2025) *Email to Scott Miller*, 26th September.

Jabi, W. (2006) *Digital Tectonics: The Intersection of the Physical and the Virtual*. ACADIA Conference Proceedings, Louisville, KY. Available at: https://papers.cumincad.org/data/works/att/acadia04_256.content.pdf (Accessed: 27 October 2025).

Mecanoo (2017) *Winners 2017 Mecanoo B.15 Modelmaking Awards Announced*. [online] 12 June. Available at: https://www.mecanoo.nl/News/ID/356/Winners-2017-Mecanoo-B15-Modelmaking-Awards-announced (Accessed: 3 November 2025).

Pitt, E. and Quinlan, K. (2021) *Impacts of Higher Education Assessment and Feedback Policy and Practice on Students: A Review of the Literature 2016–2021*. Advance HE. Available at: https://kar.kent.ac.uk/95307/1/AdvHE_Assessment%20and%20Feedback_Literature%20Review_2016-2021.pdf (Accessed: 3 November 2025).

Popa, L. (2025) *Email to Scott Miller*, 28th September.

Rehan, E. (2025) *Email to Scott Miller*, 15th October.Taylor, E.W. (2000) 'Fostering Mezirow's Transformative Learning Theory in the Adult Education Classroom: A Critical Review', *Canadian Journal for the Study of Adult Education*, 14(2), pp. 1–32. https://doi.org/10.56105/cjsae.v14i2.1929.

Technician Commitment (2024) *About the Technician Commitment*. Available at: https://www.techniciancommitment.org.uk/ (Accessed: 2 November 2025).

NOTE FROM THE EDITORS

Kasia Nawratek and Christopher Little

This concluding note is a chance to take a deep breath: to steady ourselves, to reflect on the editorial process, to look back at the hopeful and hard-won practices gathered here and to name the conditions that make their existence feel, at times, almost improbable.

Because let's be blunt: UK higher education is not going through a passing wobble. It is being restructured – financially, institutionally and culturally – into something narrower, meaner and less forgiving of the slow, labour-intensive work that creative education, educational research and scholarship require. Roper and Vorley report in their survey that 85.1% of English HEIs were operating at a deficit, breaking even, or reporting a reduced surplus, based on interviews with finance leaders at 74 institutions. More damning still, 97% of respondents understood the crisis as systemic and long-term, not a temporary difficulty to be weathered (Roper and Vorley, 2025).

The grimly familiar scenarios – recruitment freezes, voluntary severance, programme closures, restructurings and, when "voluntary" runs out, compulsory redundancies – have been playing out across the UK. Sheffield Hallam, for example, reports that around 500 staff left in 2024 via voluntary severance (Sheffield Hallam University, 2025). The University of Edinburgh lost around 350 staff through voluntary severance during the most acute phase of its recent budget reductions (Research Professional News, 2025). The University of Essex has announced plans to close its Southend campus and cut up to 400 roles as part of wider cost-saving measures (University and College Union (UCU), 2025b). Lancaster University's proposed cuts of hundreds of posts became the focus of industrial dispute, with compulsory redundancy threats later halted after union pressure (University and College Union (UCU), 2025c).

Architecture, with its space- and time-hungry studio culture, extensive contact hours and material resources, feels these shocks intensely. Even long-established schools are being forced into difficult choices. At Sheffield, the planned closure of the dual Master's in Landscape and Architecture (MALA) signalled how quickly "unique" can become "unviable" once numbers dip (Architects' Journal, 2025). At Greenwich, proposed cuts and restructuring have threatened staff, including those teaching on precarious contracts (University and College Union (UCU), 2025a).

We have felt the same pressures in making this book: colleagues withdrawing, not because the work didn't matter, but because institutional support had become too unstable, and employment too precarious, to commit the time and attention the writing required.

That matters for how this collection should be read. Contributors' perseverance was remarkable, and our role as editors extended beyond convening a space for discussion. It involved holding a strong direction of investigation and sustaining a consistent narrative thread across chapters. It also required emotional labour: supporting colleagues when they needed reassurance that yes, this is worth it – not despite, but exactly because it is so hard to find the time, attention and institutional backing needed for extended, in-depth investigation.

The editorial process, driven by the agenda of demonstrating the creative ways architectural education is responding to institutional and professional pressures, unfolded as an ongoing conversation with authors over a year and a half: correcting course when discussions drifted, and offering mentorship as part of the scholarship. The result is a narrative comprising situated arguments that speak to one another, sometimes echoing, sometimes disagreeing, forged under pressure and with real stakes.

Across this book, different voices return to recurring themes: creativity, dialogue, care and resistance, not as slogans, but as working tools. Together, they show creative pedagogy in architecture as something more than "good practice" within a stable system. That would be a luxury. Instead, pedagogical practice becomes a form of institutional dissent: a refusal to let education collapse into compliance, metrics and managed mediocrity.

The student body, too, proves that resignation is not the only available mood. Dundee architecture students, for instance, successfully campaigned in response to staffing shortages that threatened delivery and potentially the accreditation of their courses (Architects' Journal, 2026). These actions do not solve the structural crisis, but they disprove the complacent assumption that nothing can be done.

This collection is not an argument for hope in the abstract. It is a record of practice under pressure: decisions made, risks taken and new approaches built, always through care, sometimes through sheer stubbornness. If it offers hope at all, it is this: that such practices can be shared, adapted and used. In short, we dare to hope this book becomes a manual for resistance: a little punk book for the hopeful.

References

Architects' Journal (2025) 'Outrage as Sheffield Uni plans to scrap architecture and landscape combined Masters'. *The Architects' Journal*, 20 January. Available at: https://www.architectsjournal.co.uk/news/outrage-as-sheffield-uni-plans-to-scrap-architecture-and-landscape-combined-masters (Accessed: 22 January 2026).

Architects' Journal (2026) 'Dundee architecture students win fight against course-threatening staff shortages'. *The Architects' Journal*, 6 January. Available at: https://www.architectsjournal.co.uk/news/dundee-architecture-students-win-fight-against-course-threatening-staff-shortages (Accessed: 22 January 2026).

Research Professional News (2025) 'Scotland mulls university reforms as Edinburgh loses 350 staff'. *Research Professional News*, 25 April. Available at: https://www.researchprofessionalnews.com/rr-news-uk-universities-2025-4-scotland-mulls-university-reforms-as-edinburgh-loses-350-staff/ (Accessed: 22 January 2026).

Roper, S. and Vorley, T. (2025) 'Counting the cost of financial challenges in English higher education'. *WonkHE*, 2 December. Available at: https://wonkhe.com/blogs/counting-the-cost-of-financial-challenges-in-english-higher-education/ (Accessed: 22 January 2026).

Sheffield Hallam University (2025) 'Financial position'. Sheffield Hallam University. Available at: https://www.shu.ac.uk/news/all-articles/latest-news/financial-position-updated (Accessed: 22 January 2026).

University and College Union (UCU) (2025a) '"Rogue employer" University of Greenwich could axe over 300 staff'. UCU, 15 May. Available at: https://www.ucu.org.uk/article/14019/Rogue-employer-University-of-Greenwich-could-axe-over-300-staff (Accessed: 22 January 2026).

University and College Union (UCU) (2025b) 'Staff fury as University of Essex threatens to slash 400 jobs'. UCU, 2 December. Available at: https://www.ucu.org.uk/article/14277/Staff-fury-as-University-of-Essex-threatens-to-slash-400-jobs (Accessed: 22 January 2026).

University and College Union (UCU) (2025c) 'Strikes off after union forces Lancaster University to withdraw compulsory redundancy threat'. UCU, 20 November. Available at: https://www.ucu.org.uk/article/14267/Strikes-off-after-union-forces-Lancaster-University-to-withdraw-compulsory-redundancy-threat (Accessed: 22 January 2026).

INDEX

Note: *Italic* page numbers refer to figures.

For Product Safety Concerns and Information please contact our EU representative GPSR@taylorandfrancis.com Taylor & Francis Verlag GmbH, Kaufingerstraße 24, 80331 München, Germany

Batch number: 10476271

Printed by Printforce, the Netherlands